IMAGES
of America

AROUND ORANGE LAKE

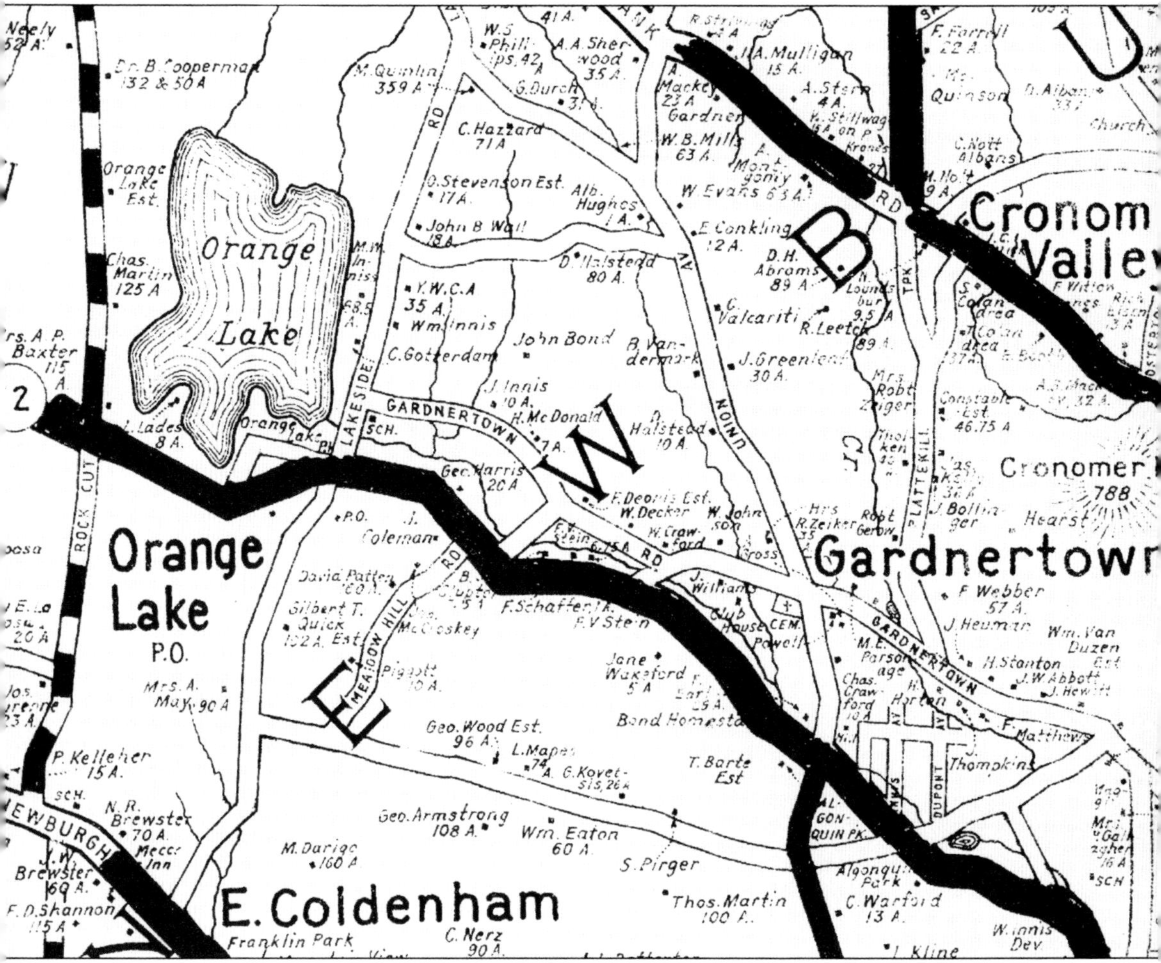

This map is a real estate map published in the mid-1930s. It shows the name of the farm owner and the acreage of each farm. There are also a number of other places listed, for example, the Orange Lake Amusement Park and the YWCA camp on Lakeside Road. (Author's collection.)

On the cover: The Crescendo Club was a well-respected group of young women singers from Newburgh. Each year it held a picnic at the home of George Peck on Orange Lake. Among those identified are, from left to right, (first row) George Peck (holding the broom), Clara Lamb, two unidentified persons, Dora Townsend, an unidentified child, Madeline Rose, unidentified, Flora Terpenning, Mrs. Doty, and Alice Hitchcock. (Courtesy of the Historical Society of Newburgh Bay and the Highlands.)

IMAGES
of America

AROUND ORANGE LAKE

Patricia A. Favata

ARCADIA
PUBLISHING

ISBN 978-0-7385-4952-1

Published by Arcadia Publishing
Charleston, South Carolina

Printed in the United States of America

Library of Congress Catalog Card Number: 2006934012

For all general information contact Arcadia Publishing at:
Telephone 843-853-2070
Fax 843-853-0044
E-mail sales@arcadiapublishing.com
For customer service and orders:
Toll-Free 1-888-313-2665

Visit us on the Internet at www.arcadiapublishing.com

This book is dedicated to the following people who have preserved the history of Orange Lake so that this volume could be written: Marguerite Harris McDermott, Ilene Patton Siegman, Mae Innis Kaiser, Kathryn Gatterdum Monti, Janette Gillispie Sylvester, Gordon Anderson, and Robert Lawrence.

Contents

Acknowledgments 6

Introduction 7

1. Early History, Agriculture, and Industry 9
2. Getting There 19
3. Schools, Churches, and the Fire Department 29
4. Hotels and Restaurants 43
5. The Amusement Park 55
6. Early Cottages and Homes 77
7. Camps, Events, Celebrations, and People 89
8. The Sporting Life 101
9. A New Frontier 119

ACKNOWLEDGMENTS

The most enjoyable part of working on this book was the time spent renewing old friendships and meeting new people, all with one common interest: their love of the Orange Lake area. I am very grateful for the help I received in completing this project.

For their generous donations, photographs, and other materials used in this book, I thank the following Orange Lake Civic Association members: Arthur Nugent and Sheila Gage Nugent, Kathleen Martel Sileno, David and Carole McDermott, Anthony and Laraine Esposito, Richard and Marguerite Lease, James and Jennifer Moore, and Charles and Cheryl Bivona. A thanks is also given to the following members for their donations in the beginning of this project: Gregory Langer, Michael and Amy Esposito, Marina Markey, Dorothy Esposito, Majorie Pimm, Chuck Bonis, Jay and Rita Coppola, Mark Tierney, Lana and Michael Gesmundo, Richard Clarino, and Karen and Donald Dubois Jr. There are many wonderful stories, family and local lore, that were told during the time it took to complete this book that unfortunately cannot all be documented here. For those stories and accompanying photographs I wish to thank: Gordon Anderson, Robert Lawrence, Marguerite Harris McDermott, Mae Innis Kaiser, Janette Gillispie Sylvester, Ilene Patton Siegman, Kathryn Gatterdum Monti, Susan Carroll, Marsha Tenny, Sr. Mary Sheppard, John Clark, Robert and Vivian Goodbread, Sharon Nichols Formato, Paul Yablonsky, Jane Grimley McCaw, Anna Auchmoody, Walter Whitehill, Karol Gee Gibson, Janice Ruggiero and Kathy Gee Kobeliski, Glenn Marshall, Arlene Hughes, George Linton, Elizabeth McKean, Roy Nagl, Stuart Berg, James and Tori Carter, Victoria Palkovic, Dorothy Tyler, Edward Stump, Jeffery Goulding and the *Times-Herald Record*, Dennis Collins, Louis Catulusci and Ilene and Russell Lange, and Vincent Forriester.

Contact people and those who helped with access to other photographs and materials also deserve thanks. They include Peter Fogarty, Suzanne Dawes, Beverly Mennerich, Mary McTamaney, Monsignor Budwick, William McQuillan, Franz Clough, Charles Lanzer, Kelly and Kevin Patton, June Rudia, Sally Lease, Edward Kennedy, Agnes Pilus, and the Newburgh Free Library staff in the Local History Room—Rita Forrester and Charles Thomas. I am also very grateful to Arthur Nugent, who proofread the text. And of course many thanks to my daughter, Buffey, and her family; my sister, Mary Murphy; my mother, Margaret Tompkins-Dillon; and my husband, Alfred, for living a chaotic life while this book was assembled on our dining room table.

INTRODUCTION

For most of my life, I have had a fascination with Orange Lake. Maybe it stems from the occasional day trips I made there as a child to spend time with friends. The rustic cottages, the bobbing up and down in the cool water to avoid touching the rocky bottom of the lake, the rare rowboat ride around its shores were all new experiences for a young girl from the city of Newburgh.

As a young adult I spent more time there and really began appreciating the beauty of the lake. Later our small family attended picnics, Fourth of July parties, and ice-skating get-togethers at the lake.

So when I was approached by members of the Orange Lake Civic Association many years later and asked to write a book about the lake, I had some very fond memories to look back upon.

As I began to read more about the lake and listen to the stories of its oldest inhabitants, I began to realize that Orange Lake had two histories, one involving its residents, the other its visitors. Both were intertwined to give Orange Lake its unique character.

The first people to call the lake their home were the Native Americans. They took only what they needed to survive from the fertile land and pristine waters, leaving only remnants of their stone tools behind.

As the Europeans came to the lake region, they began to farm the land. Others built and operated mills at the lake and along its tributaries. One enterprising man even began minting coins at the lake after the American Revolution. The area changed little for 100 years. At the end of the 19th century, about 40 hardworking families lived around the lake. They built a one-room school for their children and a church.

Small numbers of visitors had fished and hunted in the area for years. Some used the lake for boating and swimming. Eventually summer bungalows began to appear around the shoreline of the lake, but transportation to and from the lake was by horse or horse and carriage, thus limiting the area's accessibility.

A revolutionary event in the lake's history took place in 1895 when an electric railway, a trolley line, was built from the city of Newburgh waterfront to Walden. It had a stop at Orange Lake. Now access to the lake was only 10¢ away. Residents and visitors began to see the beauty and the opportunities the lake could offer.

The following passage, describing the trolley's entrance into the station at Orange Lake, is from a 1906 advertising brochure published by the trolley company:

> As you first come into view of the lake you may be disappointed as to its size, but, you only see one arm of it. Soon your idea will be changed when a full view is obtained of the various

> bays, coves and inlets, giving you a greater variety of contoured shore line more than is possessed by many larger lakes. Although only four miles of shore line exists you will find this makes up in beauty what it lacks in size. The variety of its outline, the clear water, the bold and wooded shore, the pure and healthy air, make it one of the most attractive spots in New York State.

Imagine the effect such a description had on people who lived 100 years ago and who worked six days a week in factories and lived in congested cities.

To make the lake an even more enticing destination, the trolley company built a 30-acre amusement park at the Orange Lake trolley stop. It was not long before the lake and its amusement park became known as the "Playground of the Hudson Valley." Thousands of people came to the park each year, many from faraway places, and the notoriety of the area grew. The following description of the park was written by an unidentified *Newburgh Telegraph* reporter. He said,

> Orange Lake Amusement Park is another Coney Island, without the froth, the foam, the frankfurters, and the fakes. It does more to spread the fame of Newburgh to remote corners of the world than Washington Headquarters [the first national historic site in the United States, located in Newburgh]. The best part of the resort by the inland sea is that you get full value for your money, a startling departure from the customary summer resort.

In 1908, the amusement park had a 1,200-seat theater, bandstand, dancing pavilion, roller-skating rink, and restaurant. Attractions included a Ferris wheel, a tunnel of love called Ye Olde Mill, a merry-go-round, a scenic railway, an arcade, and a circle swing. There was also an ice-cream stand, candy stand, souvenir shop, and Japanese tearoom.

The park flourished until the mid-1920s when a series of events, including the demise of the trolley and the death of the major park owner Benjamin B. Odell, began the long process that would close the park forever.

The park was dismantled in 1941, and 10 years later, the land was bought and divided into 51 building lots, and homes replaced amusements.

The park was gone, but the beauty of the lake and its many recreational uses continued to draw people to its shores. Sportsmen, especially fishermen and boaters, increased their activity on the lake. The once-private Orange Lake Fish and Game Association opened its membership to sportsmen in three counties in 1946. While the number of the boating clubs at the lake decreased, the use of private craft increased dramatically.

By the late 1950s and early 1960s, construction of new homes on the east and west side of the lake began in earnest. Residents also began to winterize and enlarge their cottages, making them into year-round homes. Some of this construction was done by former amusement park and cottage visitors who never forgot their happy days at the lake.

This influx of people, however, caused a threat to the lake's very existence. A "mystery weed," as it was called in the newspapers of the 1950s, began taking over the lake. After many years of study by environmentalists and scientists, it was determined that phosphates and nitrates were leeching into Orange Lake, causing it to fill in at an alarming rate. The water was becoming polluted and fish kills were frequent.

A group of lake residents formed the Orange Lake Civic Association in 1952 to combat this and other issues. They were finally successful in their major goal of having a centralized sewer and water system brought to the majority of homeowners in 1992. This, and additional measures taken by residents, has assured that the improved quality of lake waters will remain for many years to come.

One

Early History, Agriculture, and Industry

The approximately 440 acres of Orange Lake waters lie in the northwestern section of the town of Newburgh. The lake is fed by small internal springs and small streams on the north end that flow into it. Its outlet is the Quassaick Creek leading to the Hudson River.

Historians believe the Native Americans called Orange Lake, Oussuk, meaning "stony pond." Later the Dutch called the lake Binnin, translated as "water between other waters" or "water within land." Mouse was the lake's next name for a short while, being named for a man of the same name who settled there.

Subsequently the name Machin's Pond was used, named for the man who had mills on the lake, including the famous coinage mint. It was then called Big Pond to distinguish it from a smaller pond in the area known as Little Pond. In the 1830s, the Reverend James B. Wilson, a minister who resided in the area for over 35 years, began calling the body of water Orange Lake. There has been speculation on why he named it that, and it is said that local residents objected at the time, nevertheless, the name took hold and remains the name of the lake today.

The land surrounding the lake was originally part of the lands purchased by Gov. Thomas Dongan from the Native Americans in 1684. The land was subsequently divided into smaller patents and eventually into smaller tracts of land. Many of these lands became farms, primarily dairy farms that surrounded the lake and adjoining hamlets.

The waterpower the lake generated made it a natural for the operation of mills. As stated, Capt. Thomas Machin had a sawmill, a gristmill, and finally a coinage mill right at the beginning of the lake's outlet. Because the lake is 800 feet above sea level, it powered many varied mills as it made its way to the Hudson River. One of the earliest that had an important connection to Orange Lake was the Newburgh Bleachery. This large mill was controlled by the Chadwick family for most of its history.

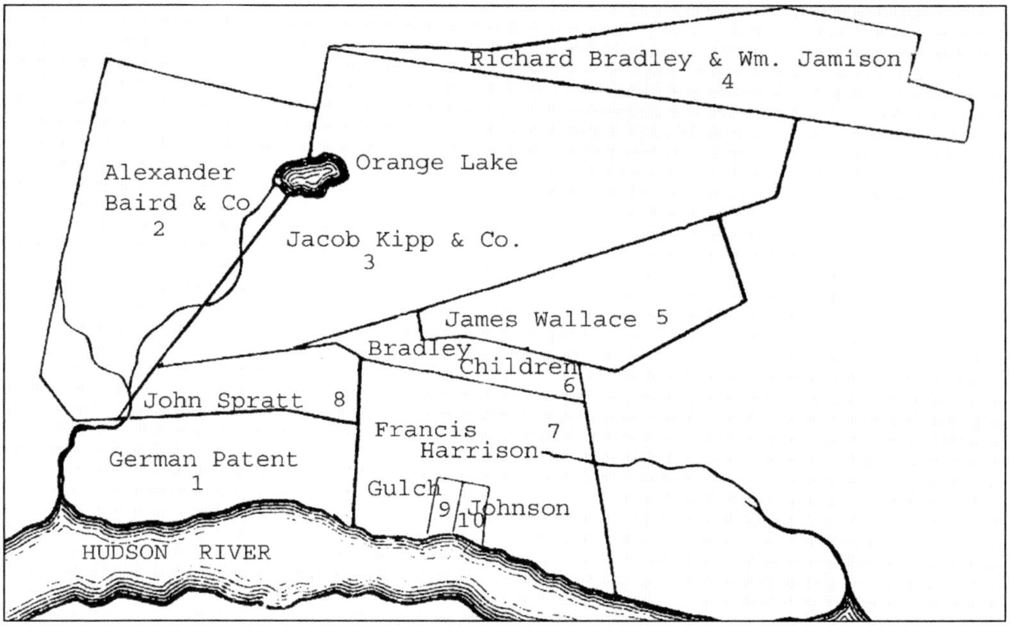

This is an early patent map of the area in 1800. These lands and others were purchased from the Native Americans by Gov. Thomas Dongan in 1684. That patent was annulled in 1699, and for the next 78 years, the land was divided into smaller patents. The lands approximate the current city and town of Newburgh. (Courtesy of the Historical Society of Newburgh Bay and the Highlands.)

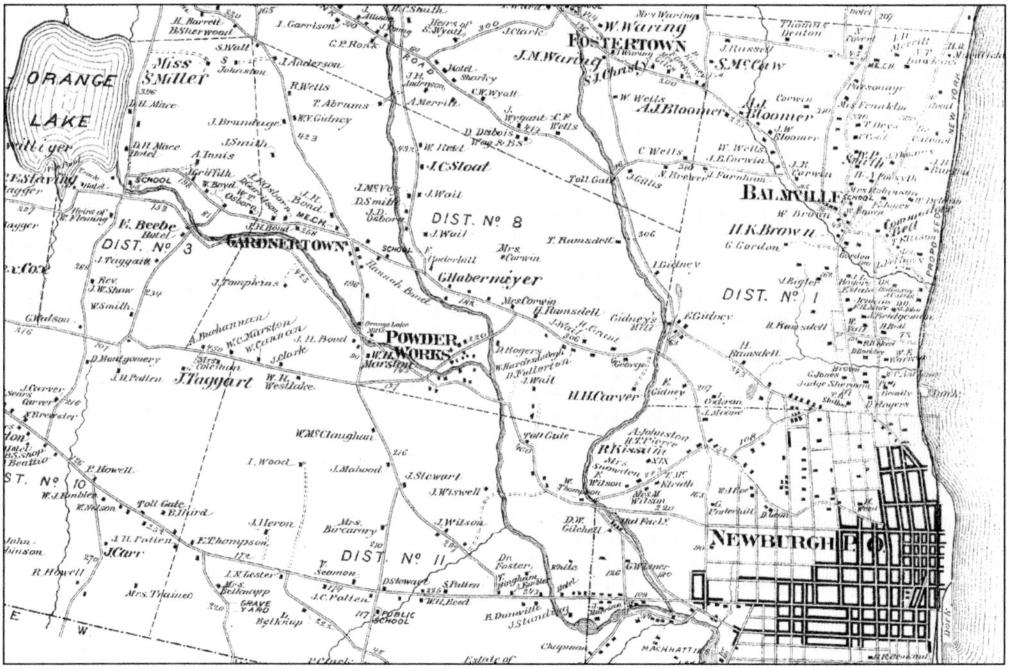

Although this map's orientation is north to south, it depicts the same lands as the patent map above. Many of the properties and locations described in this book can be found on this 1875 map. (Courtesy of the Historical Society of Newburgh Bay and the Highlands.)

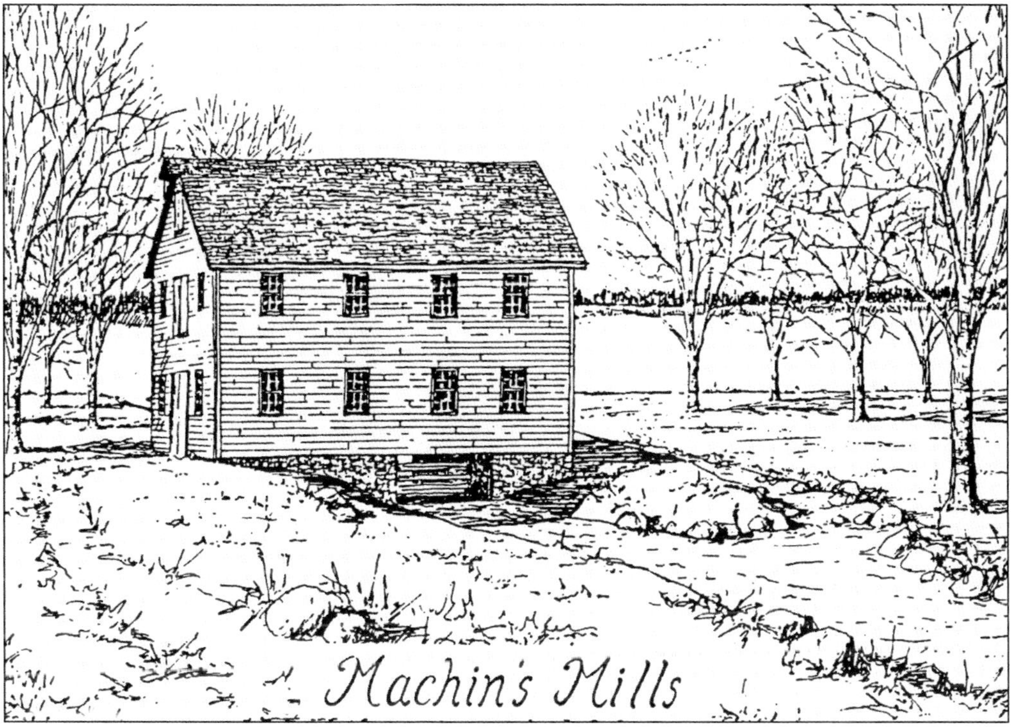

Capt. Thomas Machin, a Revolutionary War hero, settled on the eastern shore of Great Pond, now Orange Lake, in 1783. He built a grist- and sawmill that was converted into a coinage mint in 1787. Many coins were minted there; most were counterfeits. (Courtesy of the Historical Society of Newburgh Bay and the Highlands.)

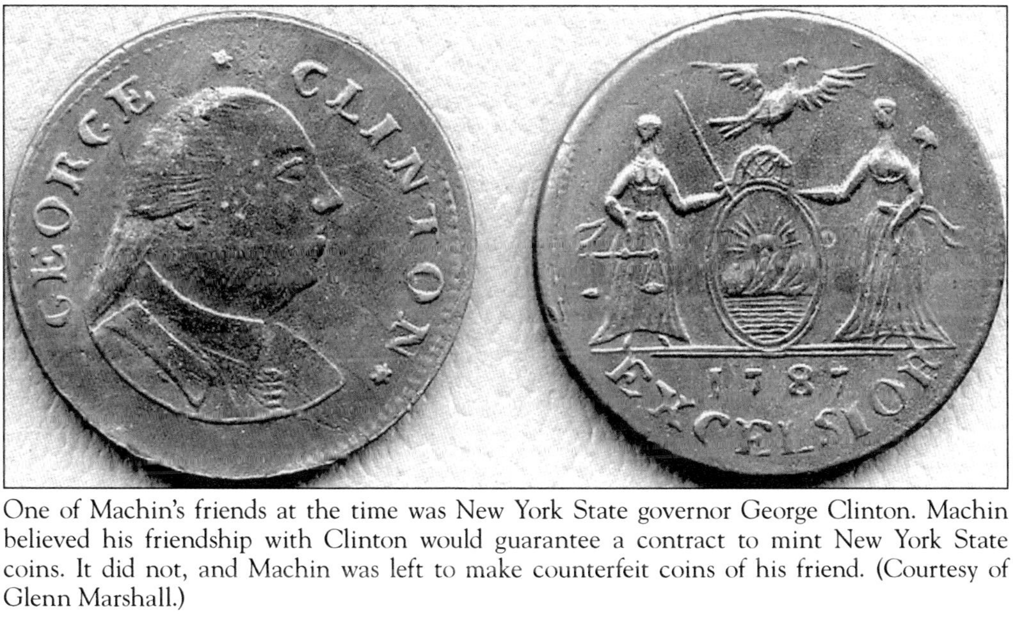

One of Machin's friends at the time was New York State governor George Clinton. Machin believed his friendship with Clinton would guarantee a contract to mint New York State coins. It did not, and Machin was left to make counterfeit coins of his friend. (Courtesy of Glenn Marshall.)

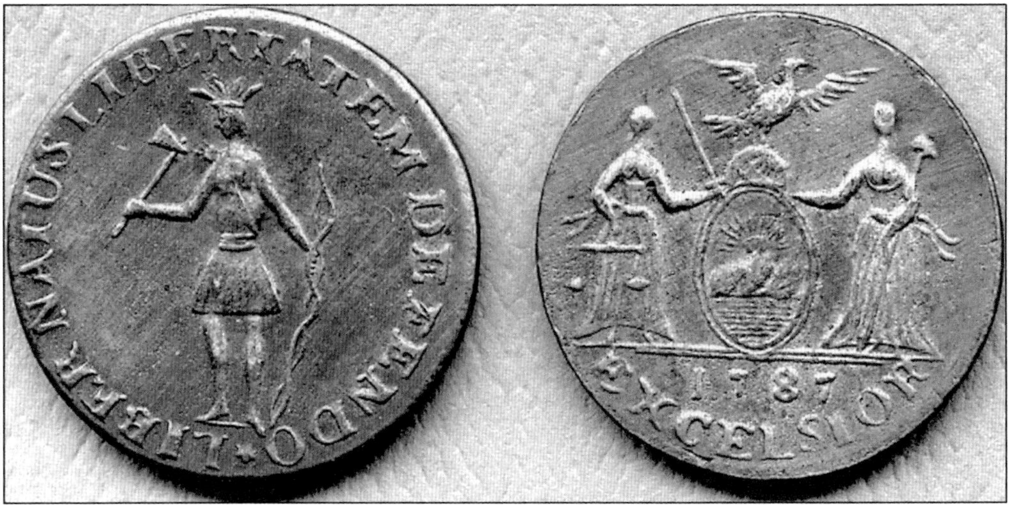

The obverse of this counterfeit New York coin bears the figure of a Native American figure with the legend meaning "born free, I defend liberty." The reverse is the same as the George Clinton coin and shows the New York State seal and its motto, Excelsior, meaning "ever higher." (Courtesy of Glenn Marshall.)

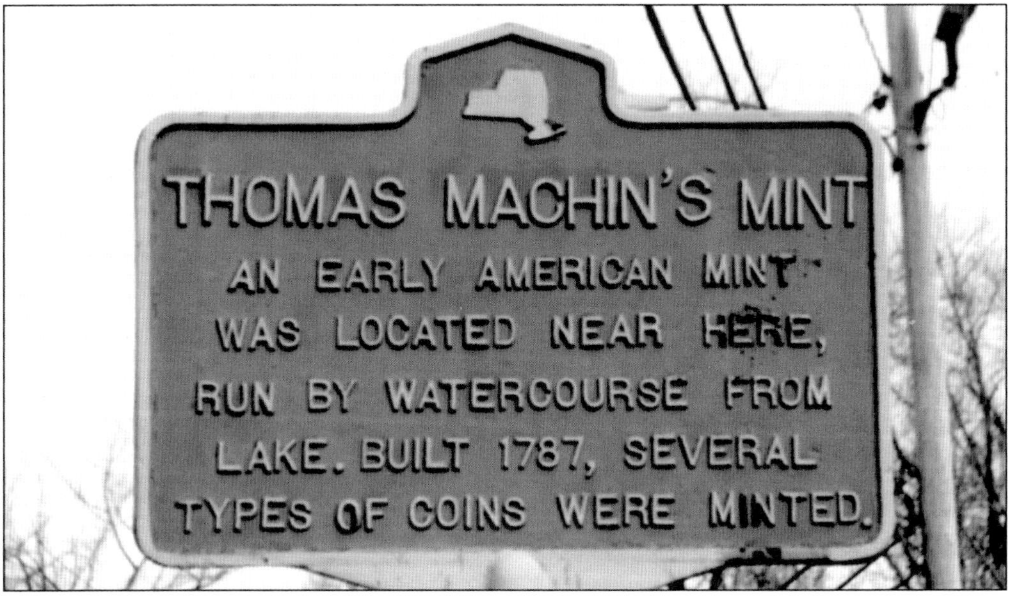

This historic marker is on Lakeside Road, just off Route 52. It shows the approximate site of Capt. Thomas Machin's mint. The sign was erected by Orange County historian Colin Faulds and his assistant, the author, in the early 1980s. (Author's collection.)

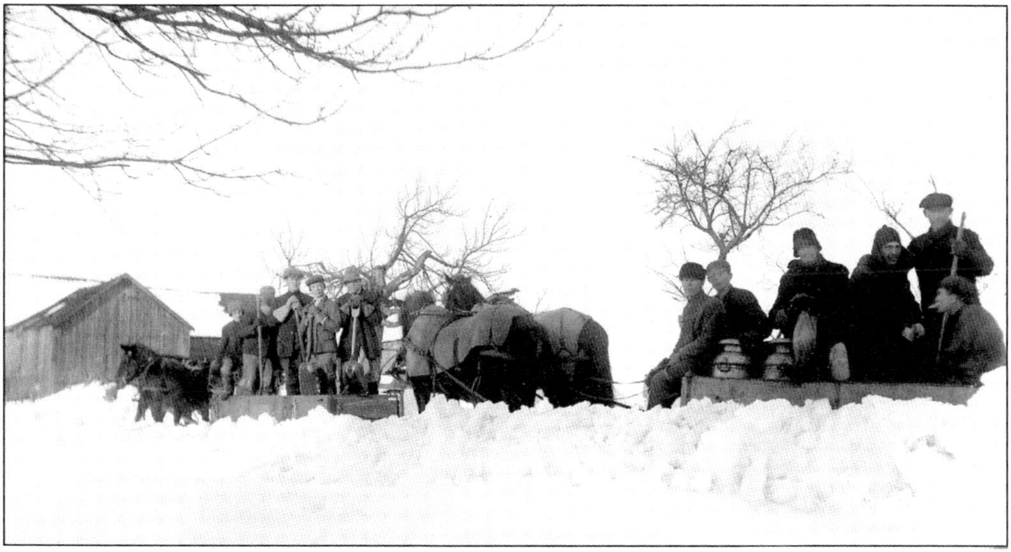

This glass negative is titled "Day of Storm. Blizzard, March 1, 1914" and was owned by Clarence Martin. The photograph shows members of Martin's family and farmworkers who had battled the elements to clear the roads, milk the cows, and bring the milk to Newburgh during the long storm. (Courtesy of the Historical Society of Newburgh Bay and the Highlands.)

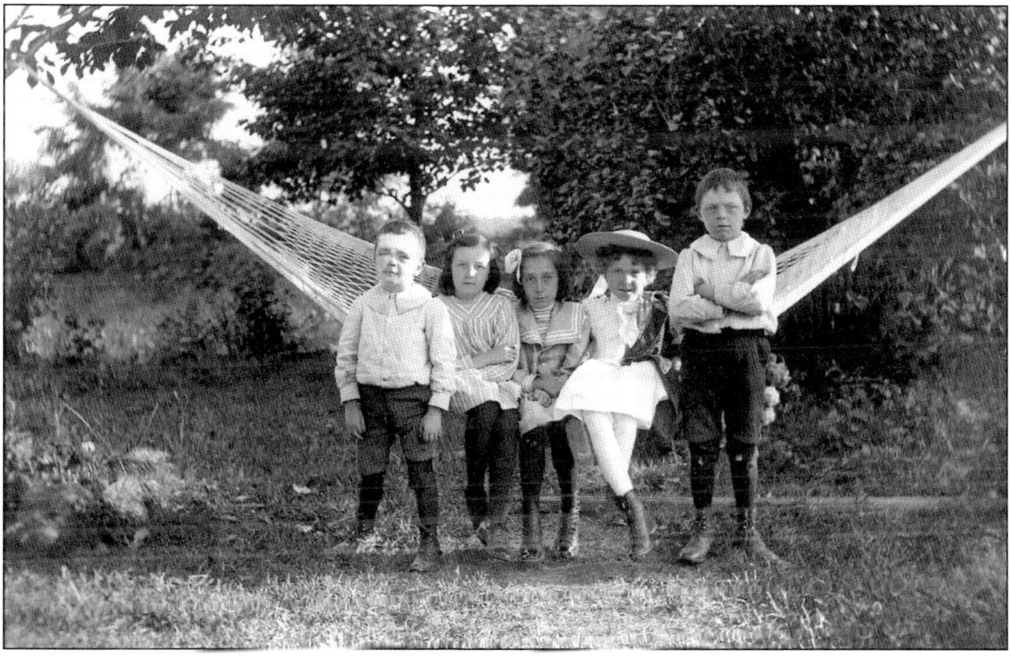

In 1870, Clarence Martin's grandfather bought the only property on the west side of the lake that was easily accessible to the water. The family farmed the land for almost 80 years before selling it in the 1940s. The children from left to right are Harold Martin, Estelle Martin, family friends Dollie Kipp and Mabel Kipp, and Clarence Martin. (Courtesy of the Historical Society of Newburgh Bay and the Highlands.)

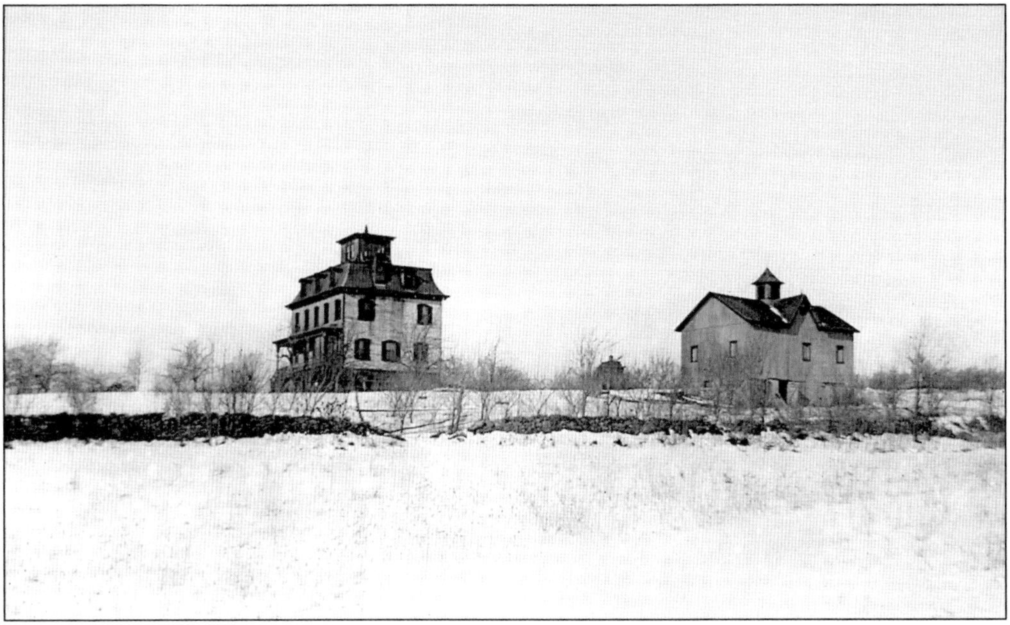

Harold Martin owned this farm next to Clarence Martin's on the same property their grandfather owned. The extant farmhouse can be seen in the background of many postcards, photographs, and some paintings, most notably in a painting by Thomas Pope that is owned by a lake resident. (Courtesy of the Historical Society of Newburgh Bay and the Highlands.)

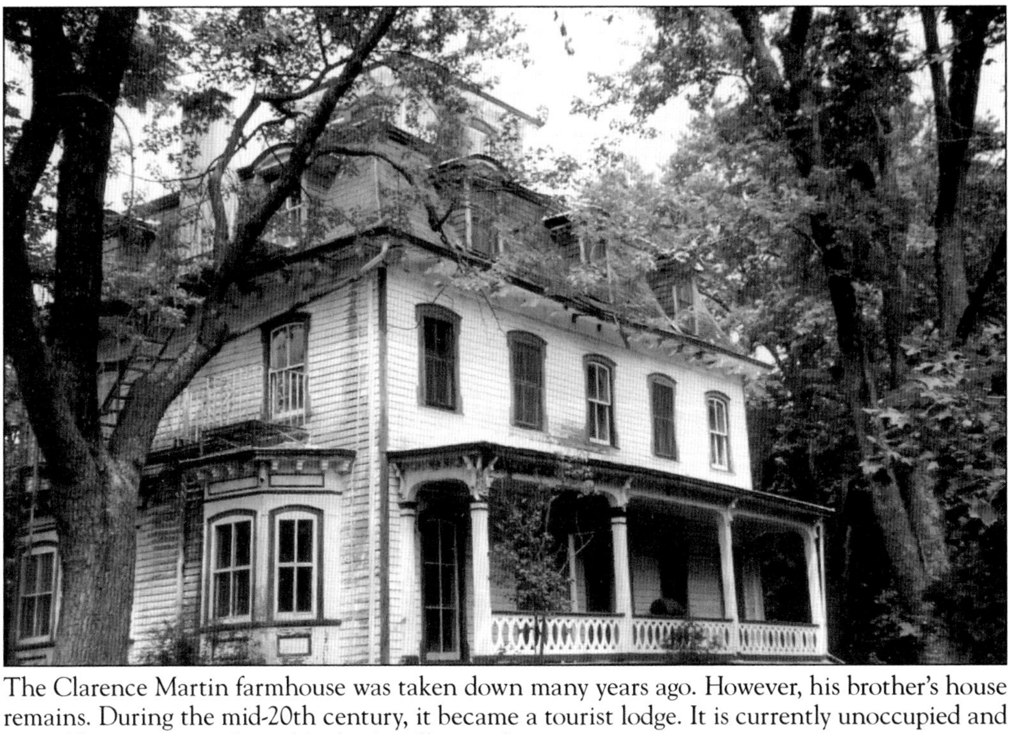

The Clarence Martin farmhouse was taken down many years ago. However, his brother's house remains. During the mid-20th century, it became a tourist lodge. It is currently unoccupied and owned by an area resident. (Author's collection.)

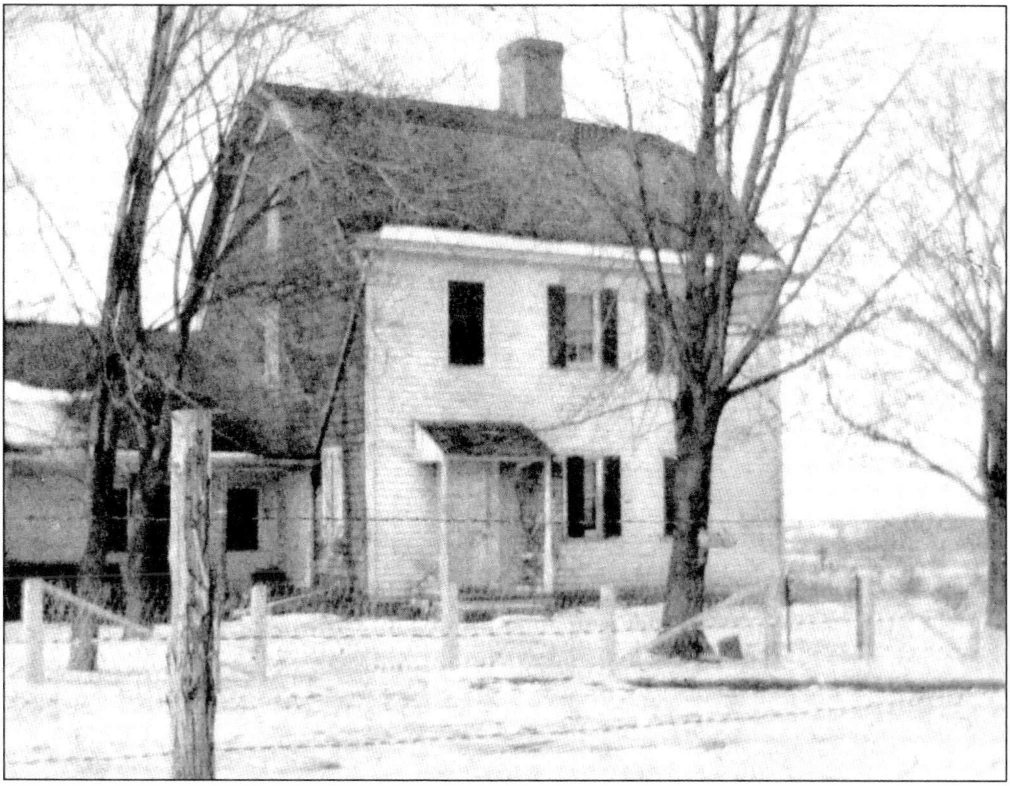

David Patton Sr. bought this farmhouse in 1887 on the top of Meadow Hill. An immigrant from Ireland, he worked for the Delano family in Balmville for 15 years to pay for the run-down farmhouse and farm. The home was enlarged over the years and is still standing. The farm became the original Meadow Hill Housing Development in 1966. (Courtesy of Ilene Patton Siegman.)

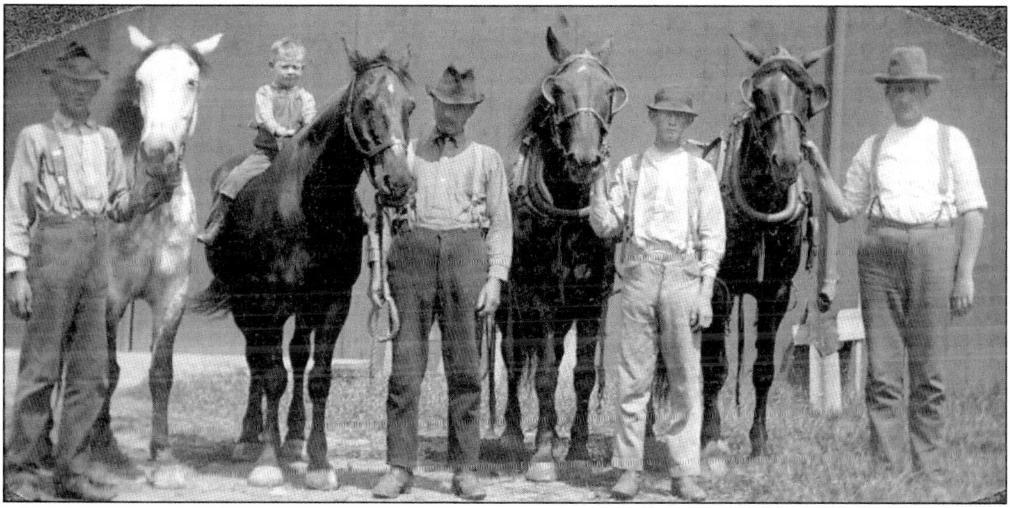

This early photograph of some of the members of the Patton family shows, from left to right, David Patton Jr., Jimmy Patton on the horse, David Patton Sr., and two unidentified farmhands. The Patton farm became very successful because of the hard work of all the family members. (Courtesy of Ilene Patton Siegman.)

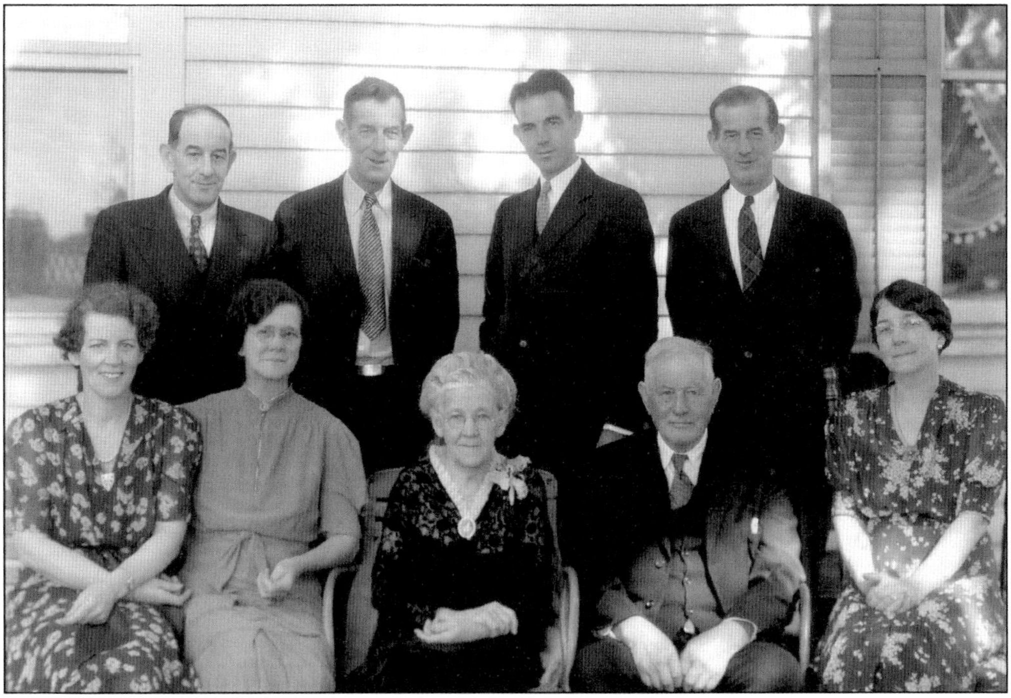

Mary and David Patton Sr. celebrated their wedding anniversary at their home with family and friends in 1938. From left to right are (first row) daughters Jennie and Velma, mother Mary, father David, and daughter Mary; (second row) sons Charles, Warren, William, and James. (Courtesy of Ilene Patton Siegman.)

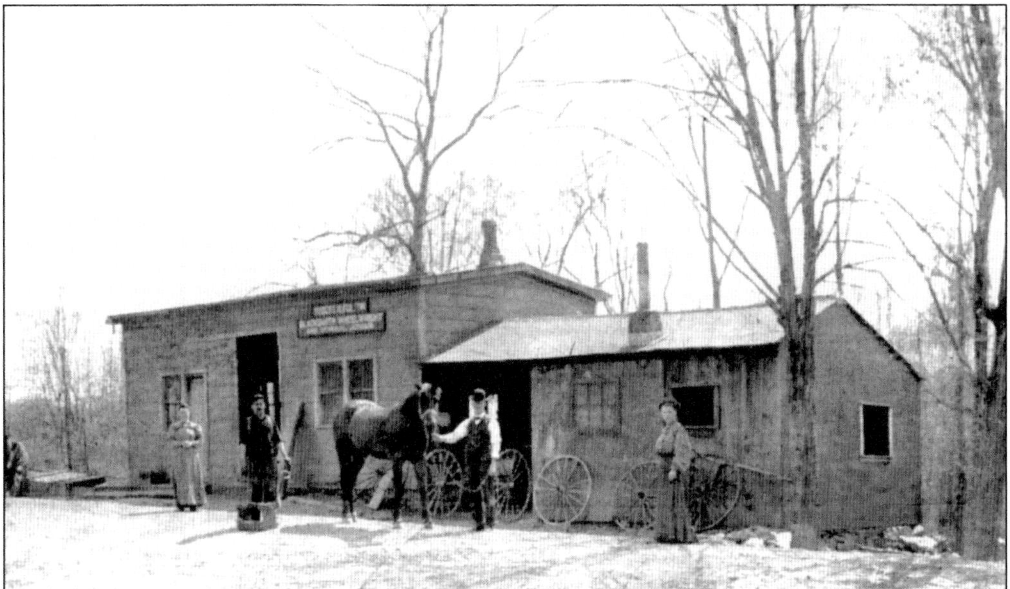

Blacksmiths were essential members of the community in farming areas up until the 1930s. This shop was located at the north end of the lake in a place known as Leptondale. It provided all the services that area farmers and residents needed. (Courtesy of David McDermott.)

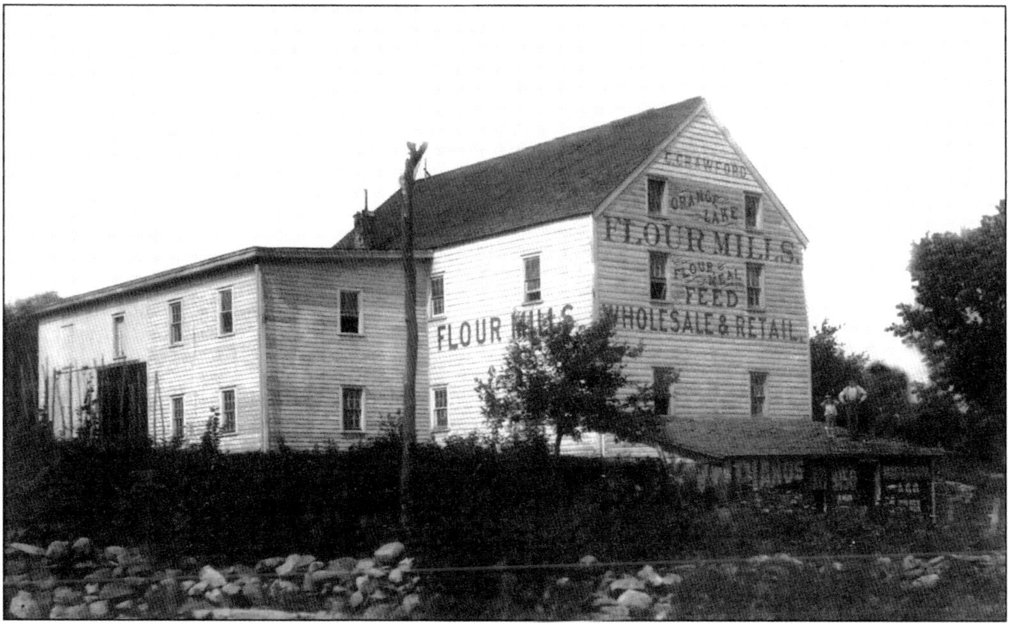

The Orange Lake Flour Mills were located at the northeast corner of South Plank Road (Route 52) and Union Avenue. They were powered by the outlet stream from Orange Lake. The mills not only processed grain for flour but provided feed for dairy farmers and others residents who raised small quantities of animals for food. (Courtesy of Paul Yablonsky.)

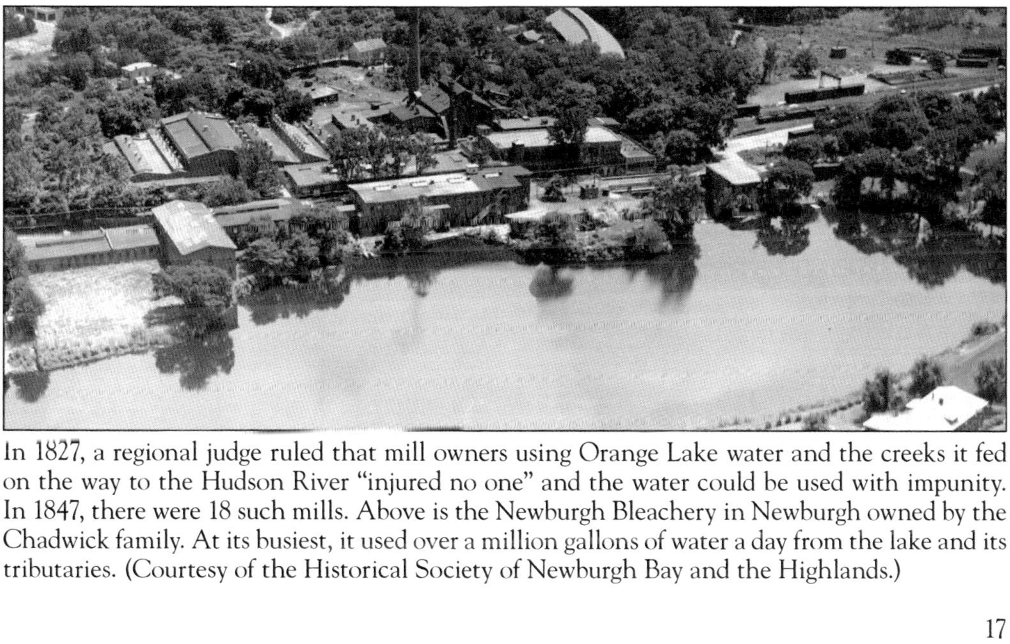

In 1827, a regional judge ruled that mill owners using Orange Lake water and the creeks it fed on the way to the Hudson River "injured no one" and the water could be used with impunity. In 1847, there were 18 such mills. Above is the Newburgh Bleachery in Newburgh owned by the Chadwick family. At its busiest, it used over a million gallons of water a day from the lake and its tributaries. (Courtesy of the Historical Society of Newburgh Bay and the Highlands.)

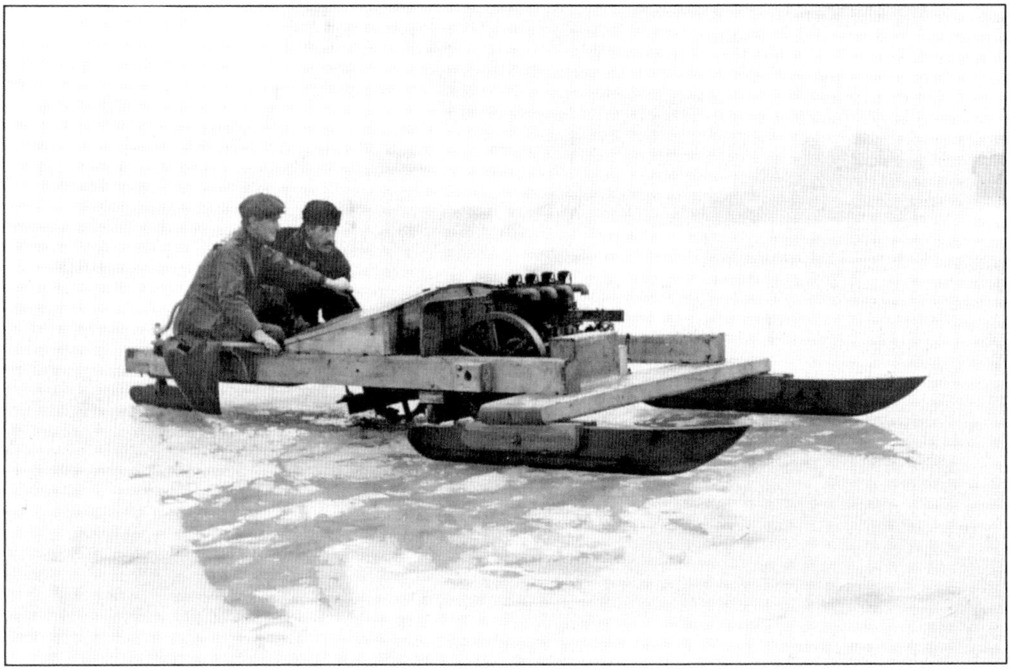

Ice was essential to the residents and summer visitors of the lake area. The Harris family on Route 52 was one the earliest families to harvest ice from their pond. The majority of ice-cutting operations in the late 1900s were small with ice being hand cut using large saws. This picture shows a motorized version of the ice harvest in the 1920s on Orange Lake. (Courtesy of Marguerite Harris McDermott.)

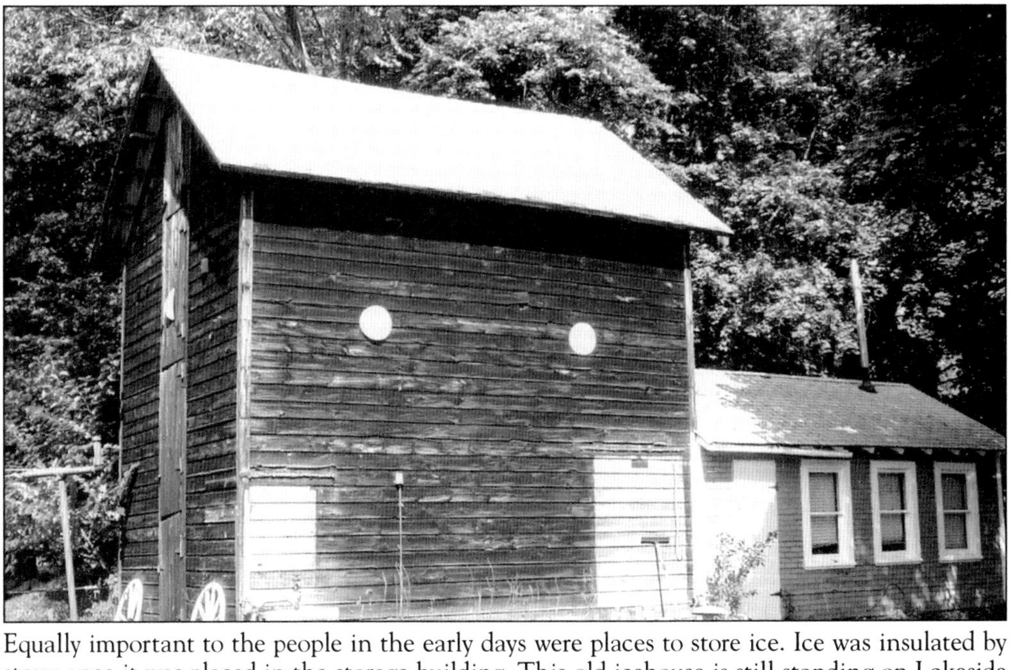

Equally important to the people in the early days were places to store ice. Ice was insulated by straw once it was placed in the storage building. This old icehouse is still standing on Lakeside Road behind the former post office. (Courtesy of Arthur Nugent.)

Two

Getting There

Orange Lake was an idyllic but remote location in the latter part of the 19th century and the early 20th century. Cottage owners, renters, tent and camp visitors, sportsmen, hotel guests, and amusement park revelers had to plan their transportation modes and routes carefully. Until the coming of the trolley line that ran from Newburgh to Walden and back, overland routes were by horse or horse and carriage.

Daily visitors and those who stayed for longer periods usually came to the city of Newburgh to begin their journey to the lake. Some of them took Dayline boats. Many of them were named for famous people. They were the *Robert Fulton*, the *Alexander Hamilton*, and the *Benjamin B. Odell*. They traveled back and forth between New York City and Albany with stops at various locations on the Hudson River. The New York Central West Shore line also stopped at Newburgh. Passengers from the ships or trains would then board trolleys at the riverfront to take them to Orange Lake.

The Newburgh and Walden Electric Railway that stopped at Orange Lake was completed in 1895. In the beginning of the 20th century, a very popular phenomenon called the trolley park was conceived. These were amusement parks constructed along trolley routes to boost ridership and freight revenues for trolley companies. Orange Lake Amusement Park was one of the most successful of these.

By 1926, strikes and other problems beset the trolley company, and it was forced to close operations. A bus company took over the trolley route but did not run as frequently.

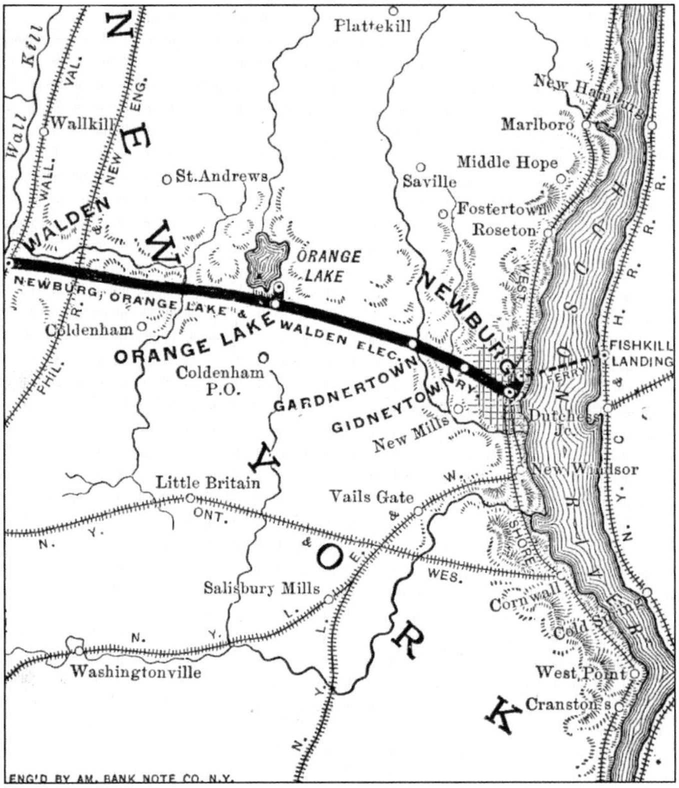

This map shows the route of the Orange Lake and Walden Electric Railway, better known as "the trolley," that took people to Orange Lake. Also pictured are the West Shore rail lines and the ferry connection from the east side of the river at Fishkill/Beacon that took thousands to Orange Lake each year. (Courtesy of Paul Yablonsky.)

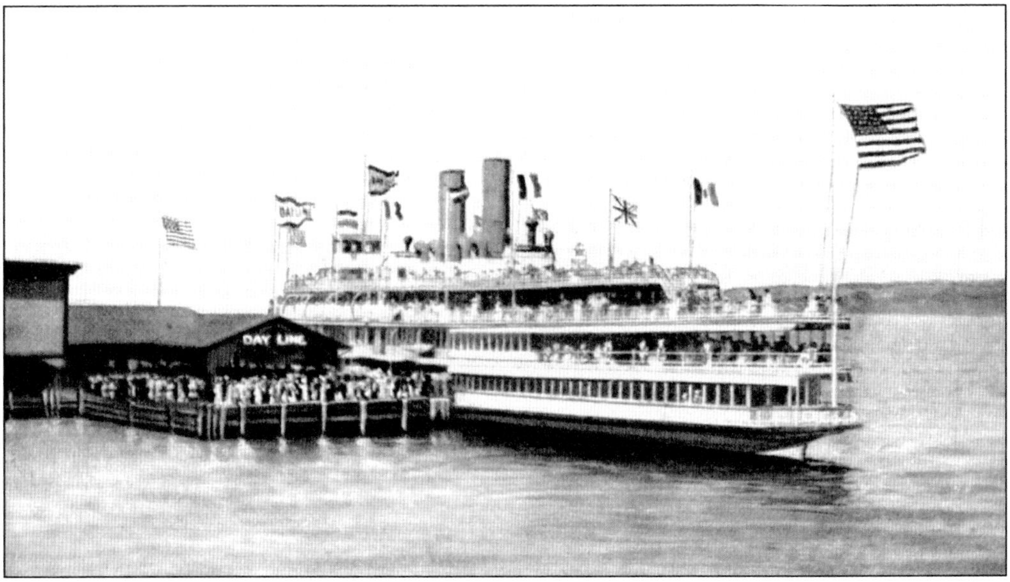

Passengers disembark from the Dayline at the Newburgh pier while others wait to board and go elsewhere. Six days a week (excluding Sundays) the Dayline boats made excursions from New York City to Albany and back, carrying as many as 8,000 passengers a day. Many visitors and summer residents made their way to Orange Lake this way. (Author's collection.)

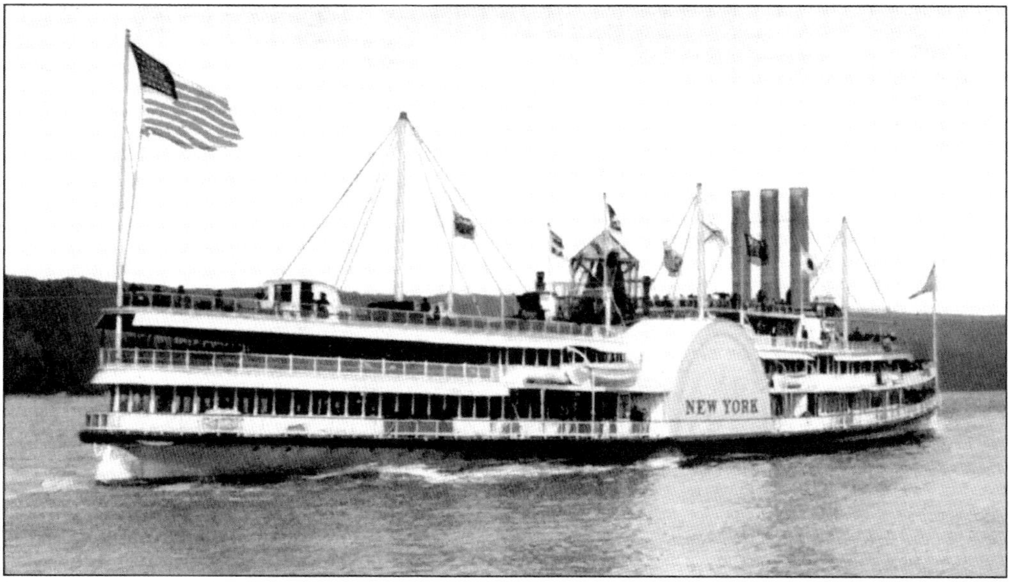

One of the first Dayliners to bring crowds from faraway places to go to Orange Lake Amusement Park was the *New York*. Built in 1887, the *New York* burned at Newburgh in a spectacular fire in the summer of 1908. (Author's collection.)

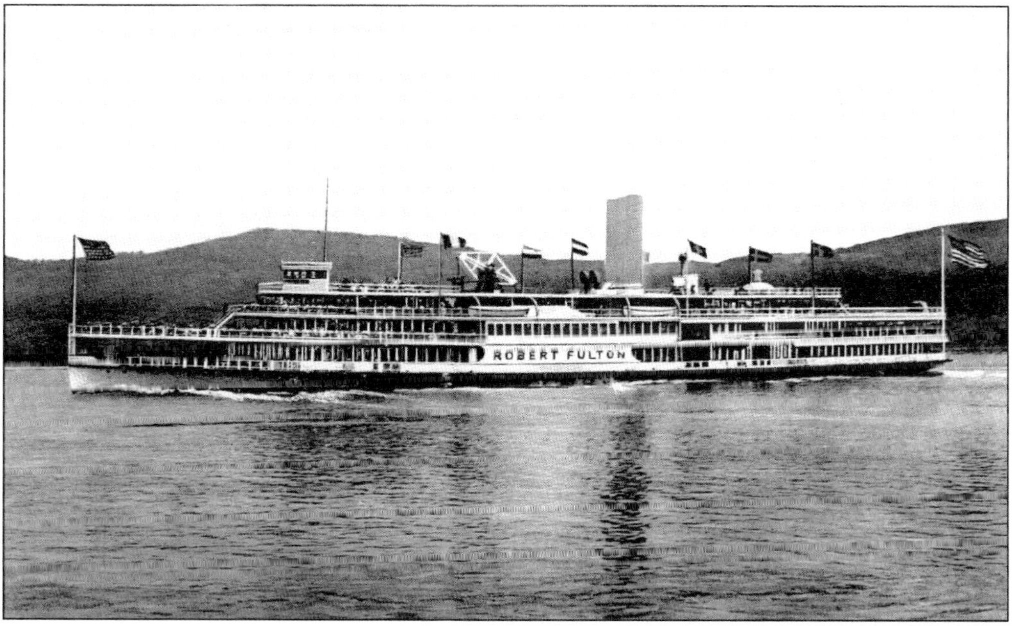

The *Robert Fulton* was a side-wheeler built from salvaged pieces of the *New York*. Licensed to hold 4,000 passengers, the ship was a favorite of New York City visitors to Orange Lake. (Author's collection.)

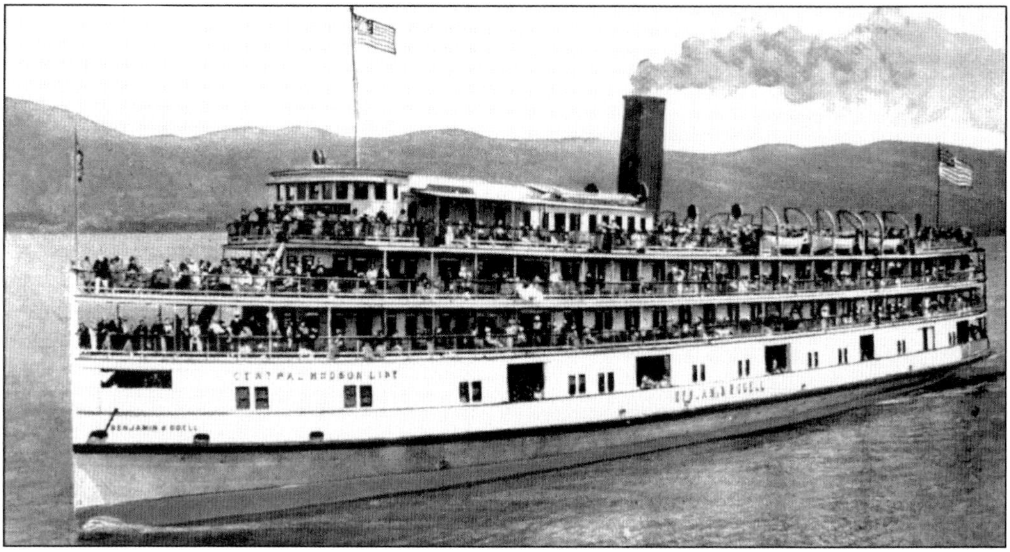

Benjamin B. Odell was instrumental in organizing and operating the Central Hudson Steamship Company, which had a fleet of 10 boats. The boat above was named for Odell and carried passengers to his trolley to visit his amusement park. He was a legendary 20th-century entrepreneur. (Courtesy of the Historical Society of Newburgh Bay and the Highlands.)

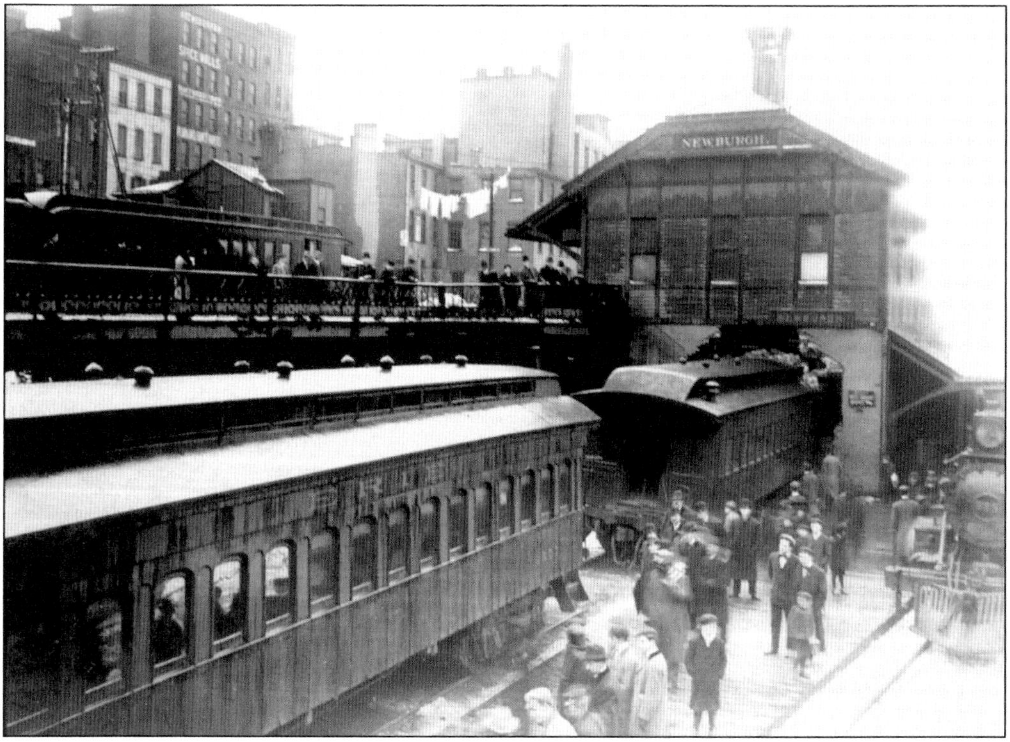

Passenger trains on the New York Central West Shore Railroad brought thousands of people to Newburgh daily. Many were destined for Orange Lake in the summer. In the winter these trains not only carried people but also iceboats from many places to compete in races on a frozen Orange Lake. (Courtesy of Paul Yablonsky.)

Former New York State governor Benjamin B. Odell, a Newburgh native and, as mentioned, a very successful businessman, acquired Orange Lake Traction Company (the former Orange Lake and Walden Traction Company) in 1906. His goals were to improve service on the trolleys and create the finest amusement park in the northeast United States. (Courtesy of the Historical Society of Newburgh Bay and the Highlands.)

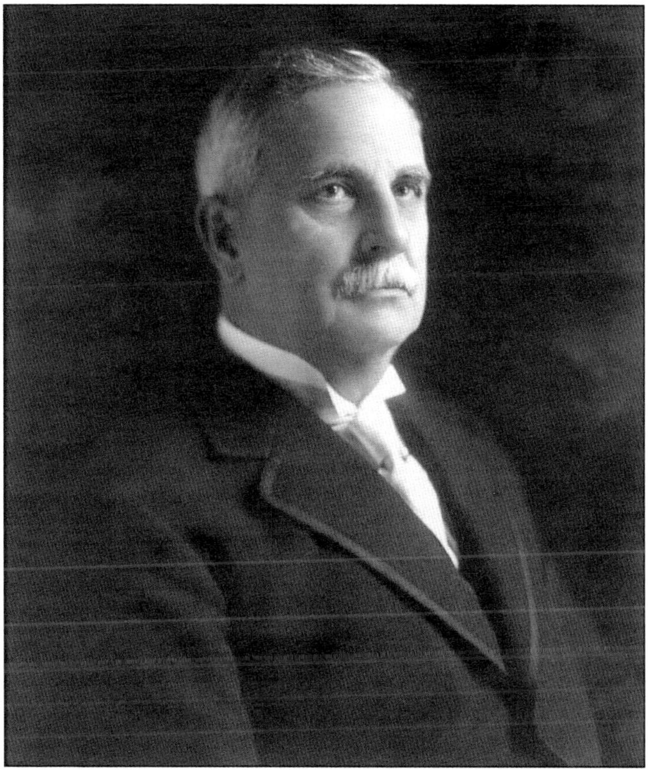

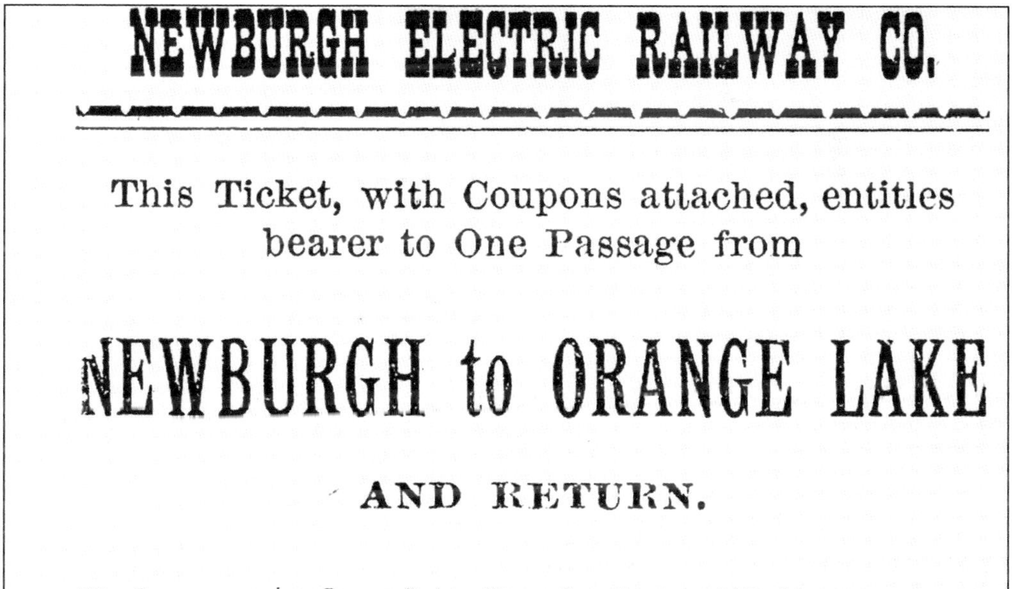

NEWBURGH ELECTRIC RAILWAY CO.

This Ticket, with Coupons attached, entitles bearer to One Passage from

NEWBURGH to ORANGE LAKE

AND RETURN.

To be surrendered to Conductor with last coupon

This is one-half of the ticket one passenger used to get to Orange Lake Amusement Park. This section was to be used for the return trip to Newburgh. Did the ticket holder become a permanent resident of Orange Lake? (Courtesy of Walter Whitehill.)

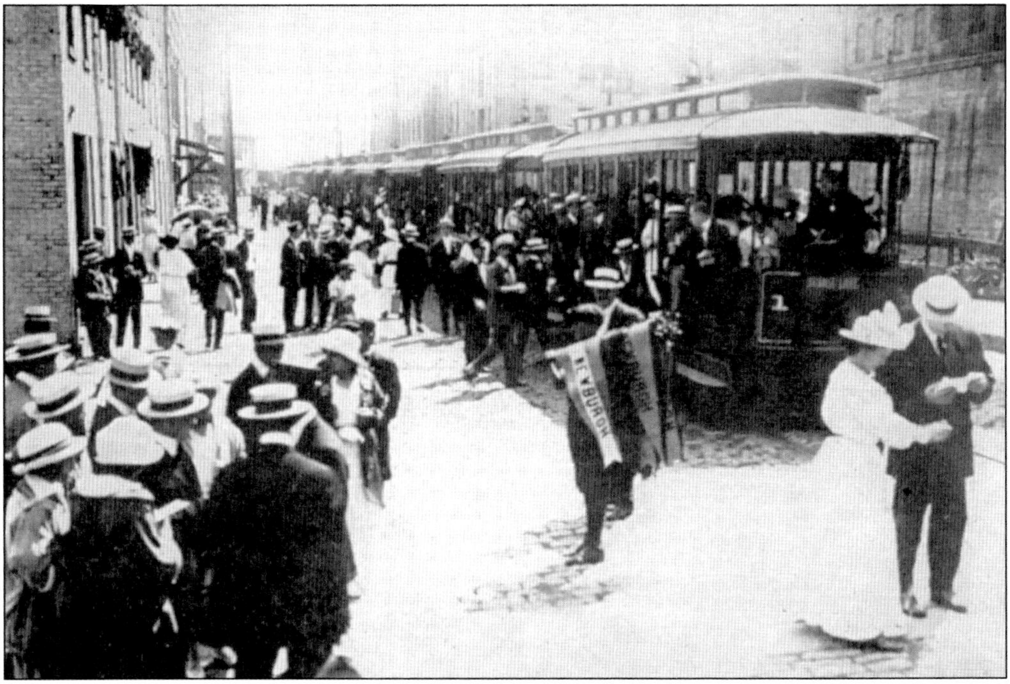

In this photograph, people are boarding the trolley at South Water Street and First Street on the Newburgh waterfront to travel to Orange Lake Amusement Park. Some have come from the New York Central train station (back, far left) while others have disembarked from the Dayliners, whose docks were slightly north of the buildings on the left. (Courtesy of Dennis Collins.)

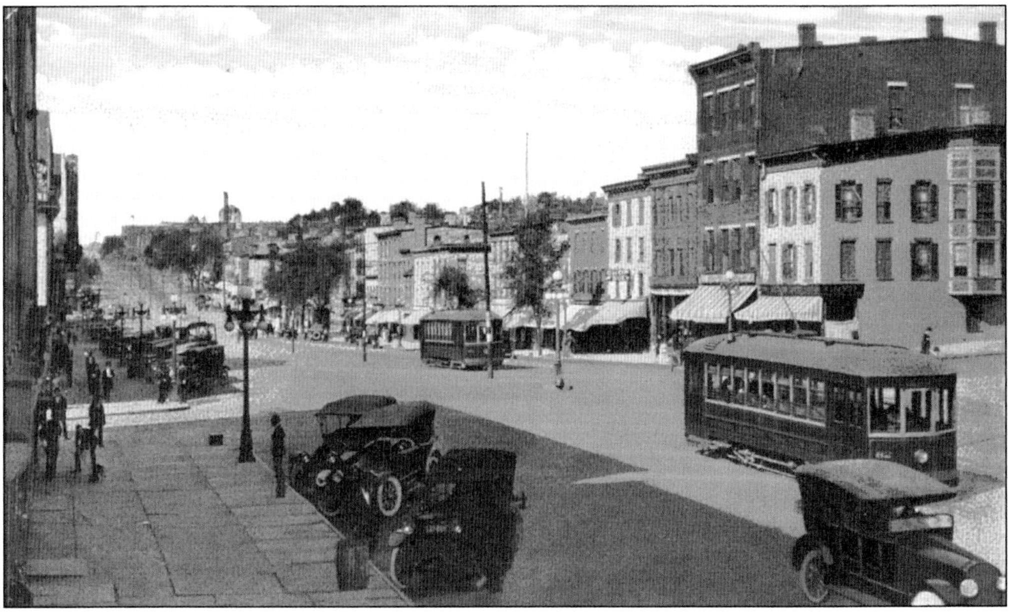

The trolley is seen here edging up the hilly waterfront to enter Broadway in Newburgh. From there it traveled to a switch station at Broadway and Wisner Avenue, eventually making its way to South Plank Road where it continued on Route 52 to Orange Lake Amusement Park in the town of Newburgh. (Author's collection.)

Erven Whitaker, pictured here, was a railroad man who was brought to Newburgh with his crew to build the new Orange County Traction route to Orange Lake and Walden. After completion, he became the chief dispatcher for the entire trolley system. In this advertisement photograph, he is dressed as tillerman. (Courtesy of Elizabeth McKean, City of Newburgh Records Management Office.)

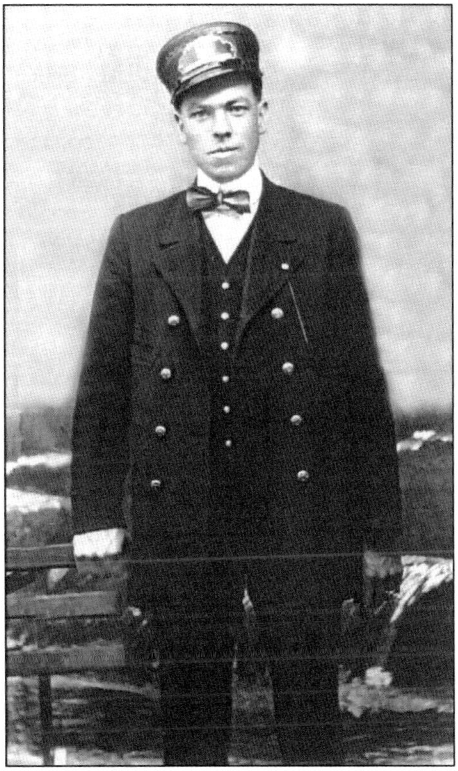

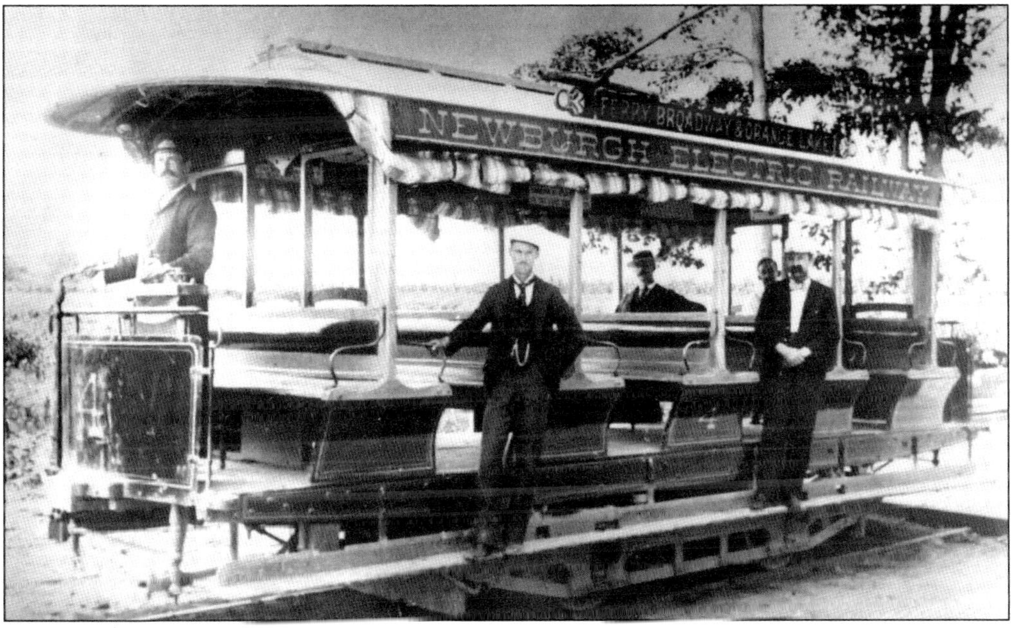

This posed photograph was used in many trolley advertisements and in amusement park literature before World War I. At the time, many newspapers, among them the *Newburgh Telegraph*, described crowded trolleys with passengers clinging to side rails and grounding themselves on sideboards as they made their way to the Orange Lake park. (Courtesy of the Historical Society of Newburgh Bay and the Highlands.)

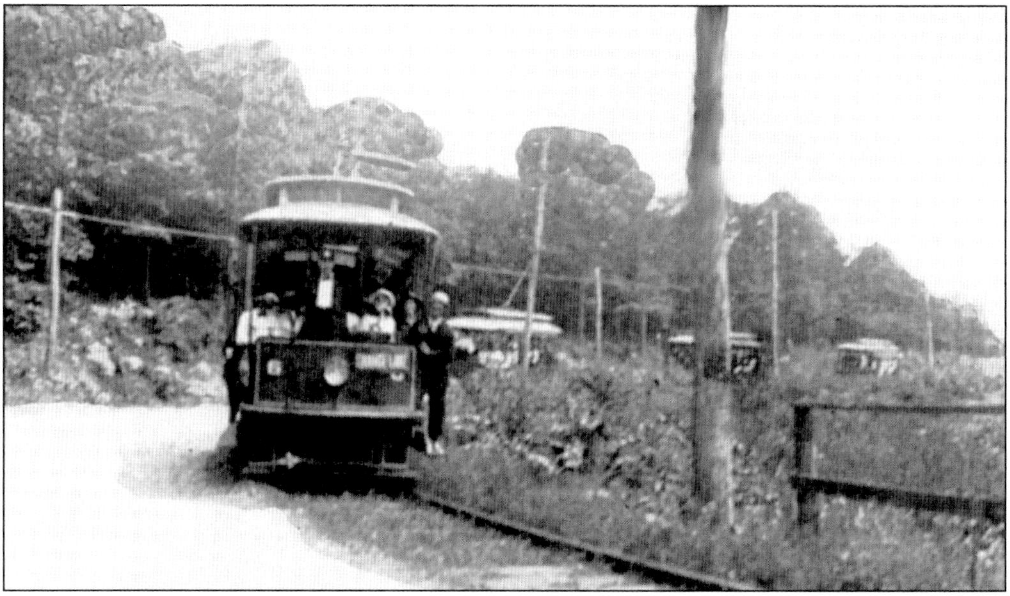

The trolley car rounds a bend in the area known today as Winona Lake as it makes it way west toward Orange Lake and Walden. There were no homes in that area then. Winona Lake is a small swamp at the right of the photograph. The lake was created in the 1930s when the larger swamp on the left was drained and cut through to the dug-out smaller swamp. (Courtesy of the Historical Society of Newburgh Bay and the Highlands.)

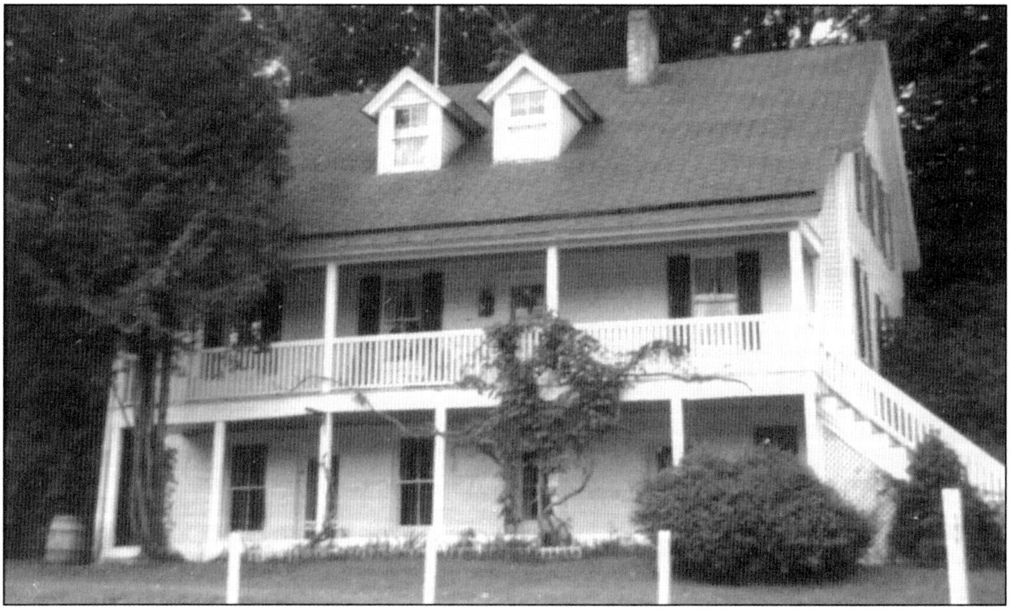

For most of its history, this building on Route 52 was known as the Half-Way House because it was an inn and watering hole located about halfway between Newburgh and Walden. Being along the trolley route, it was rumored that many passengers on the way to the amusement park often stopped here for a beer or two, sometimes taking a later trolley to the park, often just returning home after too long a stay at the house. (Courtesy of the Historical Society of Newburgh Bay and the Highlands.)

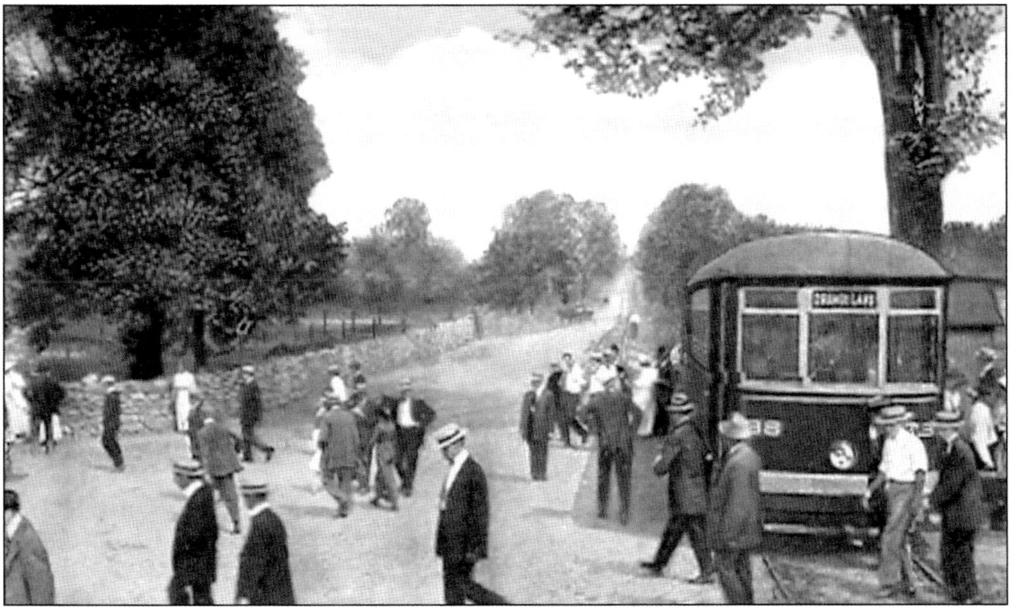

Amusement seekers are shown leaving the trolleys and walking the short distance to the park's entrance in this late-1920s postcard view. Most people always wore their Sunday best to the park, as was the custom at the time. (Author's collection.)

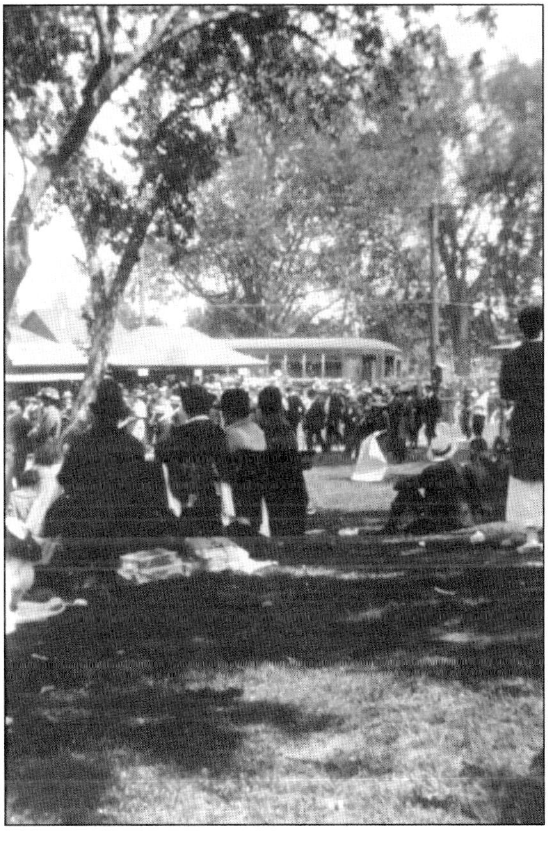

Overcrowding on the trolleys and at the park entrance were common occurrences on busy weekends. Extra trolleys were put on as demand increased but were often insufficient to handle the crowds. Likewise the park entrance was jammed on many of these weekends. This photograph shows the difficulty amusement goers encountered at the park gate. (Courtesy of Sharon Nichols Formato.)

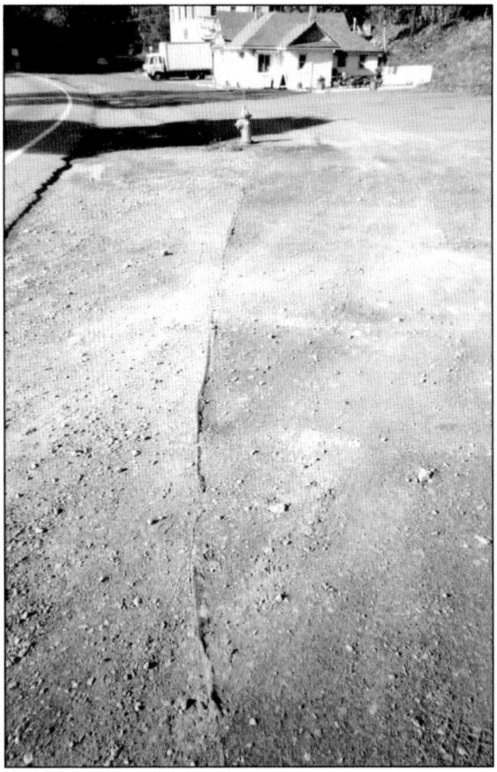

By 1926, the trolley ceased operations and the car became the popular mode of transportation. However, some vestiges of the trolley remain. In 2001, when roadwork was being done on Route 52, George Linton snapped this picture of the remaining tracks in the Winona Lake area. (Courtesy of George Linton.)

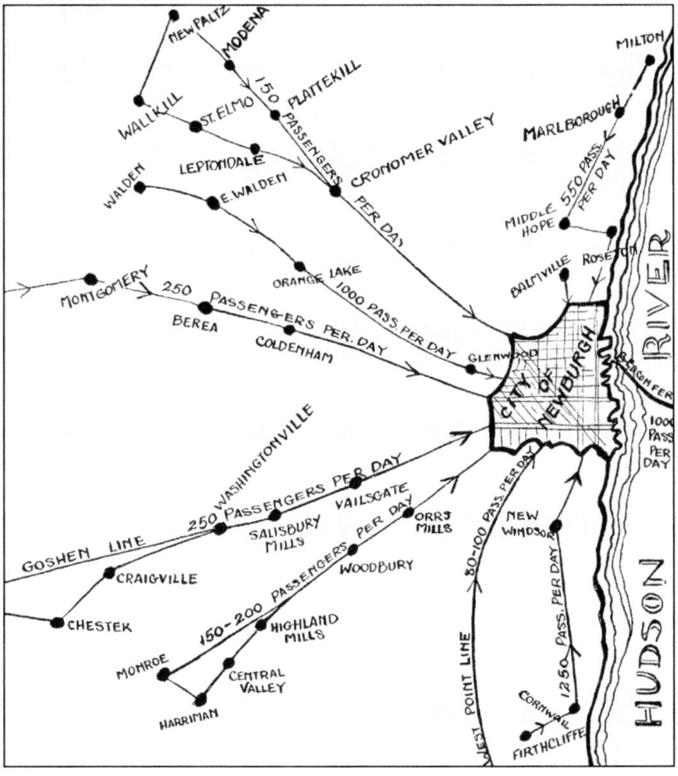

For those people who could not afford a car, buses replaced the trolley. This map of the bus routes shows the average number of passengers who rode the bus to their destination each day. (Courtesy of Walter Whitehill.)

Three

Schools, Churches, and the Fire Department

The one-room Orange Lake School was 25 feet by 25 feet and had wooden desks, a woodstove, and two outhouses, one for boys and one for girls.

Orange Lake School opened its doors for the first time in 1849. It is not known how many students attended nor their genders. What is known is that there were eight grades in the school, and the children, if they were needed at home, did not have to attend. They were, however, expected to know any work they missed.

No major improvements were made to the building until about 103 years later, in 1952, when running water and indoor sanitary facilities were installed. The building housed kindergarten through sixth grade, although some children attended classes in the firehouse next door in the 1950s. After a vote to merge with the Newburgh City School District in 1963, the school closed and was sold.

Religious institutions were very important to citizens in the area. The Gardnertown Methodist Church was the earliest of these with its foundations being established in 1788 when George Stanton, a layman, organized classes in Methodism in local homes. In 1825, a church was established, and in 1858, the present church was built. A fellowship hall was added in 1957.

Roman Catholics in the area had to rely on a priest to come to Orange Lake from Walden to say mass on residents' front porches before the owner of O'Malley's Hotel gave them an old icehouse that was converted into a chapel. In the 1930s, Our Lady of the Lake Chapel was built and continues to serve the spiritual needs of Catholics in the area.

The Dan Leghorn Engine Company has a long and proud history of service to the lake community. Begun as a volunteer fire brigade in the early 1900s, it became the Orange Lake Fire Company in 1935.

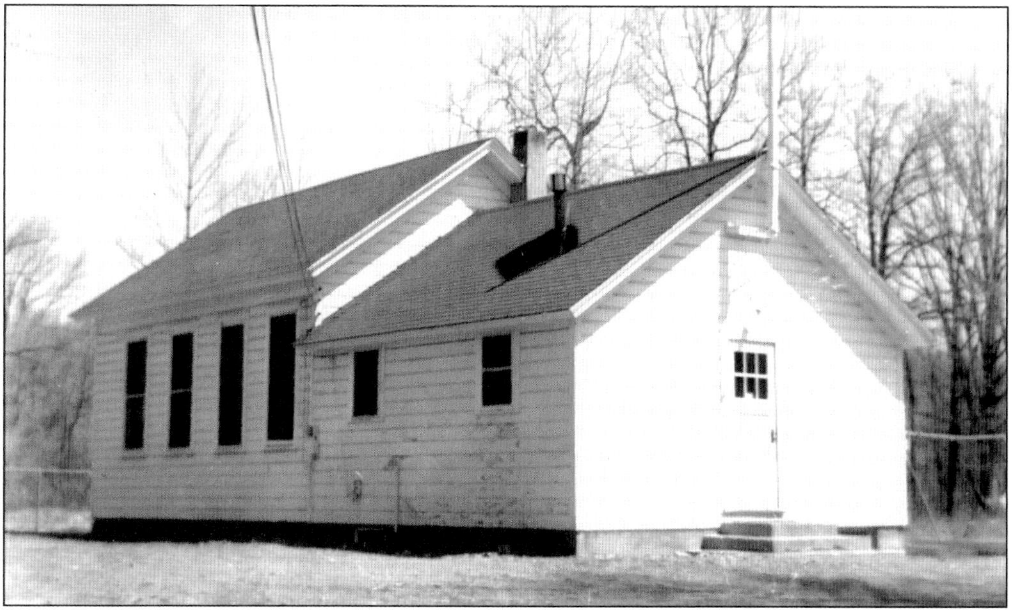

This is a photograph of the Orange Lake School in 1952. Built in 1849, the school served the population of Orange Lake and its vicinity or over 100 years before any major improvements were made. A heating system, potable water, and toilets were added that summer, making a world of difference for the students returning in September 1953. (Courtesy of Kathryn Gatterdum Monti.)

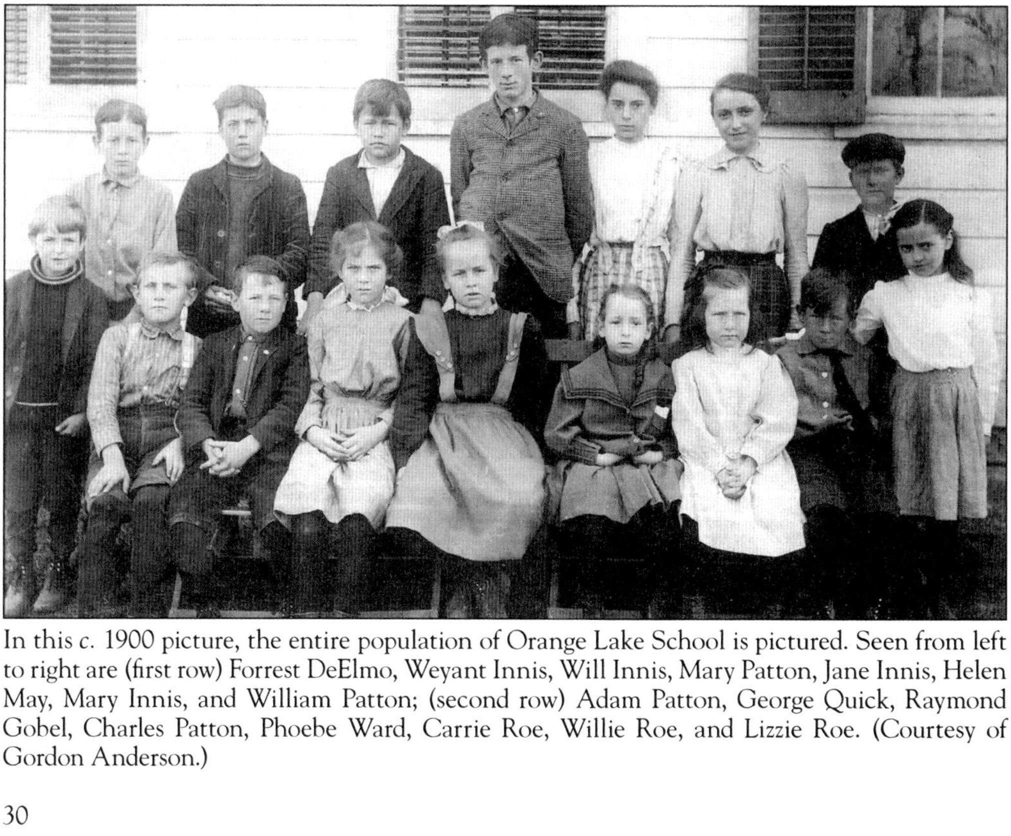

In this *c.* 1900 picture, the entire population of Orange Lake School is pictured. Seen from left to right are (first row) Forrest DeElmo, Weyant Innis, Will Innis, Mary Patton, Jane Innis, Helen May, Mary Innis, and William Patton; (second row) Adam Patton, George Quick, Raymond Gobel, Charles Patton, Phoebe Ward, Carrie Roe, Willie Roe, and Lizzie Roe. (Courtesy of Gordon Anderson.)

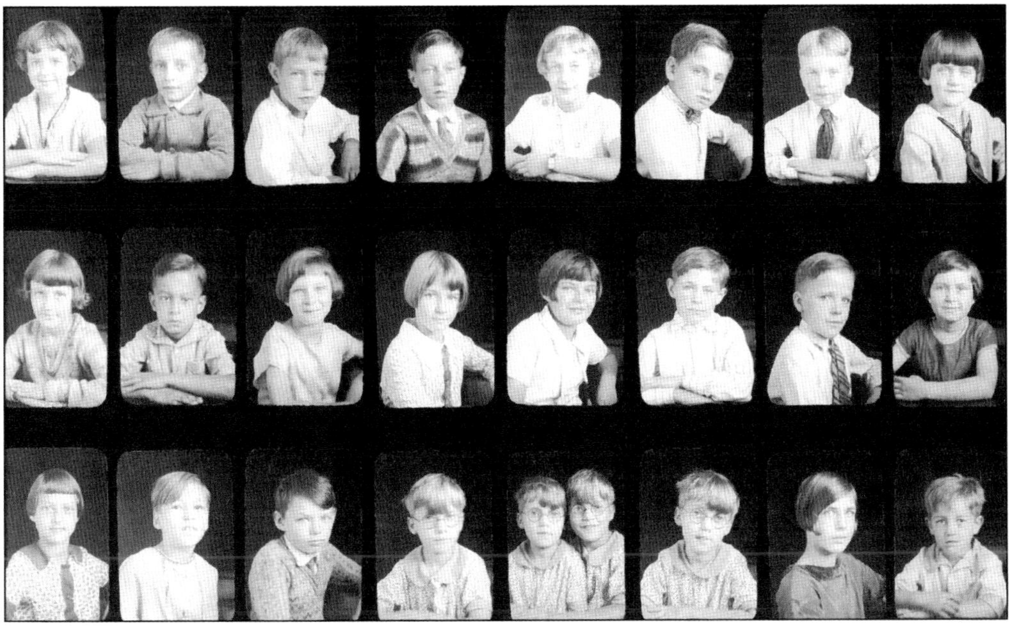

This c. 1927 photograph of the schoolchildren includes, from left to right, (top row) Helen Phillips, unidentified, Richard Bix, Ralph Nichols, Ilene Patton, William Innis, John Green, and Richard Innis; (middle row) Louise Stickley, four unidentified, John Bix, unidentified, and Julia Stickley; (bottom row) Janette Gillispie, Marguerite Harris, William Crawford, Evelyn Harris, Evelyn and Bernice Harris (together), Bernice Harris, Madelyn Gatterdum, and unidentified. (Courtesy of Ilene Patton Siegman.)

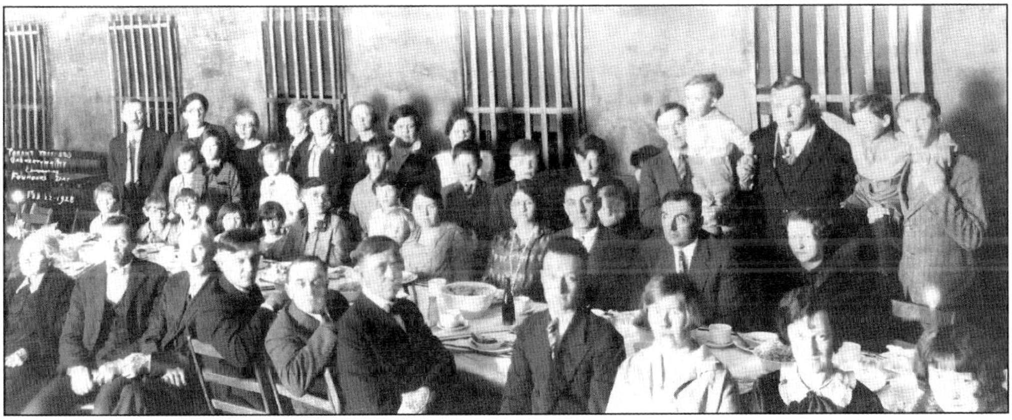

There were no meeting places to hold large gatherings in the Orange Lake and Gardnertown areas of the town. So the Gardnertown Community Center was built with the help of many lake residents in 1923, and it became both communities' social hall. This is a photograph of the Orange Lake PTA family social in 1928. (Courtesy of Gordon Anderson.)

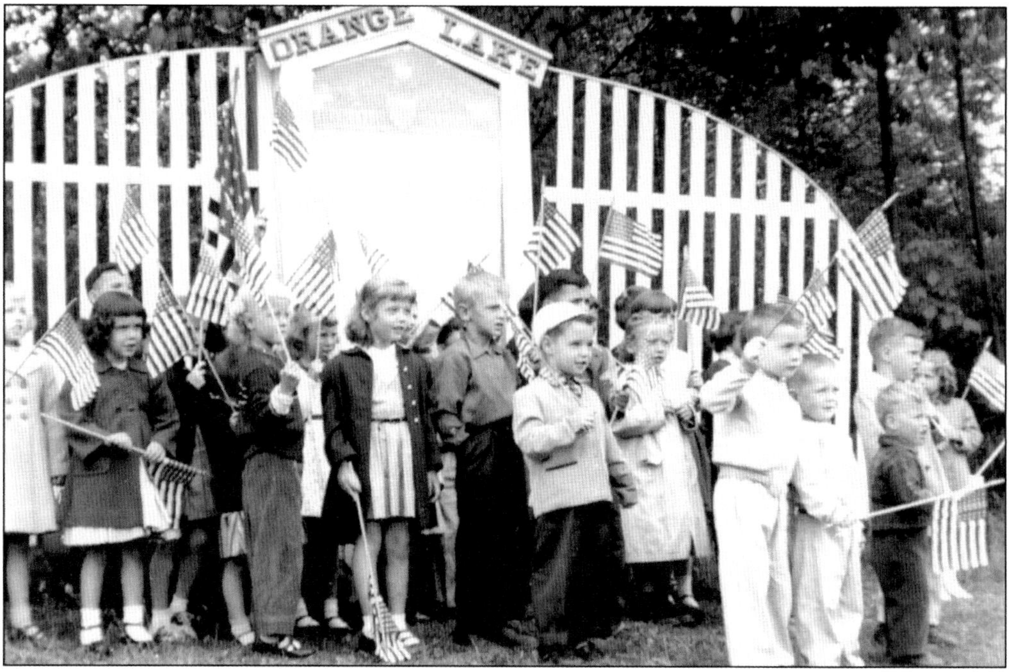

A tradition emerged at the Orange Lake School after a memorial was erected to fallen World War II soldiers. Each year students from the school would march across the street, flags in hand, to the corner of Route 52 and Lakeside Road and recite the Pledge of Alliance. This is a photograph of a class in 1953. (Courtesy of Marguerite Harris McDermott.)

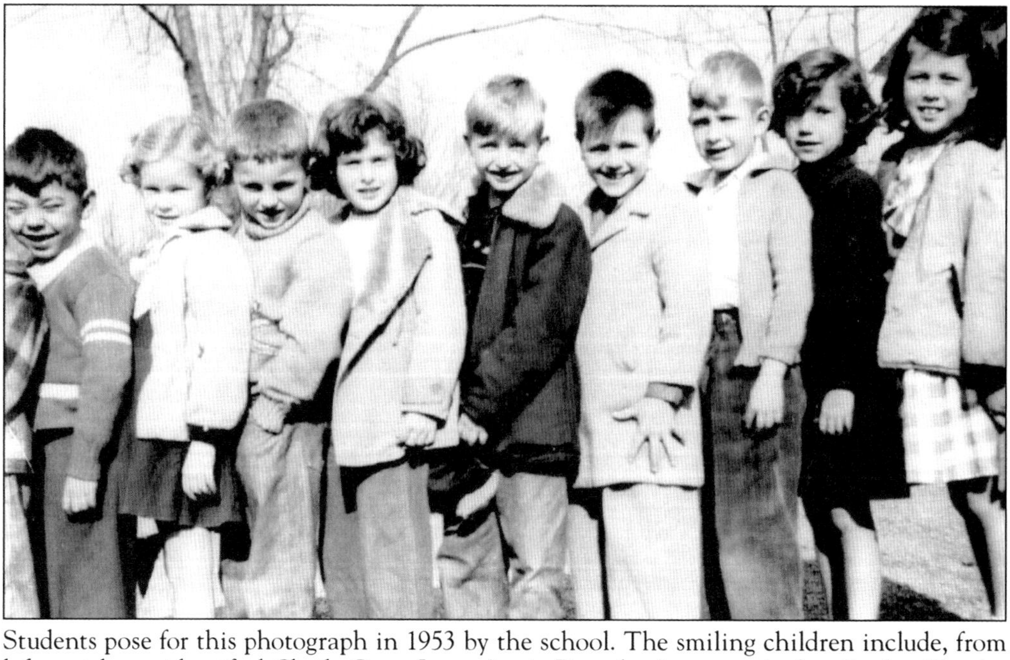
Students pose for this photograph in 1953 by the school. The smiling children include, from left to right, unidentified, Sheila Gage, James Innis, Dorothy Acquaro, Arthur Fowler, Charles Innis, Edward Armstrong, unidentified, and Beverly McDermott. (Courtesy of Marguerite Harris McDermott.)

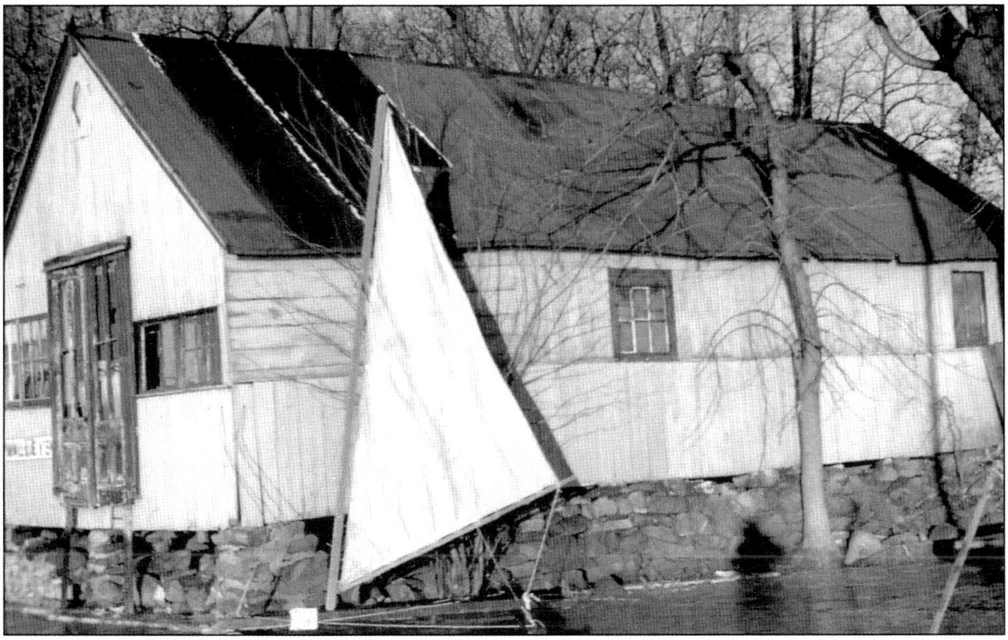

Early Roman Catholic residents and visitors had no place to celebrate Sunday mass. Belle O'Malley offered them the use of her old icehouse, and it was converted into a makeshift church. Planks were set on beer kegs as seating, and windows were cut into the building. A priest came from Walden on Sundays to hold services during most of May through September. (Courtesy of Marsha Tenny.)

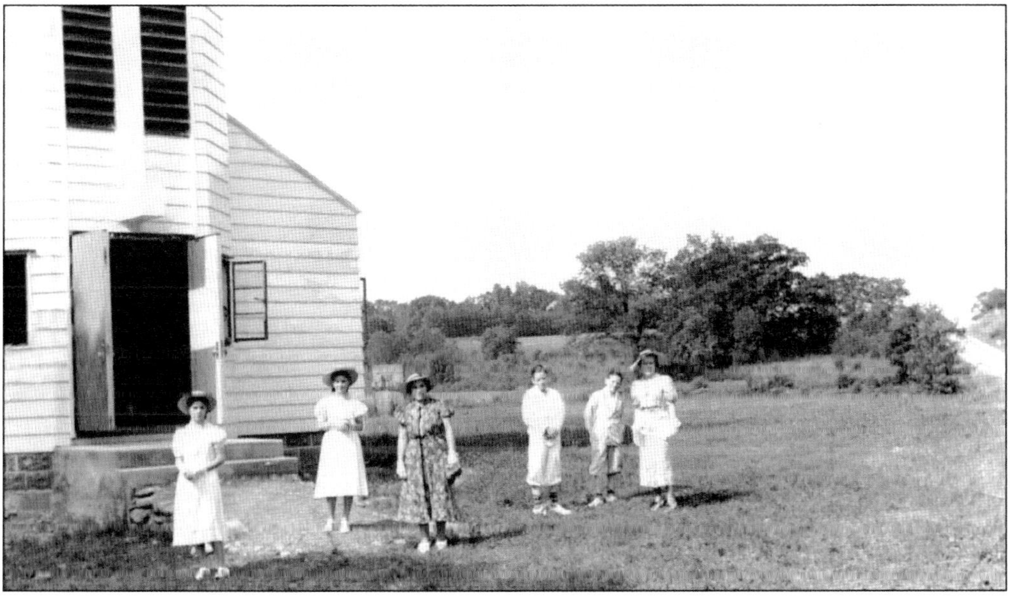

Outgrowing the O'Malley property, a church was constructed after many years of planning and soliciting donations. In the summer of 1939, Our Lady of the Lake Chapel held its first service. In this photograph, from left to right, June Grimley; Jane Grimley; their mother, Jane Grimley; John McCarthy; an unidentified boy; and Madeline Williams are seen outside the chapel on opening day. (Courtesy of Jane Grimley McCaw.)

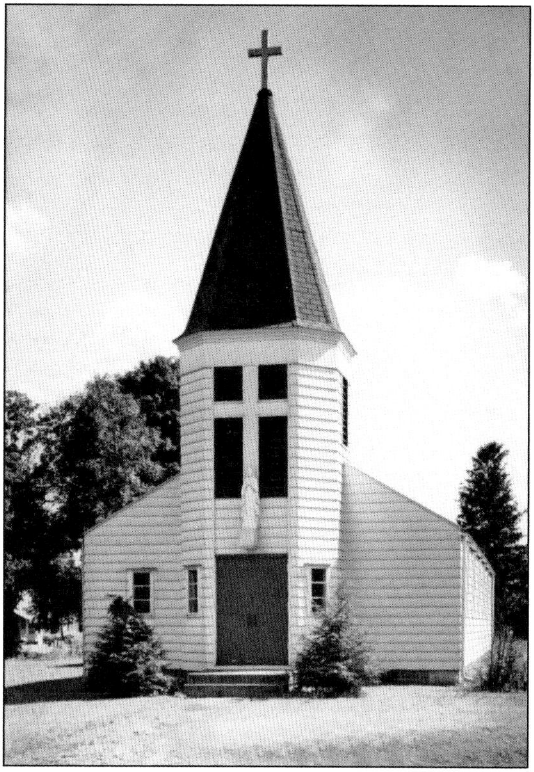

The early construction of the church was accomplished through the efforts of three men: B. Maynard Higginson, an avid duck hunter and contractor; John Clark, a lake resident and horticulturist; and Joseph Tierney, a landowner and lake resident. The church has undergone many renovations and is considered part of St. Patrick's parish in Newburgh. (Courtesy of Paul Yablonsky.)

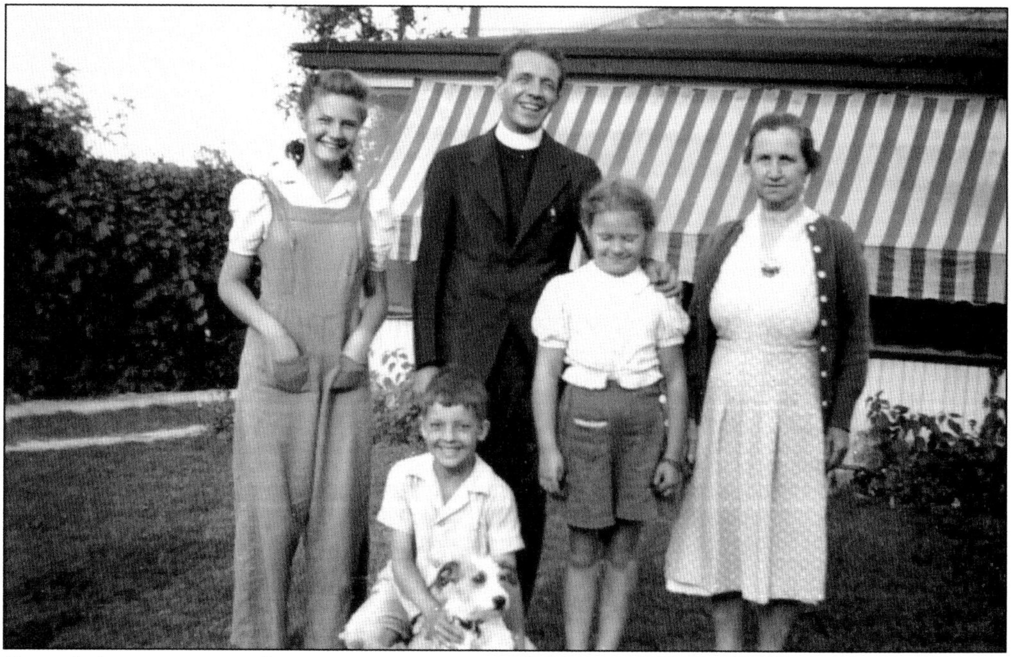

One of the most revered priests to minister to the congregation was Fr. Richard Luedke. In this photograph, he is seen with Richard Carnwright, who is kneeling with his dog in the first row. In the second row from right to left are Dorothy Tyler, Fr. Richard Luedke, Eleanor Oberle Youngberg, and Anna Lynch. (Courtesy of Dorothy Tyler.)

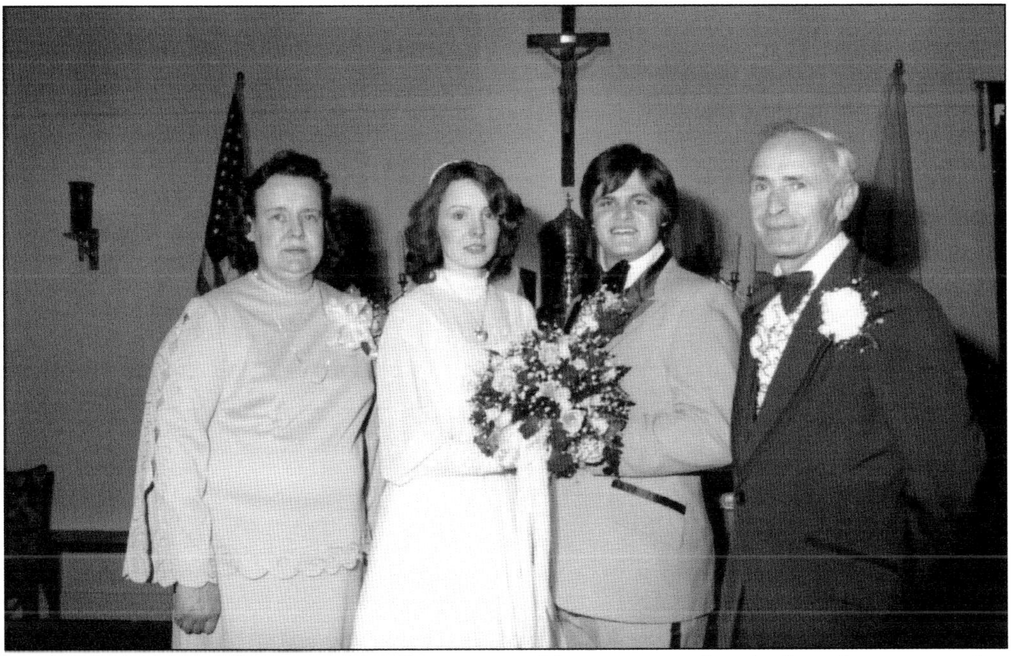

Mark Westhausser and Stacey Yablonsky are one of the many couples who have been married in the chapel. In this early-1980s photograph, from left to right are Barbara Yablonsky, mother of the bride; Stacey, the bride; Mark, the groom; and the bride's father, Stefan Yablonsky. (Courtesy of Paul Yablonsky.)

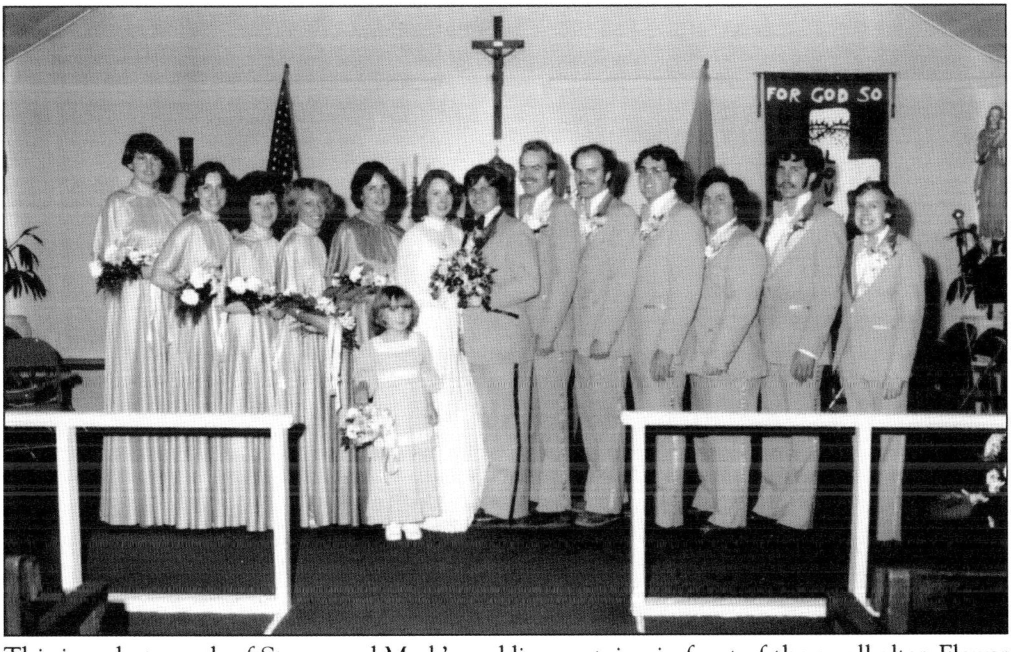

This is a photograph of Stacey and Mark's wedding partying in front of the small altar. Flower girl Justina Yablonsky is in the front row. In the second row the first five women are unidentified, Stacey and Mark Westhausser follow, the next five men are unidentified, and the last young man is Paul Yablonsky. (Courtesy of Paul Yablonsky.)

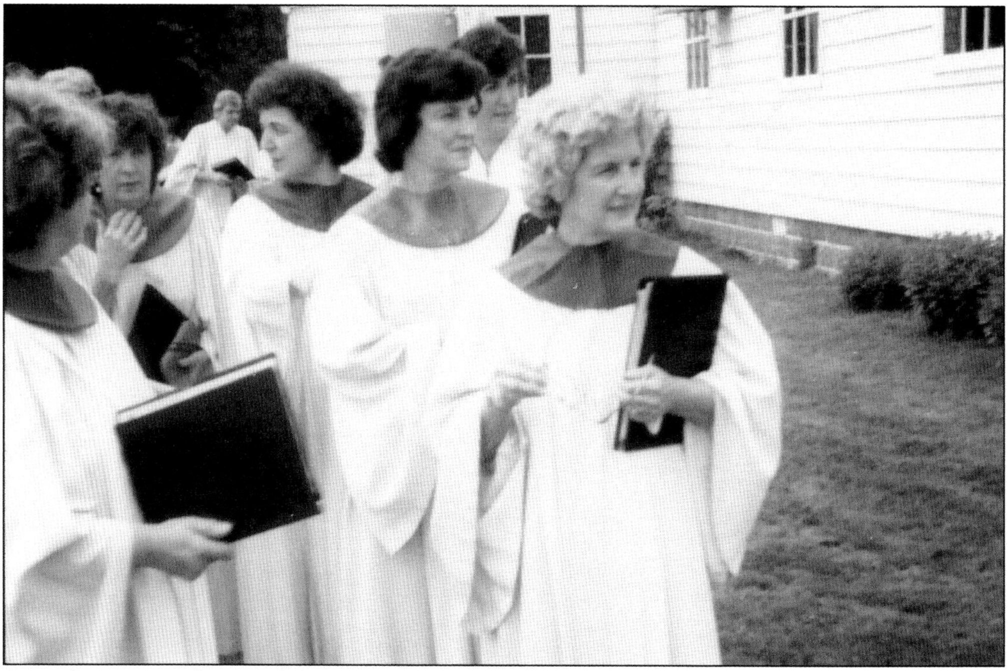

Over the years, a choir and altar society were formed at the chapel. In this 1979 photograph, the choir prepares to enter the church on Our Lady of Lourdes Day. Three members of the choir can be identified: Stella Conners is in the front center, followed by Mary O'Neil, and then Anna Auchmoody, who is looking to her right. (Courtesy of Anna Auchmoody.)

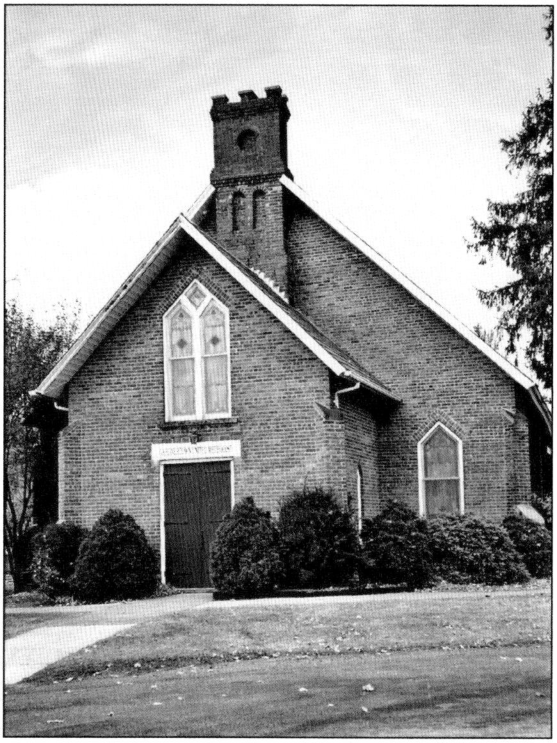

The Gardnertown Church Society (Methodist) was formed in 1825. The present structure, at left, was built as the Gardnertown Methodist Church in 1859 and replaced an earlier wooden one. It continues to serve the spiritual needs of both Gardnertown and Orange Lake residents. (Author's collection.)

In 1909, this cartoon titled "The Orange Lake Fire Brigade" appeared in a local newspaper. It has the names and caricatures of the original members. Dr. Henry Stock, whose family owned the property that Pennsylvania Station in New York City was built on, was a very generous man who fought to establish an early fire brigade. (Courtesy of Marguerite Harris McDermott.)

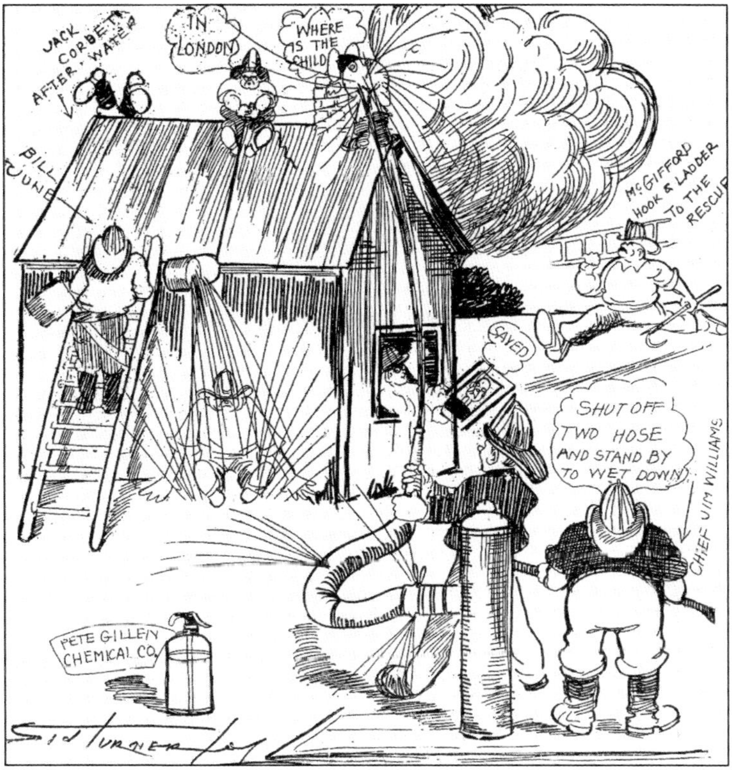

The Old Fireman's Song of the Orange Lake Fire Department (Volunteer)

Orange Lake Fire House Headquarters
Special Meeting
September 15, 1911
Roll Call: 18 Present

Fireman's Song

"AS WE RAN WITH THE OLD MACHINE"

Through fire and flame
Through sunshine and rain
Through zephyr wreaths
May never rise again
As we ran with the old Machine
(repeat forever)

"The Old Fireman's Song" is one of the remnants of the original fire brigade. Some of the early members of the department also tried to start a rescue unit that would specialize in water rescues, but that idea did not take hold until many years later. (Courtesy of Susan Carroll.)

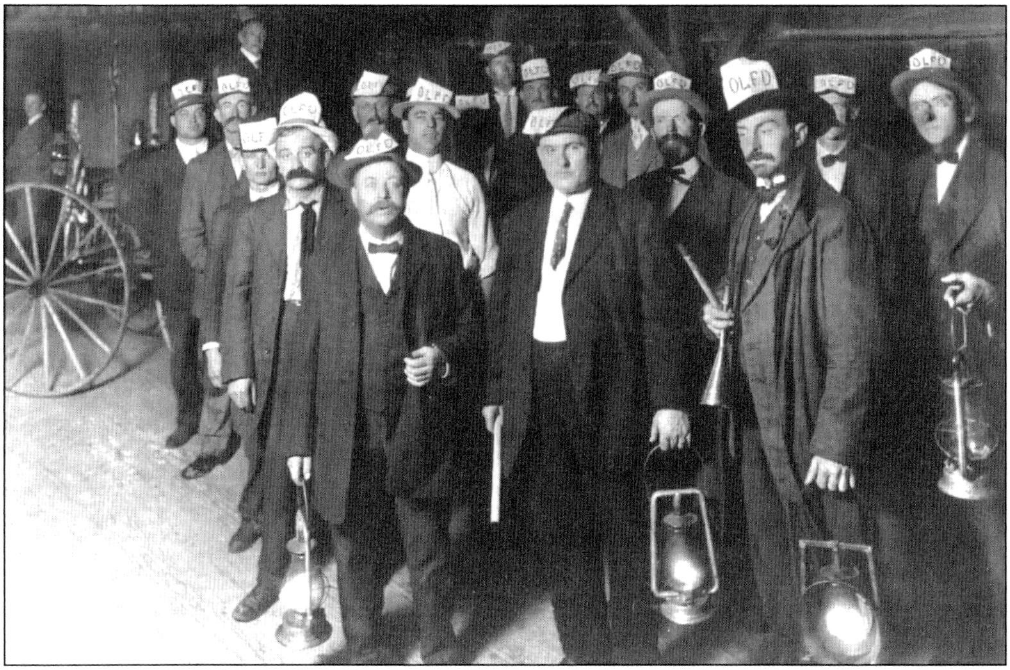

Only two men are identified in the September 11, 1909, photograph above: James Williams is the first man on the left with the lantern in hand and Dr. Henry Stock is in the first row on the right with a lantern and small horn. Others who are in the picture include Peter Gillen, William Tibbs, "Dad" Hammond, George Ronk, John Kessler, and Daniel Leghorn. (Courtesy of Gordon Anderson.)

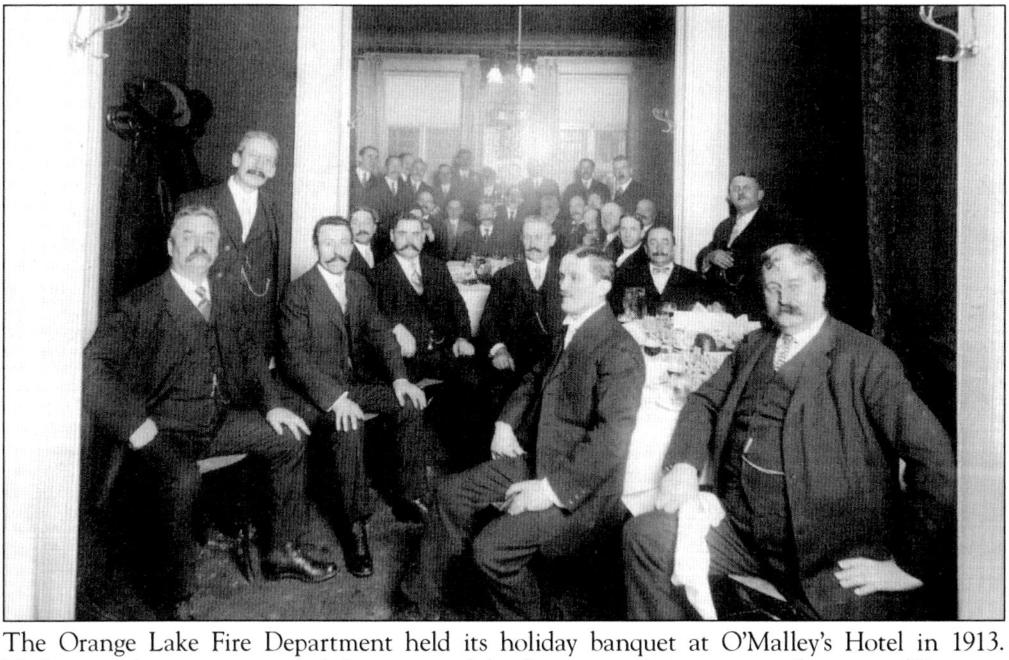

The Orange Lake Fire Department held its holiday banquet at O'Malley's Hotel in 1913. Unfortunately no one recorded the names of the firemen or their guests at the event. (Courtesy of Gordon Anderson.)

Daniel Leghorn owned the local general store. The first organizational meeting of the current fire company was held there on September 3, 1935. Leghorn was very active in the department and was elected its first chief. After his untimely death in 1936, the name of the company was changed to the Dan Leghorn Hose Company of Orange Lake. It was later known as the Dan Leghorn Engine Company. (Courtesy of Susan Carroll.)

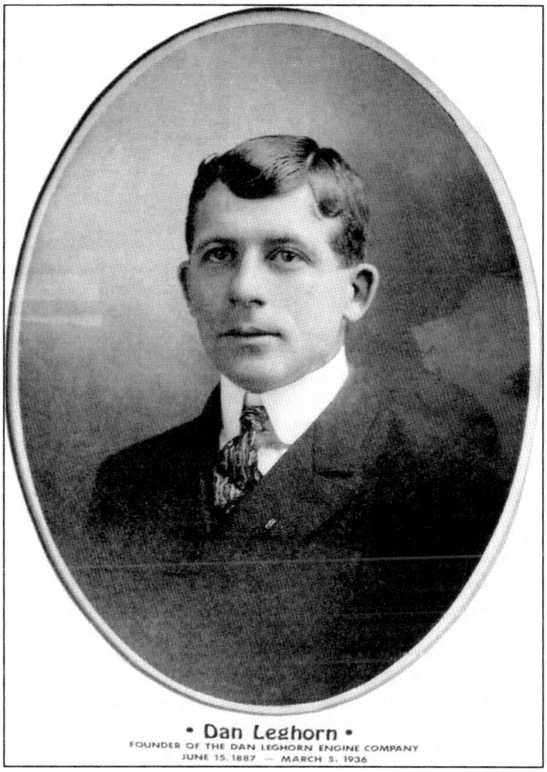

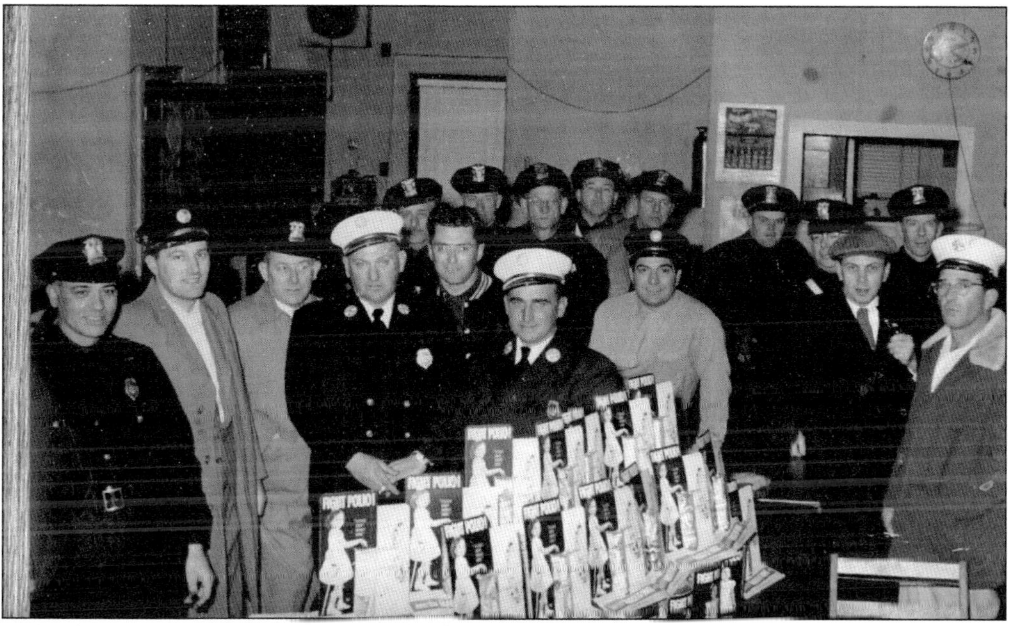

This photograph has members of both the Dan Leghorn and the Winona Lake companies. Winona was formed as a sister company of the Orange Lake company in the mid-1950s. Some of the people in the photograph include Rocky Sinisgalli, Herbert Deil, Anthony Colandrea, David Ryan, Samuel Darrigo, Maury Middleton, James Ruggiero, William Dillon, James Morrill, Stanley Lewis, and Arthur Kasink. (Courtesy of Susan Carroll.)

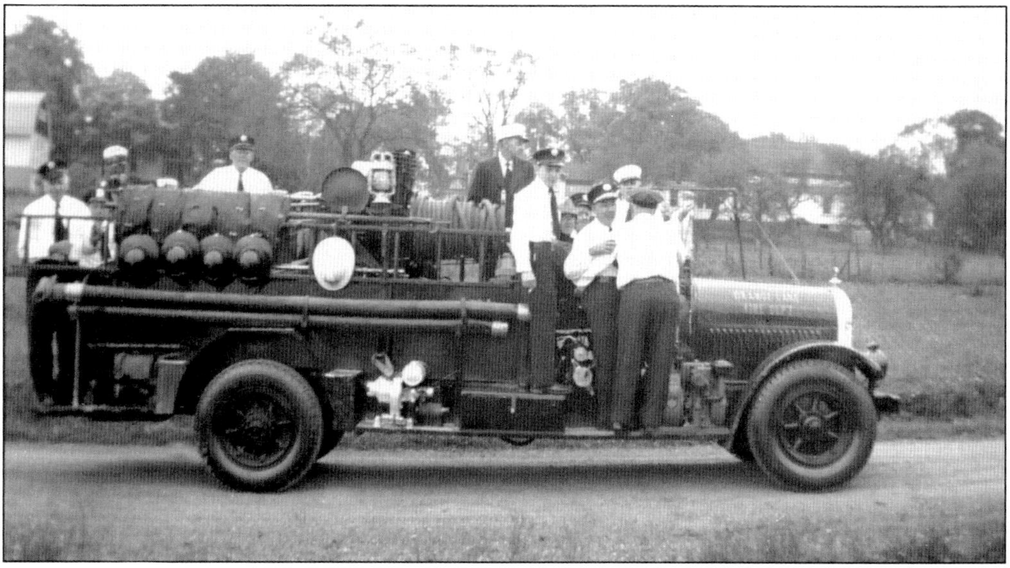

The Dan Leghorn Engine Company has a proud history of taking part in area parades. The photograph above shows firemen getting ready to march in a Walden parade in the 1950s. (Courtesy of Susan Carroll.)

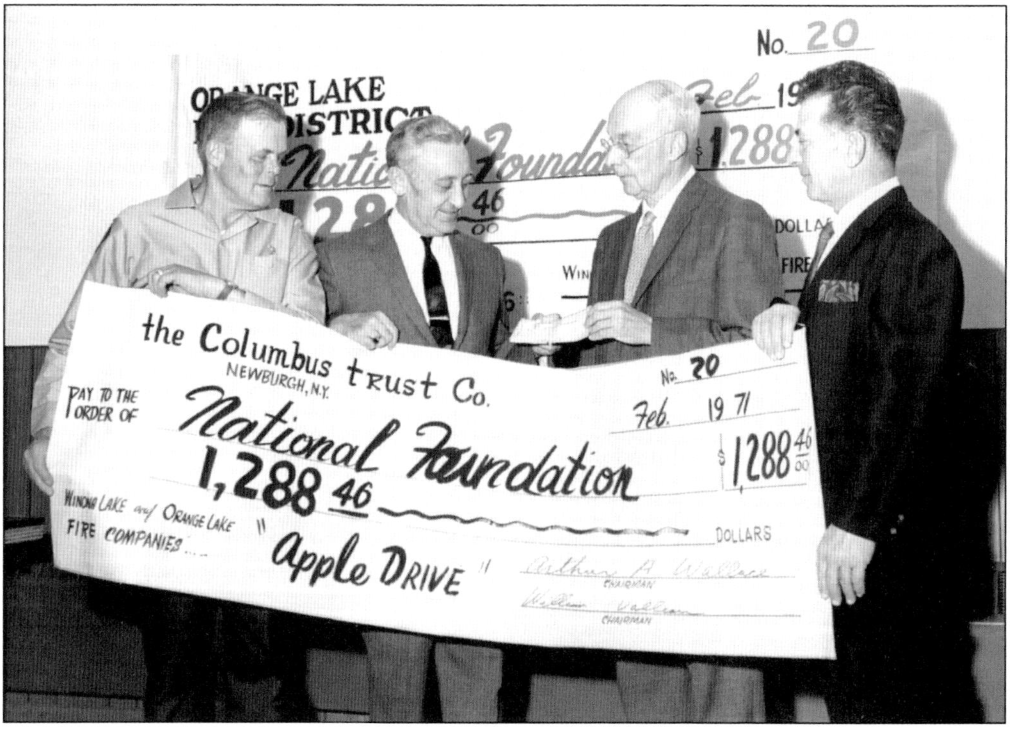

In early 1971, firemen from the Dan Leghorn and Winona Lake companies sold apples at the intersection of Route 52 and Union Avenue to raise money for polio victims. Above, members hand a check for $1,288.46 to representatives of the National Polio Foundation. From left to right, they are Maury Middleton of Winona Lake, unidentified, unidentified, and James Ruggiero of Dan Leghorn. (Courtesy of Susan Carroll.)

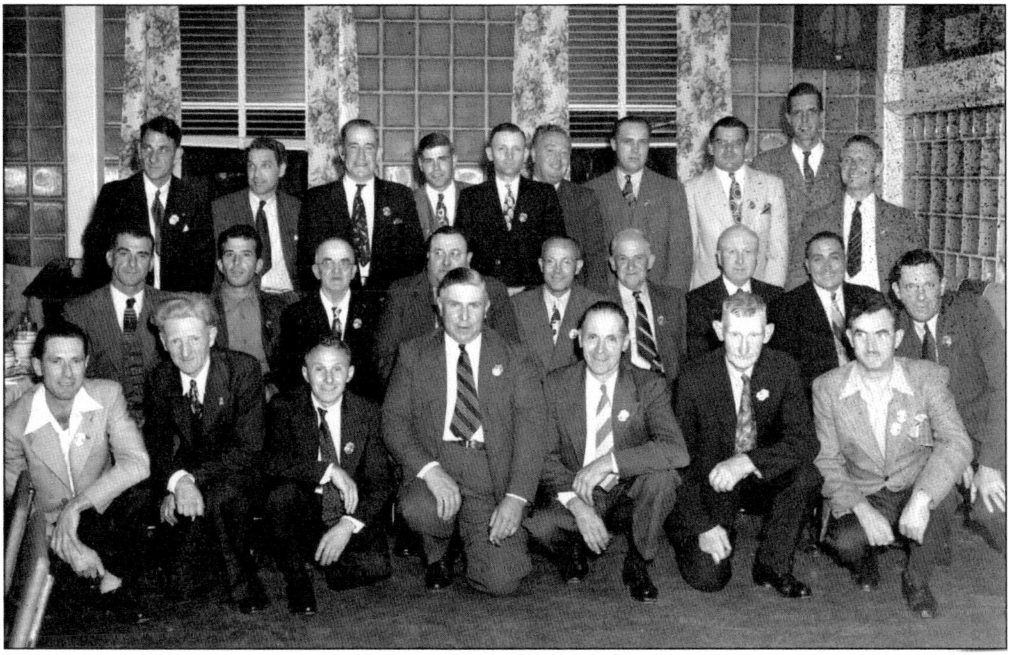

The fire department held many of its social events at O'Malley's. In this water-damaged photograph, from around 1950, from left to right are (first row) Ralph Nichols, ? Innis, William Bartholmes, ? Woods, Clarence Martin, ? Ford, and Murl Perry; (second row) Francis and James Ruggiero, three unidentified, ? Elmsly, and three unidentified; (third row) Leo Stepski, Karl Jurgens, ? Wilheim, five unidentified, Stanley Urban, and unidentified. (Courtesy of Susan Carroll.)

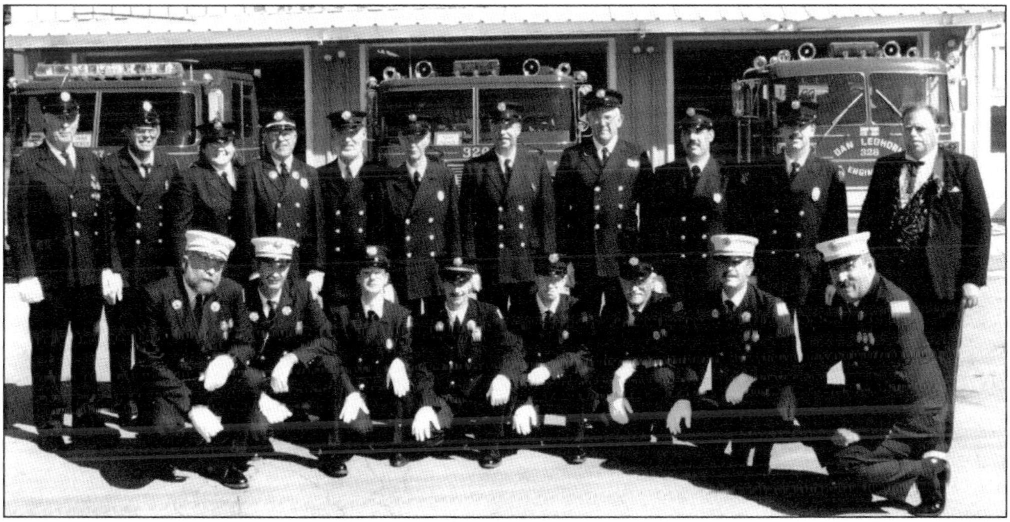

Members of the Dan Leghorn Engine Company pose in front of their firehouse in this 1990s photograph. From left to right, they are (first row) Al Christein, Eric Christein, Della Peel, Jeffery Rock, David Randolph, Frank Angelo, Dennis Spampinato, and Percy Ennist; (second row) Ronald Joy, Thomas Kramer, Susan Carroll, Charles Piper, Frederick Hall, Bud Lent, Chip Trojan, James Bondur, James Steltz, Charles Lanzar, and Lawrence Eckert. (Courtesy of Susan Carroll.)

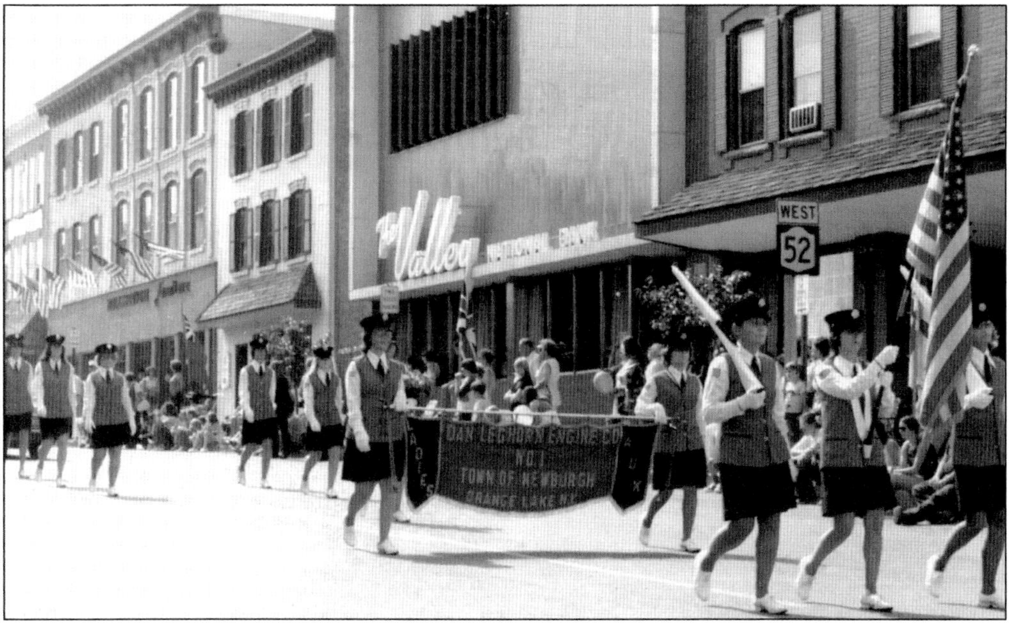

In May 1938, the ladies' auxiliary of the fire company was organized. It held bingo nights and other events to raise money for the department. Eventually it purchased its own uniforms and marched in parades. Thelma Bondur, right front holding a rifle, is the only auxiliary member identified in the 1971 Walden parade pictured above. (Courtesy of Susan Carroll.)

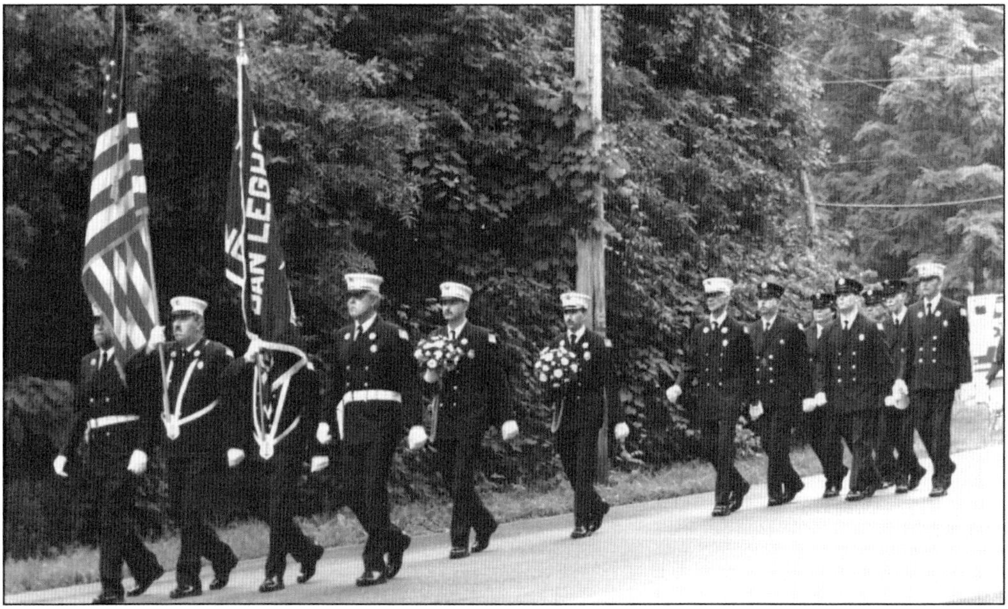

The Dan Leghorn Color Guard leads its unit in the 1996 parade at Hillcrest in this picture. From left to right, the color guard members are (first row) Al Christein, Reynolds Randolph, and unidentified; (second row) Chief Eric Christein; (third row) Assistant Chief George Woolsey Jr.; (fourth row) unidentified; (fifth row) Richard Moerman; (sixth row) unidentified and Chip Trojan; (seventh row) Susan Carroll and Anthony Ferrioulo; (eighth row) Bud Lent; (ninth row) George Woolsey Sr. (Courtesy of Susan Carroll.)

Four

Hotels and Restaurants

For over 125 years, Orange Lake's hospitality has been legendary.

The original hotel at the lake was the Orange Lake Hotel, built shortly after the U.S. Civil War. It catered to fishermen and early baseball teams. Hotel guests came by horse-drawn carriages or on horses.

Pine Point was probably the most well known of all the resorts at the lake. The *Sunday Telegram* reported its opening on Sunday, June 7, 1896, stating, "Nothing has done so much to change the character and possibilities of Orange Lake as a summer resort, as the construction of the club house at Pine Point by Higginson and Congressman Odell. The tone of the entire locality has been raised . . . it is the right thing in the right place."

The Lakeside House, a hotel and restaurant, was built by Alexander Kidd in 1880 and was a prosperous and well-established business when he sold it seven years later. Some 20 years later, the Gatterdum family took over control and ran a very successful business there for over 40 years. The Lakeside House was then converted into an apartment house. After a fire there in 1986, the building was rebuilt.

Of all the Orange Lake establishments, the Lakeview House/O'Malley's Hotel and Restaurant probably has the most colorful history. Originally opened as the Lakeview House, a boardinghouse in 1866, the restaurant's bar was a well-known watering hole for locals and visitors. In the 1930s, the former icehouse turned Catholic church, which was located on the property, was converted into a summer training facility for boxers. The name of the business changed to O'Malley's in the early 1900s. It was named for red-haired Belle O'Malley, the longtime proprietor. After a series of owners, renovations on the building began in 1991, and a sign was found in the basement. It was an early Lakeview House sign, and once again the establishment is known by that name. The current owners, James and Tori Carter, have a fine restaurant there today.

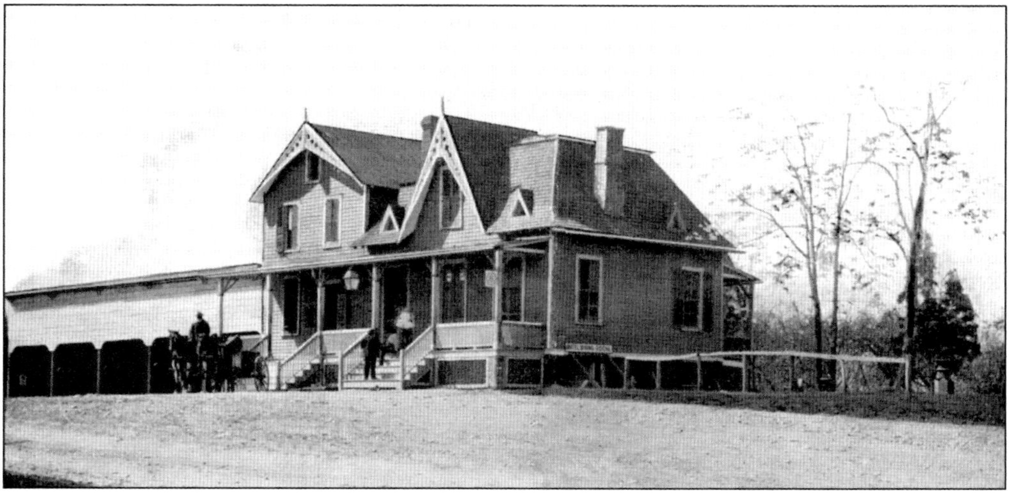

The Orange Lake Hotel was close to collapsing on its own before it was torn down in the early years of the 20th century to make way for the amusement park.

ORANGE LAKE HOTEL

and Picnic Grounds,

ORANGE LAKE, N. Y.

JOSEPH F. SCULLEY, Proprietor.

Bar in connection with the Hotel. Ample Accommodation for Horses and Carriages. Fine Grove for Picnic or Private Parties, with Race Track Connected. Boats, Bait, Fishing Tackle, etc., constantly on hand. Trolley from Newburgh and Walden Direct to the Hotel.

Also SCULLEY & DORNAN, HOTEL, 42 Liberty Street, Newburgh, N. Y.

Choice Wines, Liquors and Cigars.

The hotel catered to sportsmen, as can be seen from the 1900 advertisement below. Even though a horse-racing track was a special draw in the early years, baseball became so popular that a baseball diamond replaced the track before the hotel's demise. (Courtesy of Marguerite Harris McDermott.)

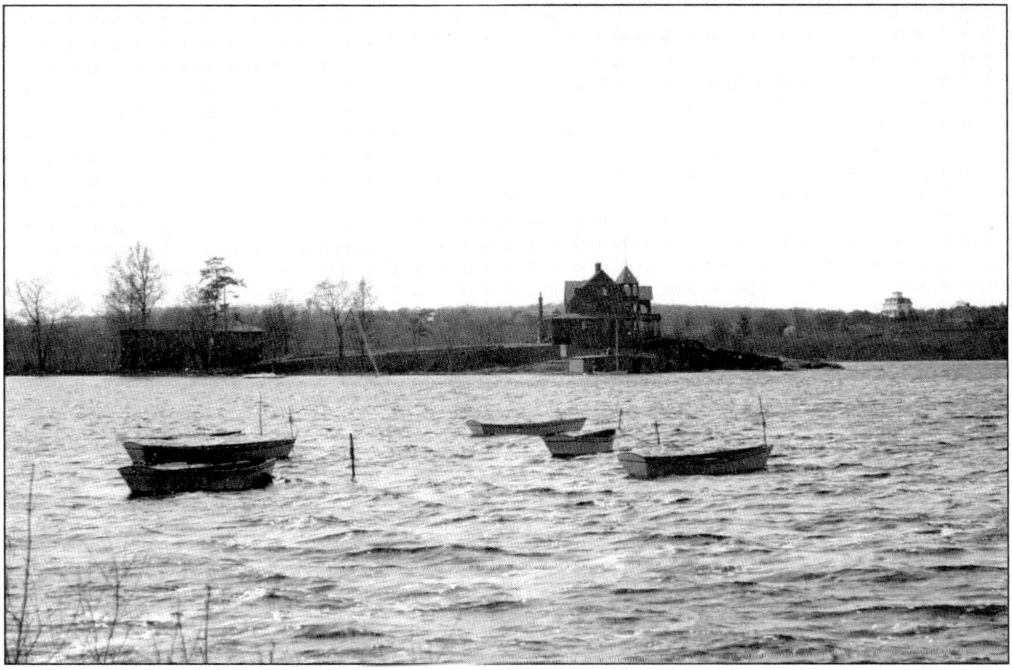

This is an early photograph of the Orange Lake Club House, which eventually became known by its location, Pine Point. The club also had another clubhouse in Newburgh. Built by Henry C. Higginson and then Congressman Benjamin B. Odell in 1896, the club was open to the public and had a fine restaurant and rooms for rent. (Courtesy of Sharon Nichols Formato.)

The Orange Lake Club,

OF

NEWBURGH, N. Y.

ORGANIZED JULY 1, 1881.

INCORPORATED NOVEMBER 21, 1881.

CONSTITUTION,

BY-LAWS,

AND

LIST OF MEMBERS.

CLUB ROOMS:

54 Water Street,

AND

Pine Point, Orange Lake.

1896.

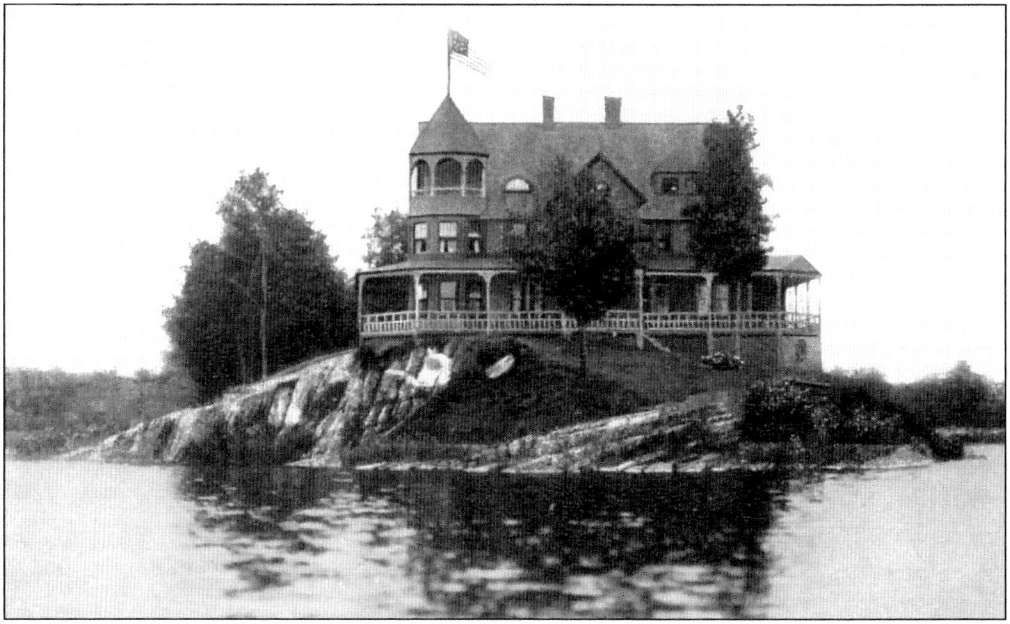

The Orange Lake Club eventually left the building, and Pine Point became a fine hotel. This postcard view shows the reason why the hotel was often called the "Little Gibraltar." Marguerite Harris McDermott, whose father was an iceman, remembers delivering ice there in the 1920s. (Author's collection.)

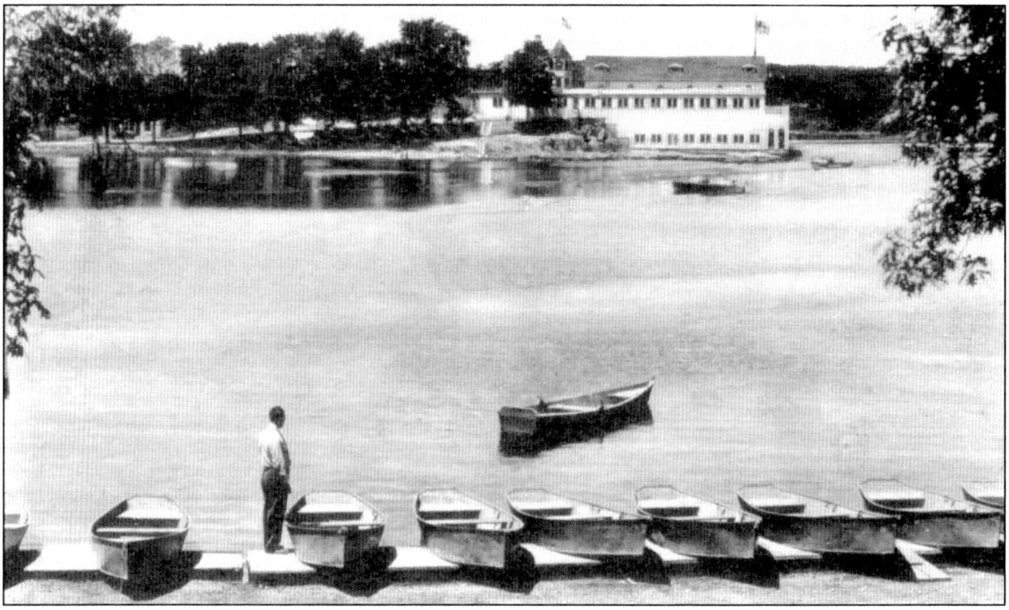

After a fire, major changes were made to the building when it became a casino and nightclub. Dance marathons were held there during the Depression, and a large restaurant provided catering for weddings, proms, and other events. (Courtesy of Louis Catulusci and Dennis Collins.)

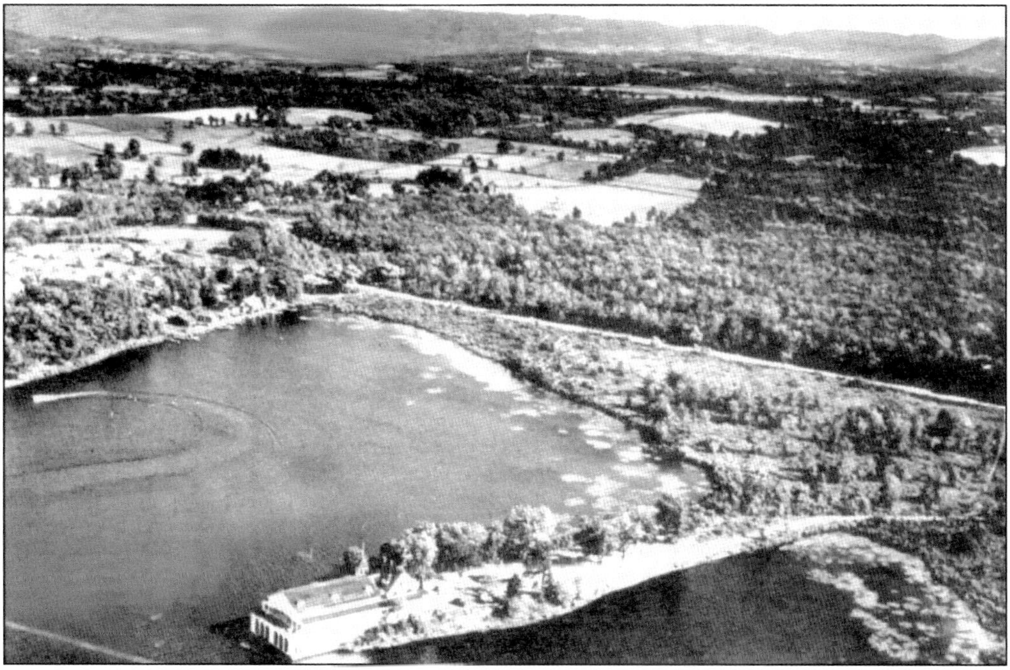

This aerial photograph of Pine Point shows the small road leading to the casino from Route 52 in about 1950. The casino at this point was owned by a man named Yank Cohen. It closed in the early summer of 1953. (Courtesy of Louis Catulusci and Dennis Collins.)

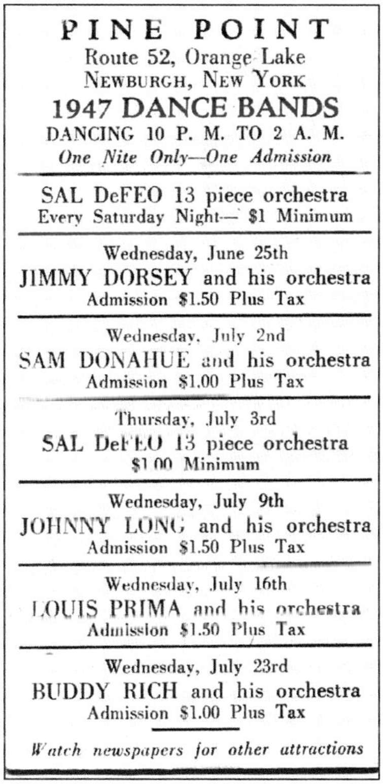

This advertising card from 1947 shows some of the big names of the time that performed at Pine Point. Others who appeared there include Johnny Mercer, Benny Goodman, Ozzie Nelson, and Frank Sinatra. (Courtesy of Walter Whitehill.)

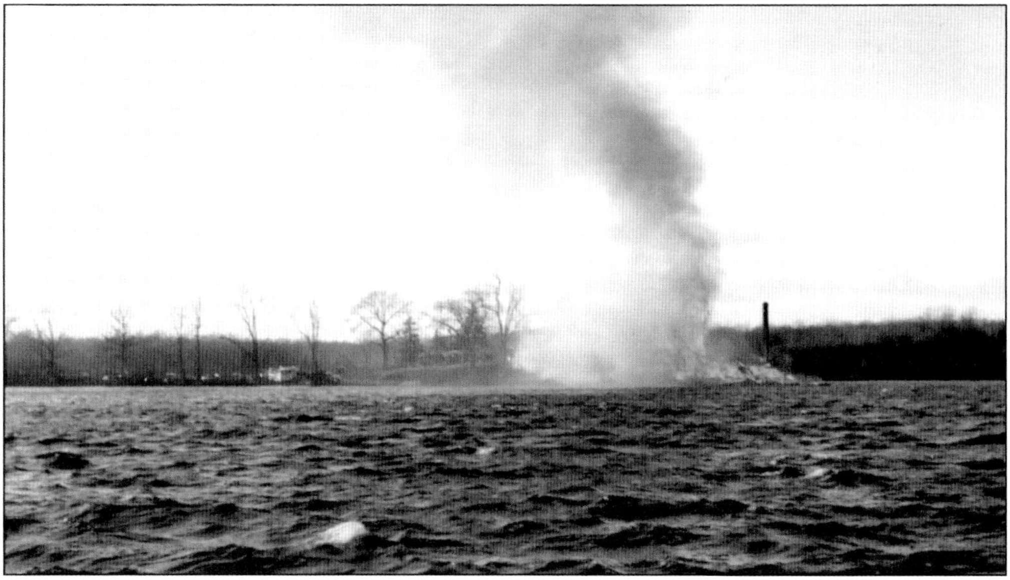

Toward evening, on a windy day in the fall of 1971, Pine Point went up in flames. The fire consumed the building within a matter of hours. This photograph is one of the few known to exist from that day. (Courtesy of Kathryn Gatterdum Monti.)

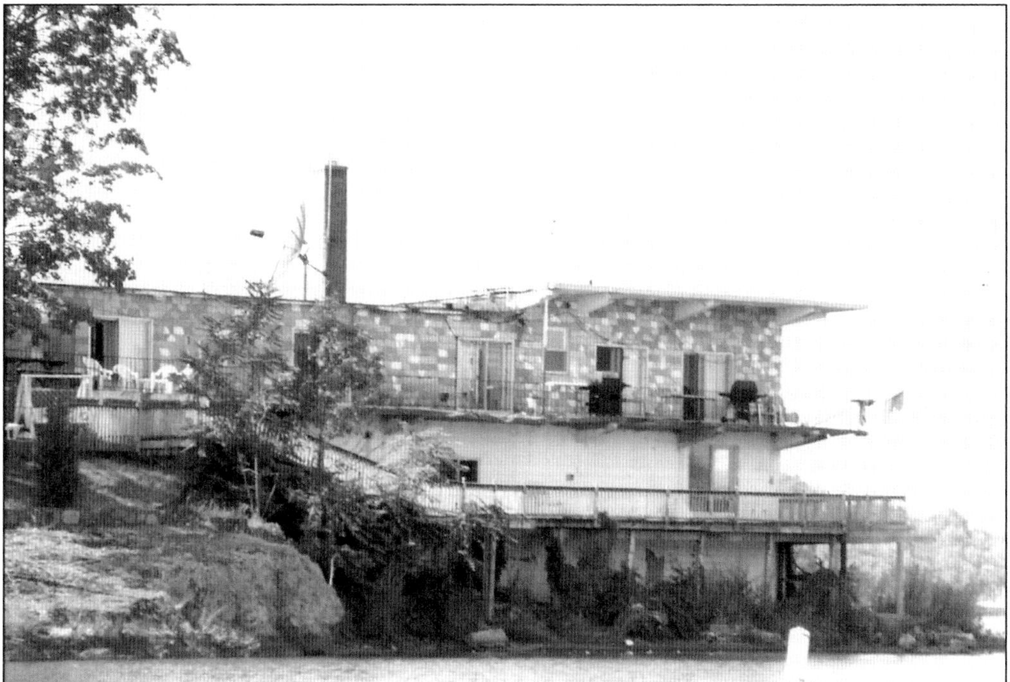

A private individual bought the remains of the building and built this structure as his home. The chimney is one of the two that were original to the Pine Point. (Author's collection.)

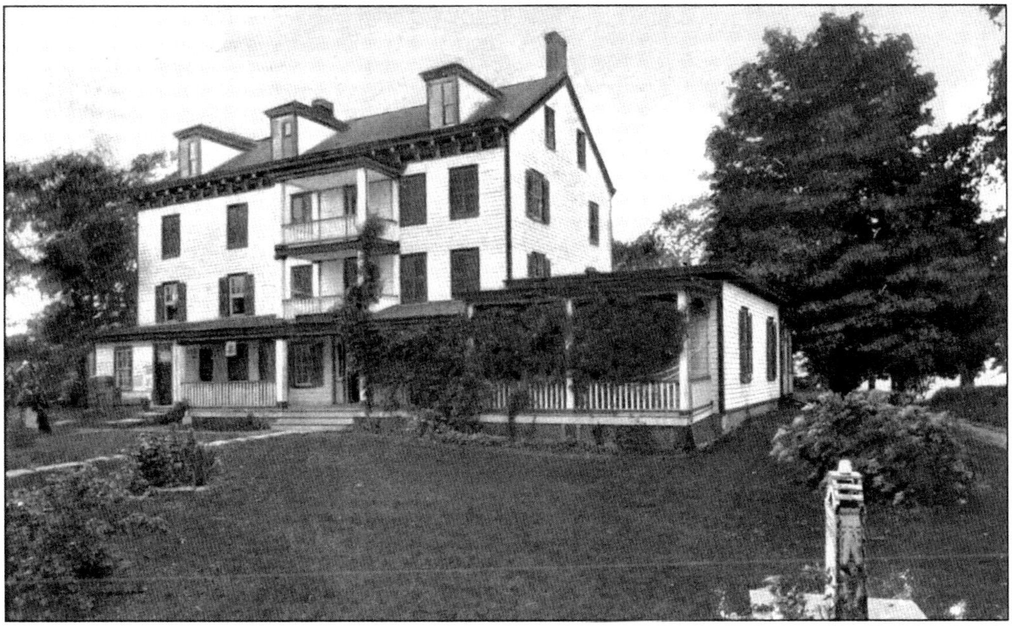

Alexander Kidd, a Newburgh grocer, built the Lakeside House in 1880 as a residence for summer tourists. He successfully managed the establishment for seven years before selling it in 1887 to build a larger hotel in Walden. (Courtesy of the Historical Society of Newburgh Bay and the Highlands.)

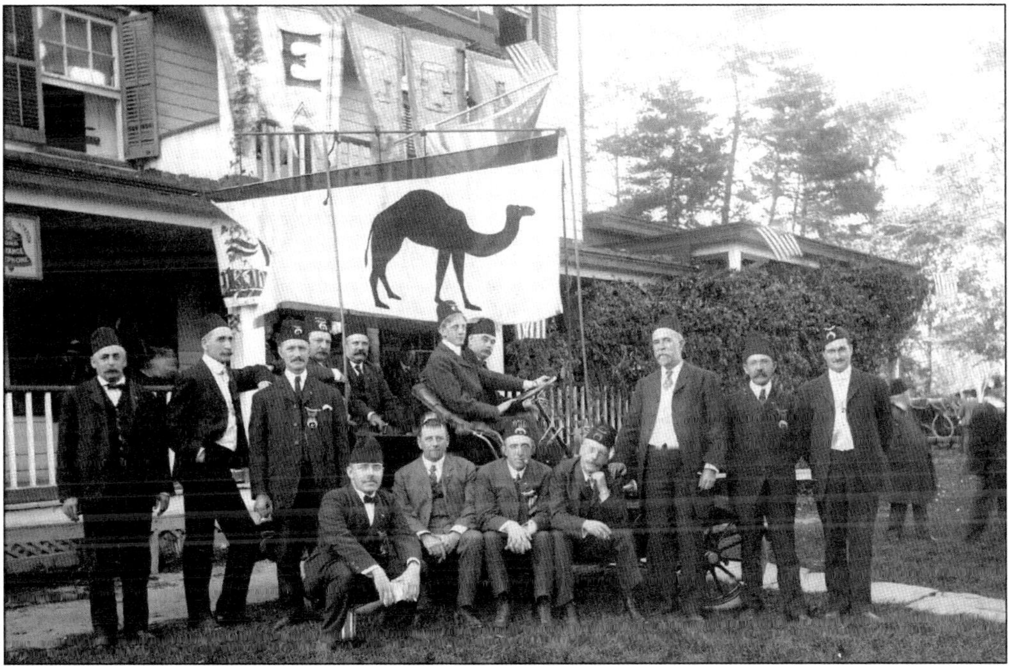

Many groups held their meetings and conventions at the Lakeside House. Above, the W. H. Weston Shriner's Association of Newburgh and its guests from Kingston gathered there in 1905. This photograph from October 19 of that year shows Walter Whitehill Sr. in the passenger seat of the car. All the others are unidentified. (Courtesy of Walter Whitehill.)

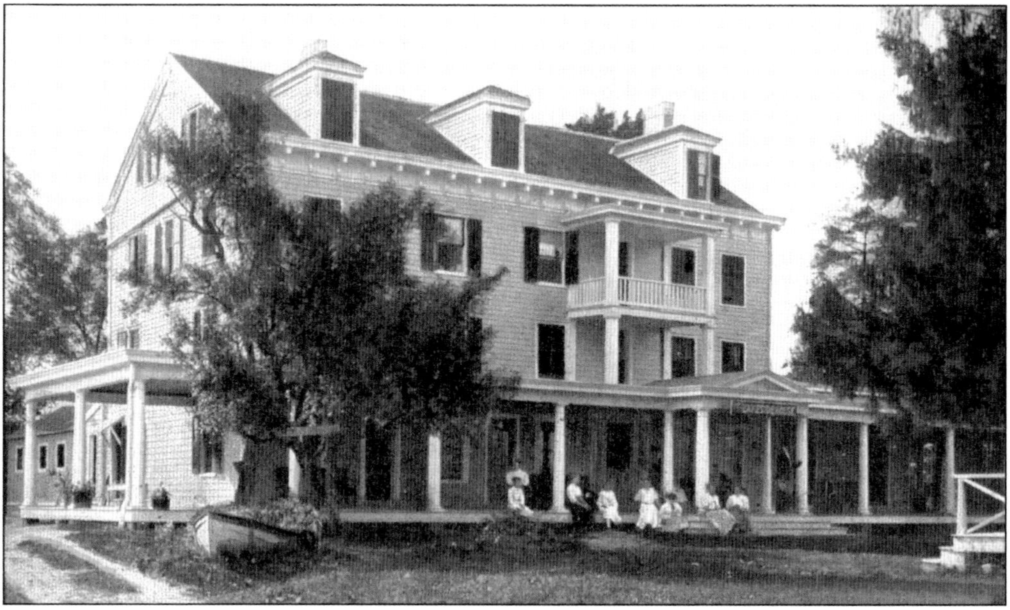

The Gatterdum family came to Orange Lake about 1917. They operated the hotel and restaurant for a few years and bought the property in 1920. The Lakeside House had large sunny rooms and offered guests the best amenities. (Courtesy of Marguerite Harris McDermott.)

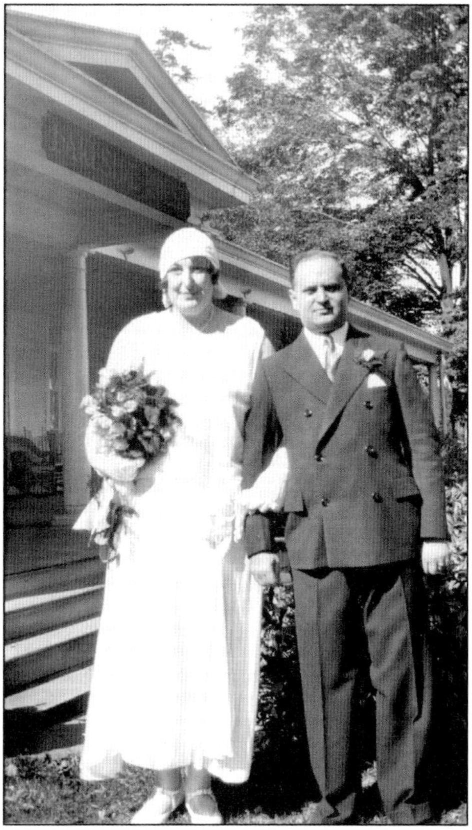

Madeline Gatterdum helped her mother run the Lakeside House. In October 1930, she married Dr. Louis Cohen in a ceremony at the Lakeside House. Cohen, a Newburgh physician, also saw patients at his home at Orange Lake. (Courtesy of Kathryn Gatterdum Monti.)

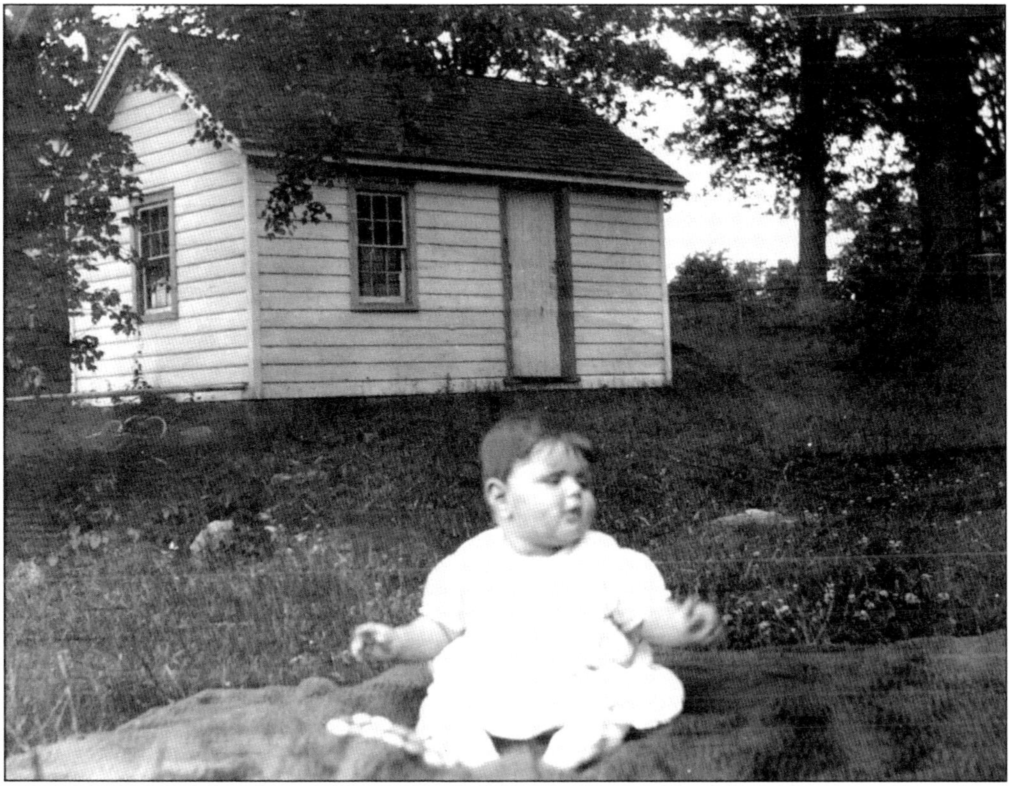

Louis and Madeline's daughter, Kathryn, is seen here in a 1934 photograph. She is seated on the lake side of the house in front of the pump house. (Courtesy of Kathryn Gatterdum Monti.)

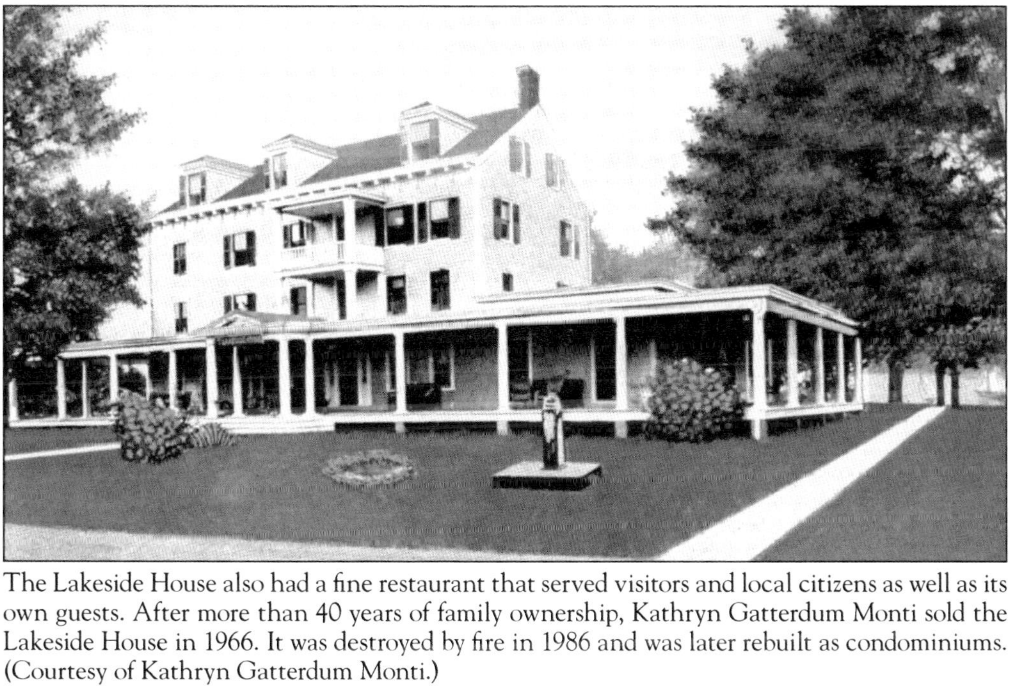

The Lakeside House also had a fine restaurant that served visitors and local citizens as well as its own guests. After more than 40 years of family ownership, Kathryn Gatterdum Monti sold the Lakeside House in 1966. It was destroyed by fire in 1986 and was later rebuilt as condominiums. (Courtesy of Kathryn Gatterdum Monti.)

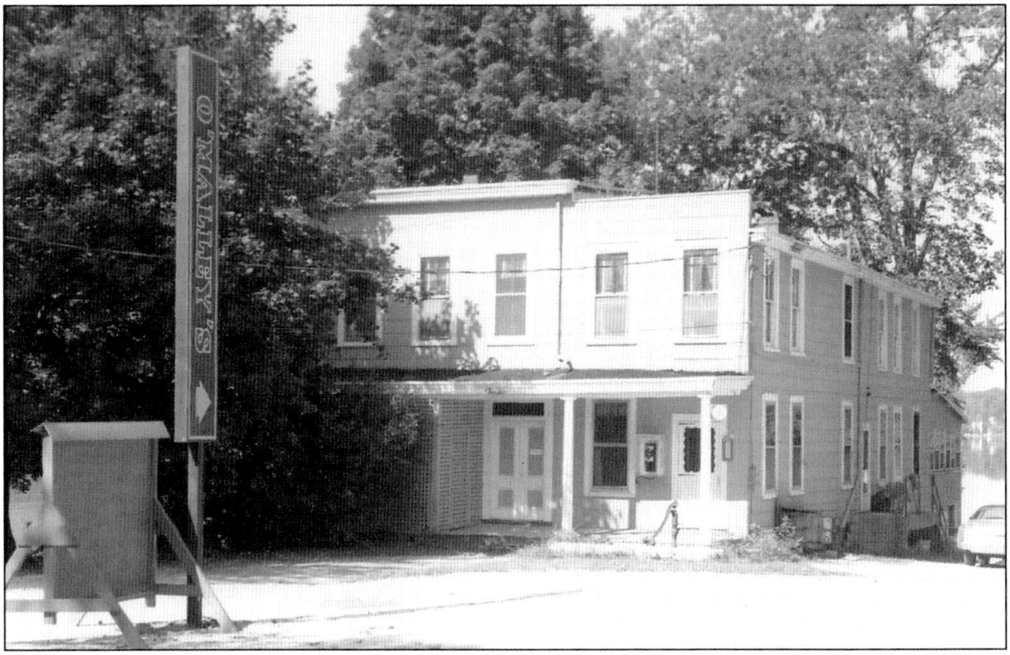

Another famous eatery and early hotel was the Lakeview House. Built in 1866, the Lakeview House was also known as O'Malley's for many years. From the early 1900s through 1934, the proprietor of the establishment was red-haired Belle O'Malley, and she is credited with the name change. (Author's collection.)

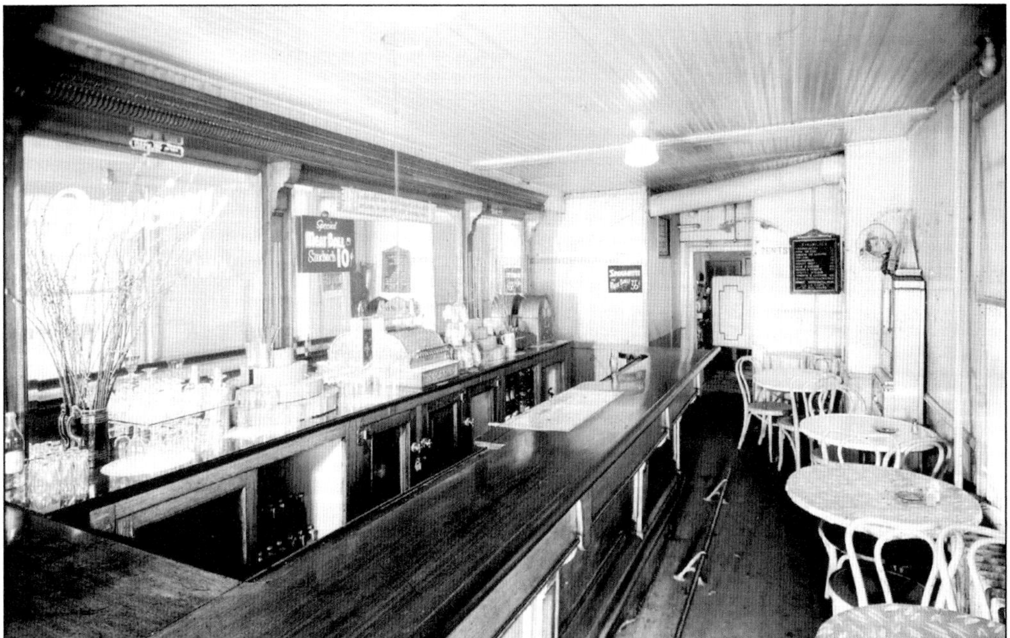

This early photograph of the bar at O'Malley's hangs in the bar of Lakeview House today. The restaurant holds the distinction of having the first liquor license issued in 1899–1900 by the State of New York. (Courtesy of Tori and James Carter.)

Frederick Sylvester bought O'Malley's in 1935 and retained ownership until 1972. He posted this list of libations available over the bar in the 1950s. (Courtesy of the Historical Society of Newburgh Bay and the Highlands.)

WINES

	glass	½ bot.	bot.		glass	bot.
Claret	20	75	1.25	Port	25	2.75
Sauterne	20	75	1.25	Sherry	25	2.75

Rhine 1.50 half bot. 2.50 bot.

COCKTAILS ETC.

O'Malley Special	25c	Gin Ricky	25c
Manhattan	25c	Dubonnet	25c
Bronx	25c	Jack Rose	25c
Dry Martini	25c	Old Fashioned	30c
Gin	25c	Bacardi	35c

Whiskey Sours 35c Tom Collins 35c Side Car 35c

WHISKIES

Rye High Ball	25c	Rye Whiskey	glass	25c
Bourbon High Ball	25c	Bourbon Whiskey	glass	25c
Scotch High Ball	35c	Scotch Whiskey	glass	35c

CORDIALS

Apricot Brandy	40c	Creme de Menthe	40c
Cognac [3 star] Brandy	40c	Benedictine	45c

Cointreau 45c

BEERS & ALES

P.O.N. Lager bot. 15 P.O.N. Lager draft 10 P.O.N. xxx Ale 15

MINERAL WATERS

Canada Dry Ginger Ale 50c White Rock Water 50c

Saratoga Vichy 50c

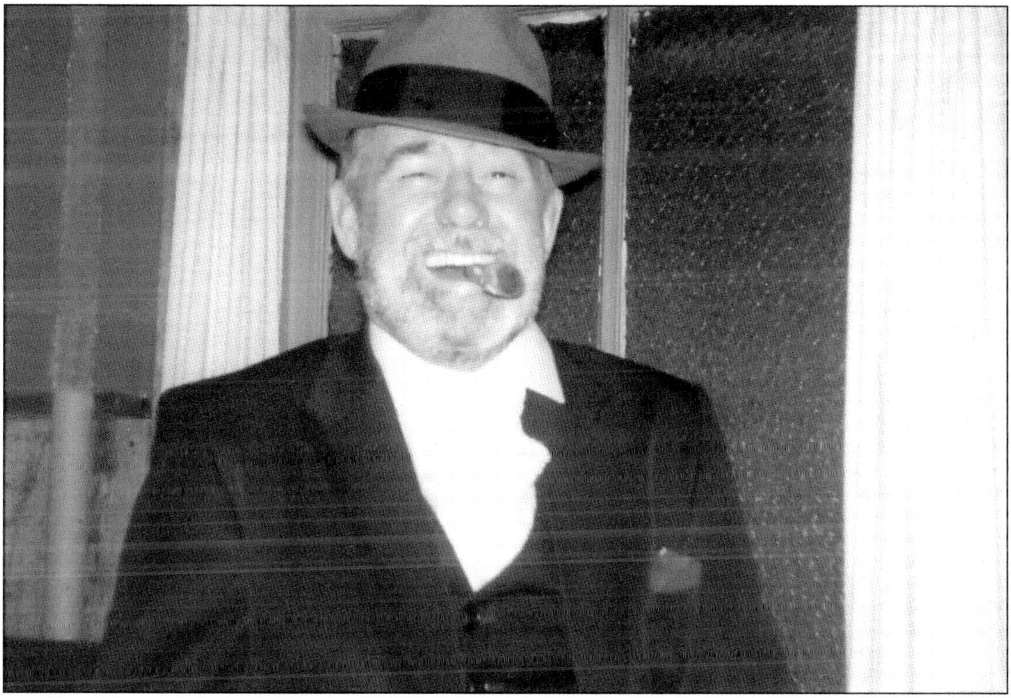

James Tenny purchased O'Malley's from Sylvester in 1972 and ran the business until 1986. A jovial man, Tenny brought a new vitality to the old landmark. Special holiday parties were frequent. Above, Tenny laughs, cigar clenched in his teeth, during a Halloween party in 1989. (Courtesy of Marsha Tenny.)

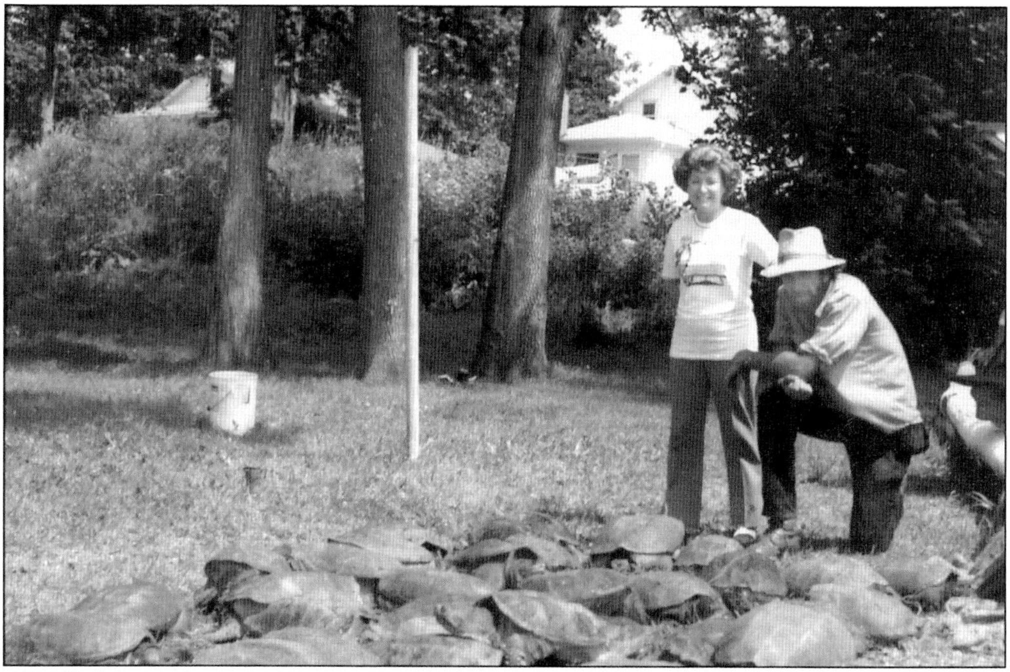

O'Malley's hosted a special visitor every 9 or 10 years. He was known as "the Turtle Man." He came from New England and would harvest turtles to bring back home and cook, selling the meat to restaurants and gourmet shops. With an unidentified woman, he looks over his catch in the 1980s. (Courtesy of Marsha Tenny.)

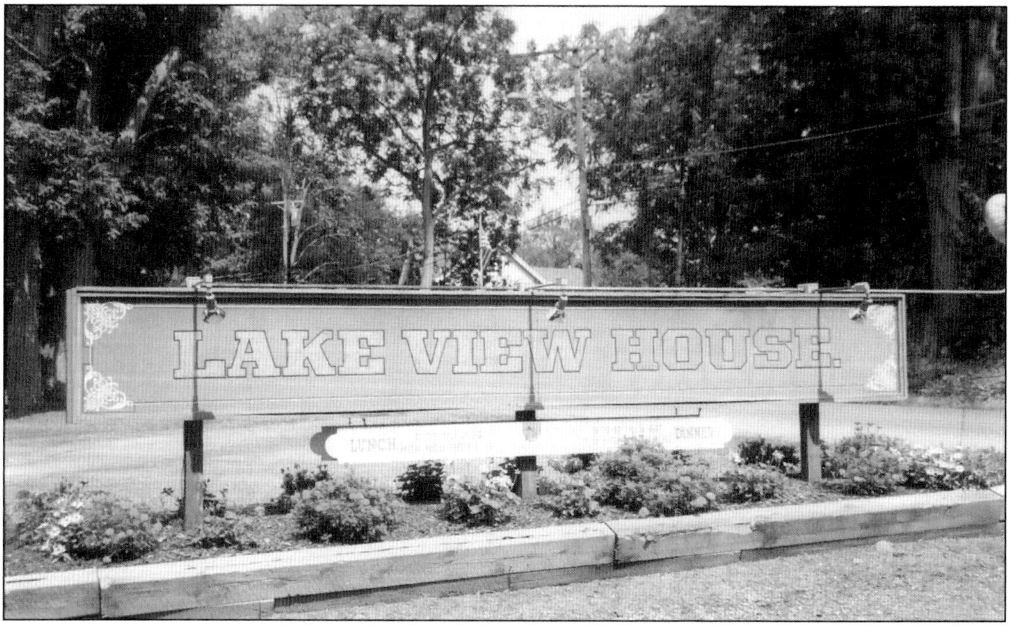

In the mid-1980s new owners took over O'Malley's. While making renovations, they found this original sign for the building. They restored the sign, and after almost eight decades, the business became the Lakeview House again. It is currently owned by Tori and James Carter. (Author's collection.)

Five

The Amusement Park

Major changes took place at Orange Lake as a result of the trolley line and the subsequent expansion of the park in 1903. Orange Lake became the "playground for the Northeast." To this day, the name Orange Lake is still synonymous with amusement park for many. On a large map called the "Grand Plan of Improvements, Orange Lake Park," dated 1903, the following are drawn in as new and improved attractions: an amphitheater, bandstand, merry-go-round, restaurant, boathouse, dance pavilion, casino, and bowling alleys. Space was also allocated for amusement features, lawns, walks, lawn tennis, and croquet. Some of these improvements were never made, as in the case of the bowling alleys and casino, and the areas reserved for lawn tennis and croquet actually became rides, a midway, and other features.

In 1908, a local newspaper reported that 15,000–20,000 people visited the park on an average weekend. Special events, especially on opening weekend, could bring crowds of 40,000 people a day. In 1918, the trolley made 21 daily trips to Orange Lake. Each year, rides were changed and enhanced and more attractions added.

So why did the park close? The answer is the same as it was for parks and other similar attractions in the United States. The automobile became reasonable for an increasing number of people. Citizens had more choices of places to go and could travel longer distances from home. Attendance at the park dropped. The trolley stopped running in the mid-1920s. In 1925, rumors circulated that the park would close.

The death of Benjamin B. Odell in 1926 complicated negotiations with vendors, some of whom had valid leases until 1934. One of these concessionaires, Harold Rhodes, bought the park but was forced to close it during the Depression. Harold Levin, who leased the park from Rhodes, eventually bought it in 1937. Financial difficulties forced him to close the park, and in 1941, the attractions were dismantled and the park demolished.

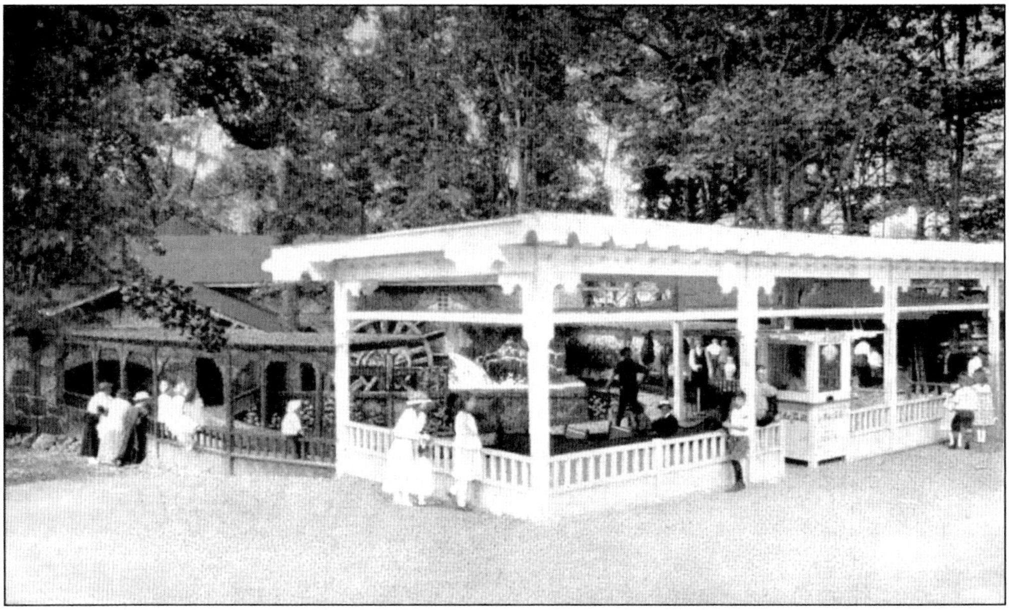

Ye Olde Mill was one of the most popular attractions at the park. The ride featured a tunnel of love. For those young lovers who were fortunate enough to know the operator, a Mr. Nichols, the ride might just have a breakdown for a few minutes while the couple was in the tunnel. (Author's collection.)

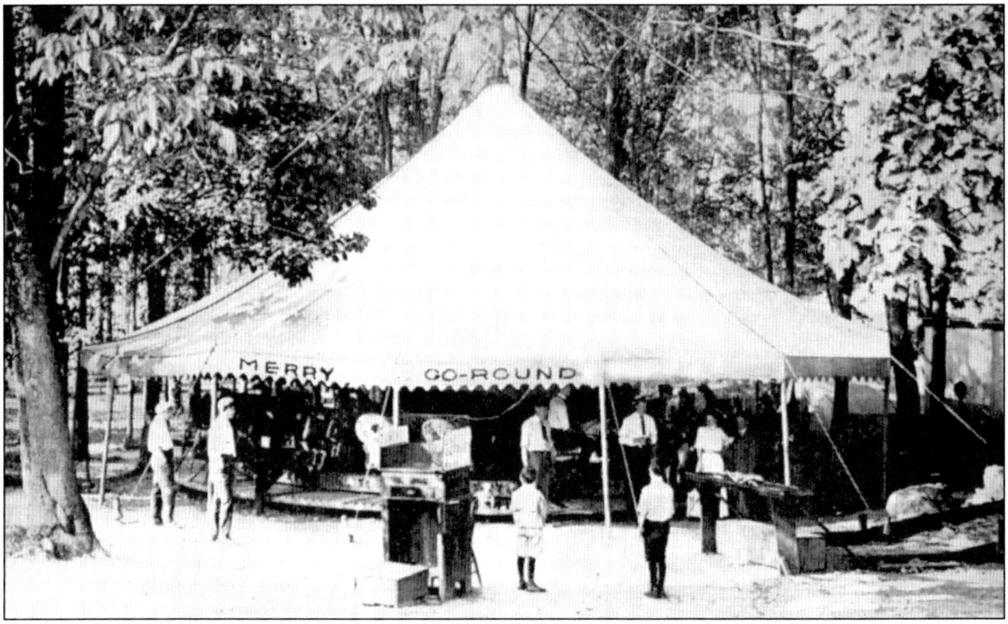

This carousel, or merry-go-round, was erected by the Philadelphia Toboggan Company located in Pennsylvania in 1927. In a twist of fate, when the park was sold, the merry-go-round was taken back to Pennsylvania to an amusement park in Reading. Its final resting place was a park in Texas. (Author's collection.)

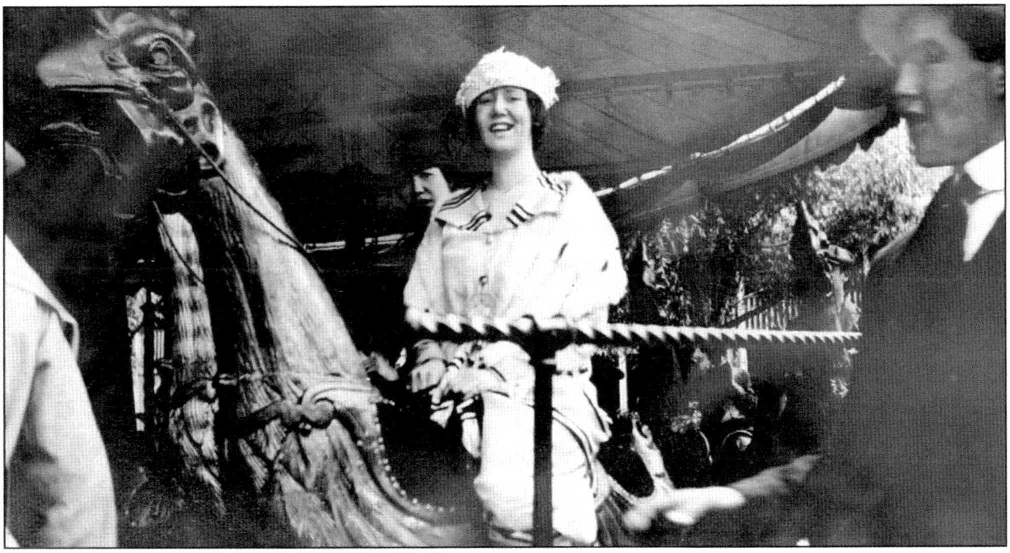

The 1927 merry-go-round at the park was outfitted with horses and brass rings. The earlier one, pictured above, had a variety of animals. This woman appears to be on an ostrich or other exotic animal. (Courtesy of Paul Yablonsky.)

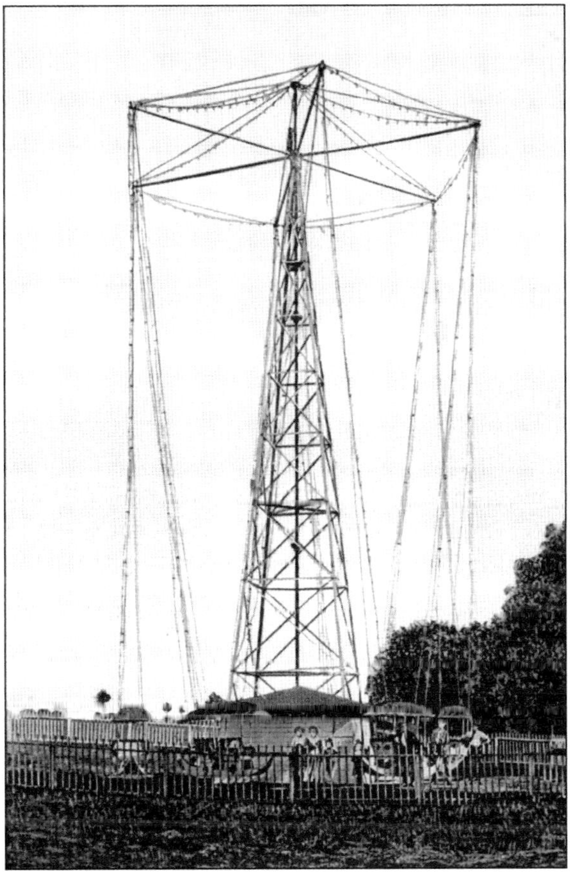

The Circle Swing was one of the first attractions at the park. It featured large wooden swings that held three to five people and swung precariously close to the lake. (Courtesy of Robert Goodbread.)

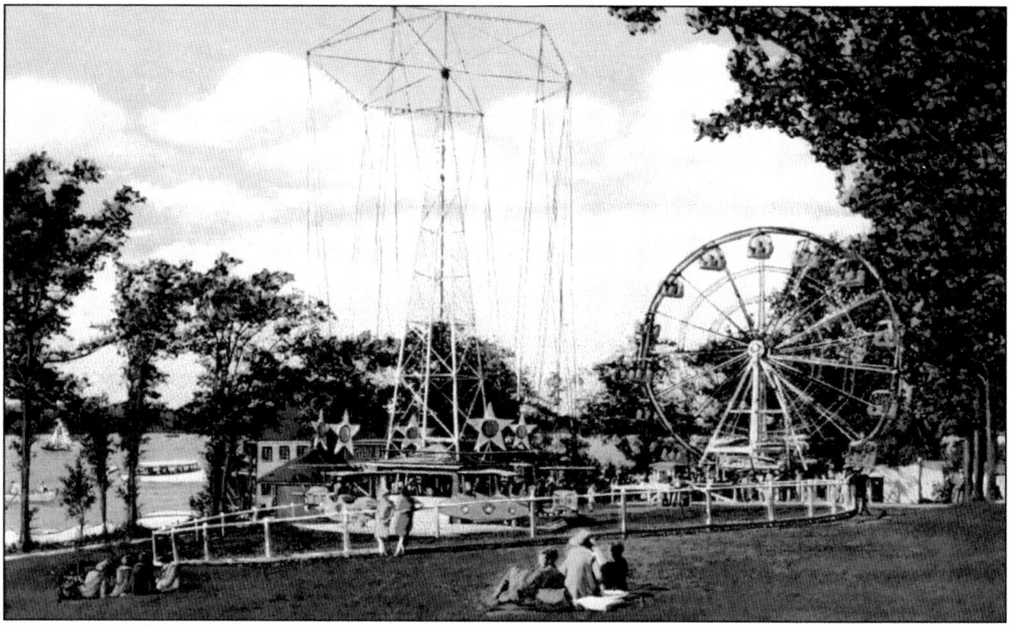

Upgrades and improvements were made to the park each season. In this postcard view, one can see the Ferris wheel and the former Circle Swing. Now called the Aeroplane Ride, the swings were changed to small airplanes. (Courtesy of Robert Goodbread.)

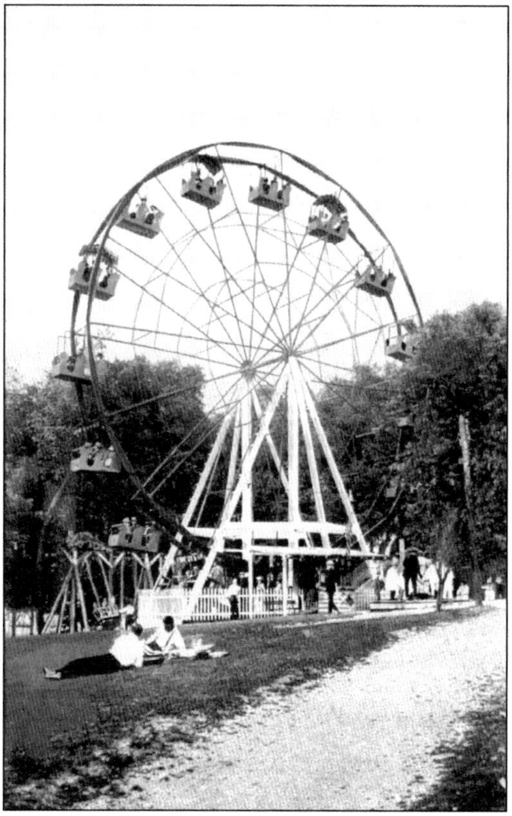

The Ferris wheel was a very popular attraction. On busy days, people waited in line for more than two hours for a ride. When the park closed, this attraction was dismantled, but its final destination remains a mystery. (Courtesy of Robert Goodbread.)

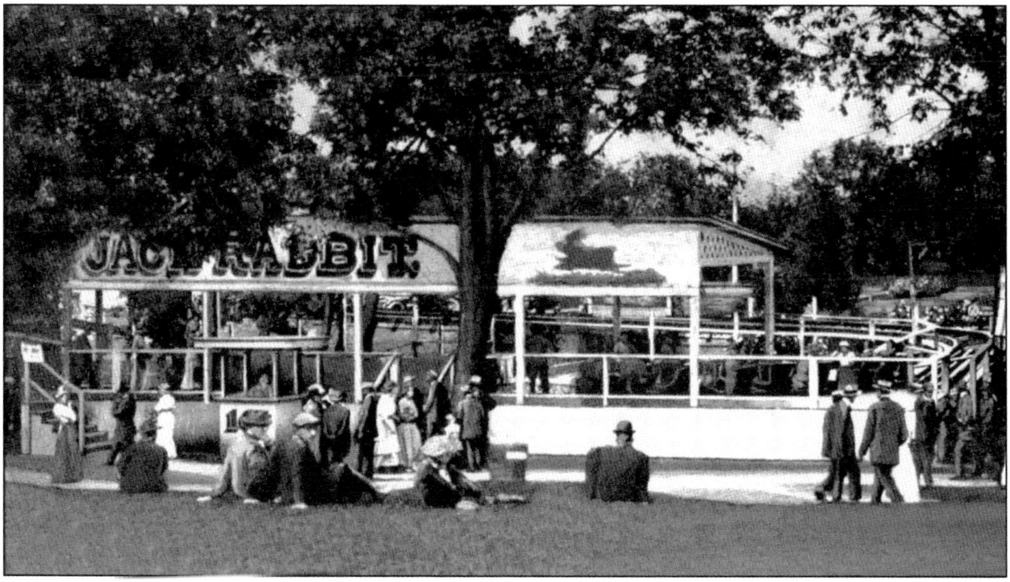

The Jack Rabbit was a scenic railway ride that took passengers on a gently sloping trip around the northern part of the park. There are advertisements and promotional materials showing a much larger roller coaster at the park; however, no original photographs or postcards have ever been found. (Author's collection.)

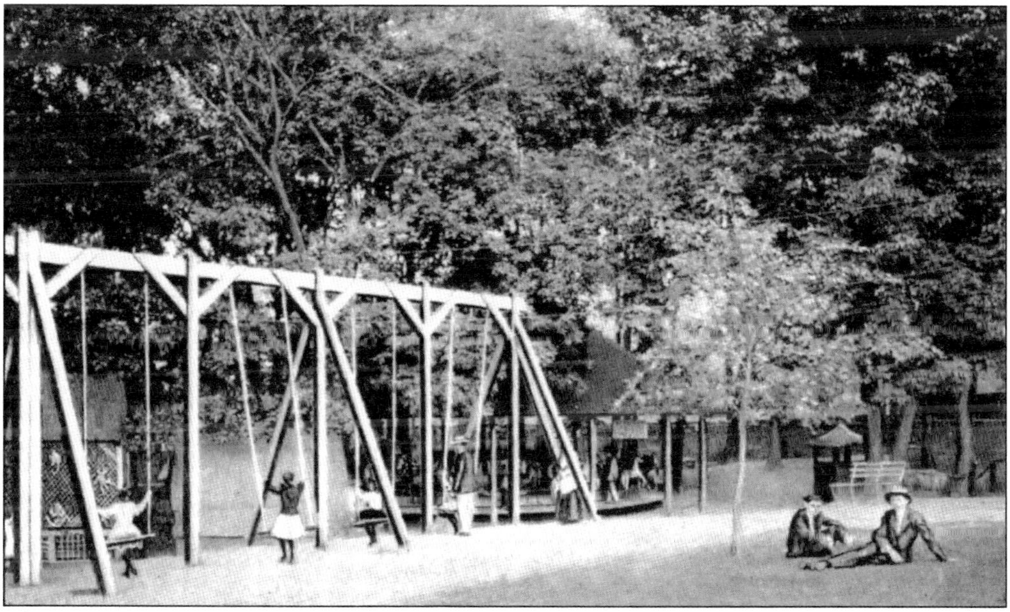

There were also traditional swings at the park located by the merry-go-round. In the far left of this postcard, behind the girl on the swing, is the Monkey House, a 1920s addition to the park. (Courtesy of Robert Goodbread.)

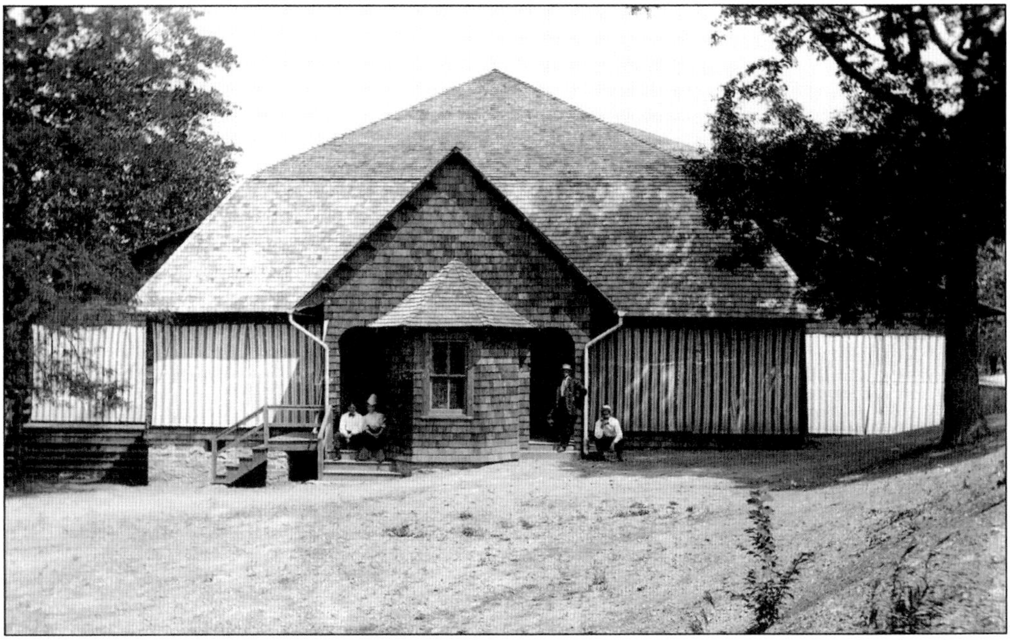

Awnings are closed in this photograph of the theater. Seating over 1,000 people, the theater had both evening and matinee performances. Some of the acts for the 1911 season opening included J. M. Moores's New Orleans Minstrels, the Globe Comedy Four, and special vaudeville "surprises." (Courtesy of the Historical Society of Newburgh Bay and the Highlands.)

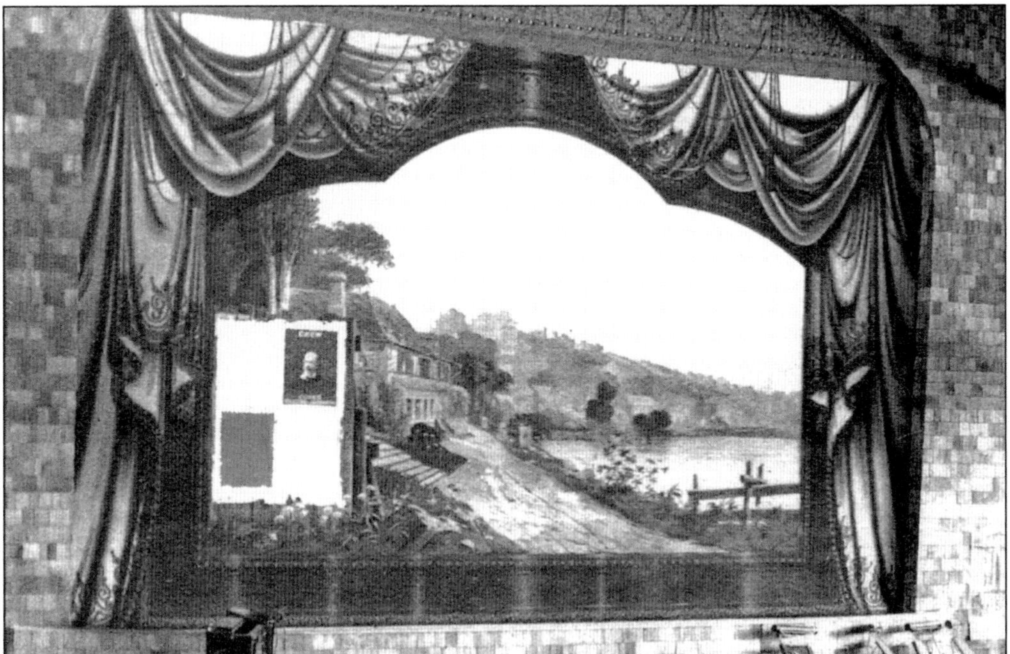

The interior of the theater was quite plush. A small orchestra accompanied many of the performances, and scenery was hand painted. Passengers showing their trolley ticket for the day were charged reduced rates for the theater events. (Courtesy of Sharon Nichols Formato.)

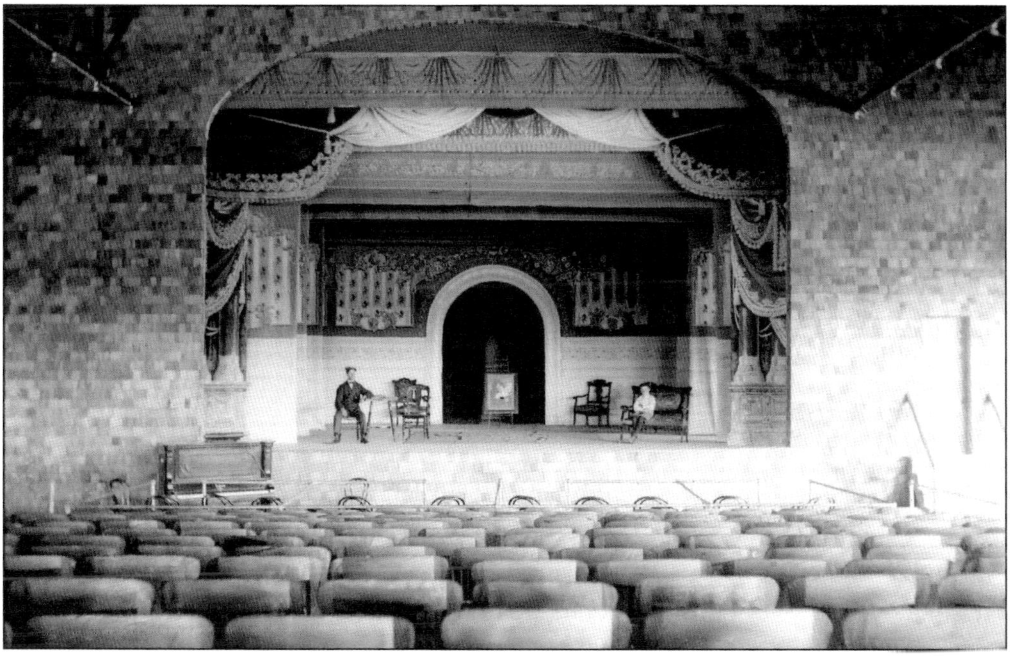

Two men practice their lines for a performance long forgotten in this photograph. In July 1908, some of the best-reviewed acts of the season included Carolyn Booth in *A Model Maid* and Sallie Randall, who did burlesque impersonations of people known on New York's Broadway. On Wednesday and Saturday afternoons, programs for children were held. (Courtesy of the Historical Society of Newburgh Bay and the Highlands.)

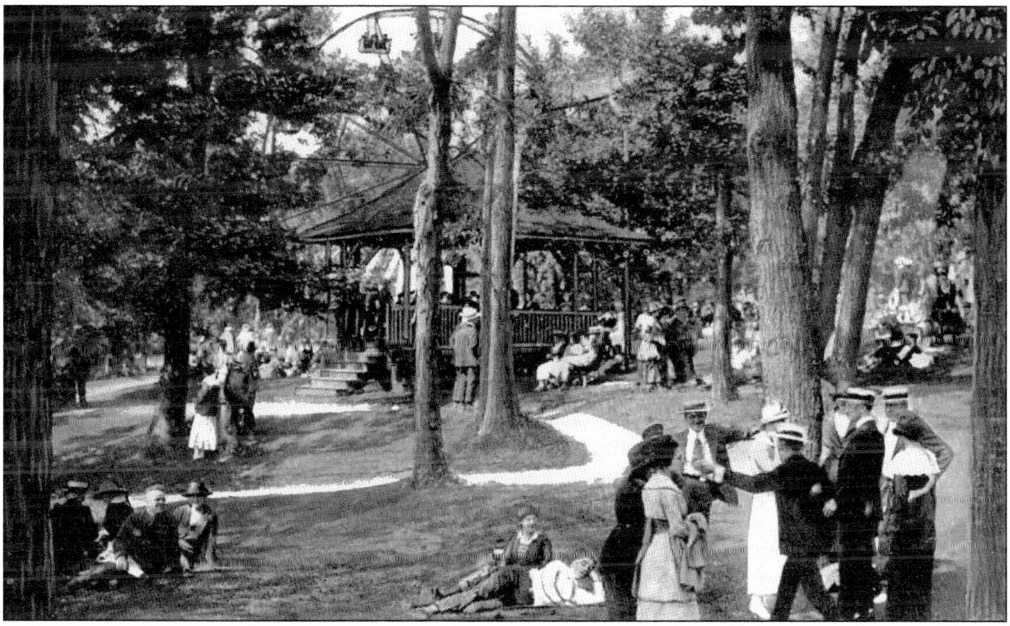

People gather around the bandstand waiting for a concert to begin. Collin's Band from Newburgh played there frequently and was always a hit with the crowds. Seating was limited, and most people, as is obvious in this postcard and others, sat on the ground. (Author's collection.)

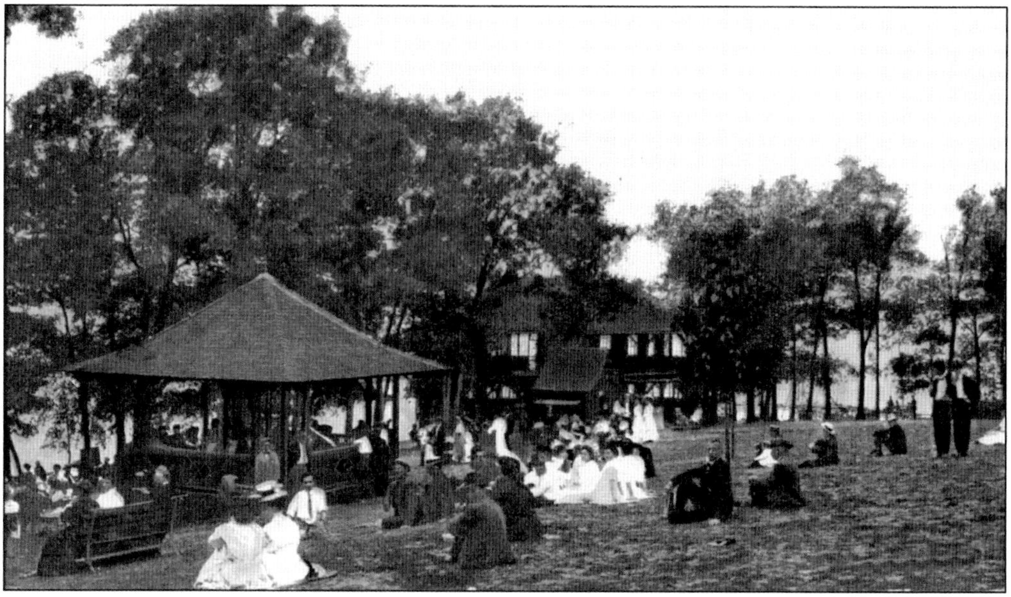

This is another shot of the bandstand and the boathouse. According to a 1925 newspaper account, visitors on their way to the borscht belt would stop by the Orange Lake park to partake of the amusements before going to hotels in the Catskill Mountains. (Author's collection.)

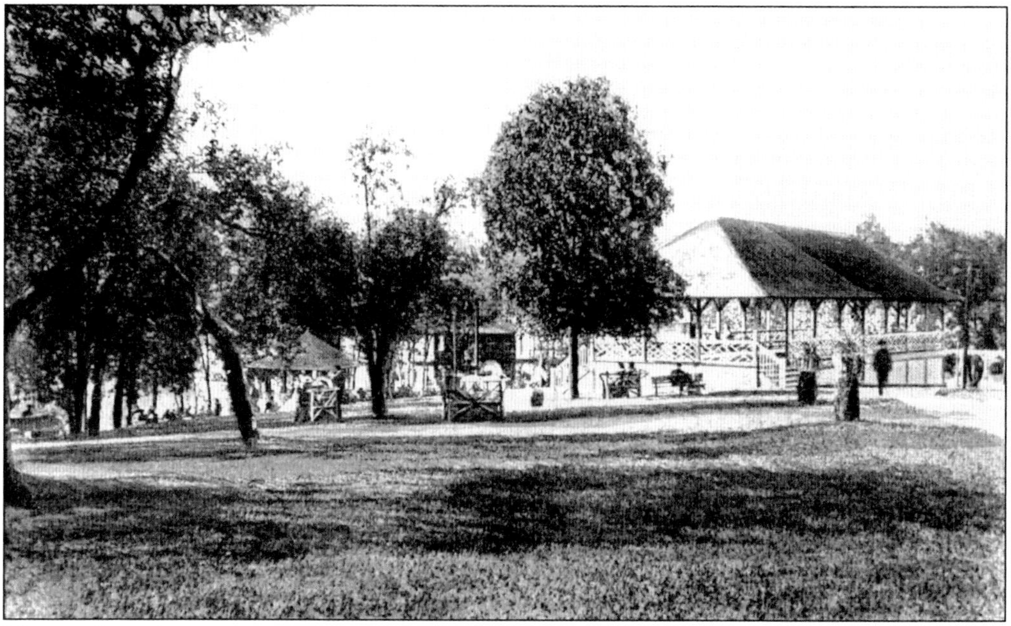

The outdoor dancing pavilion is at the right of this postcard view. Edna Smith, in a 1976 newspaper interview, told the reporter that she met her future husband there on a Sunday afternoon in the 1930s while listening and dancing to Ward Harrison's Orchestra, another Newburgh group. (Courtesy of Robert Goodbread.)

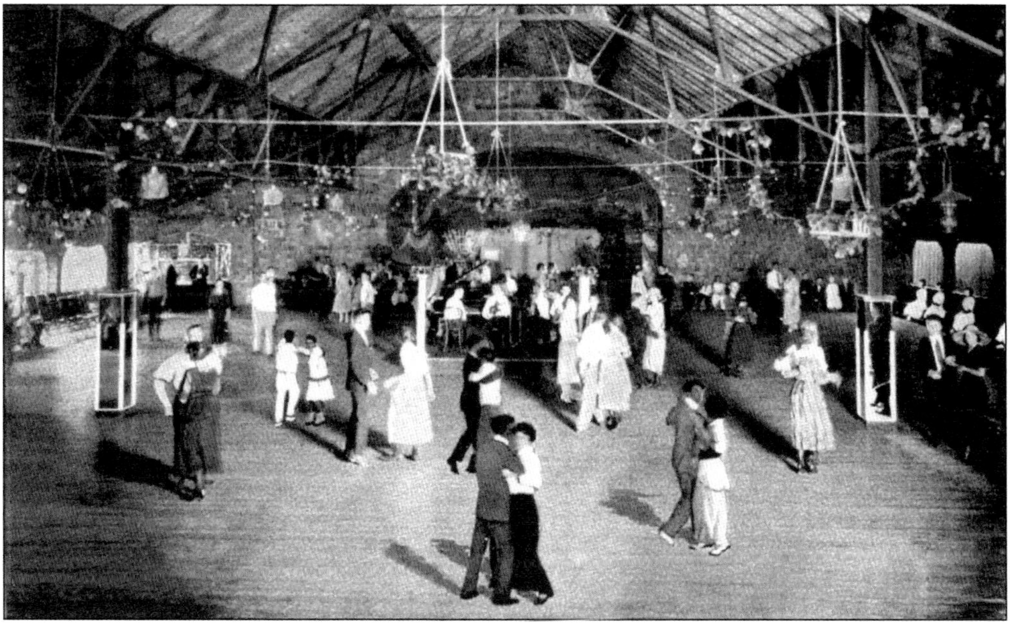

This is the interior of the dancing pavilion in the evening. According to old Orange Lake pamphlets, dances were held each afternoon and evening in the season. Electricity came to the park when it opened while lake residents had to wait more than 20 years to have it in their homes. (Author's collection.)

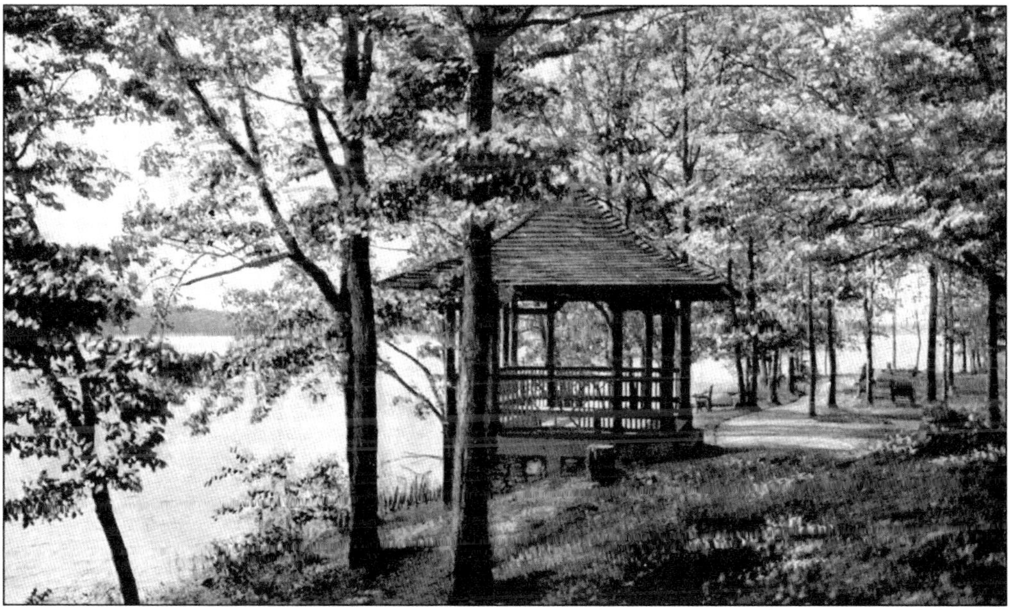

Summerhouses dotted the shores and walkways of the park. These rustic resting places were common from the middle of the 19th century until the late 1930s. They were introduced to the world by Newburgh's father of landscape architecture, Andrew J. Downing. (Author's collection.)

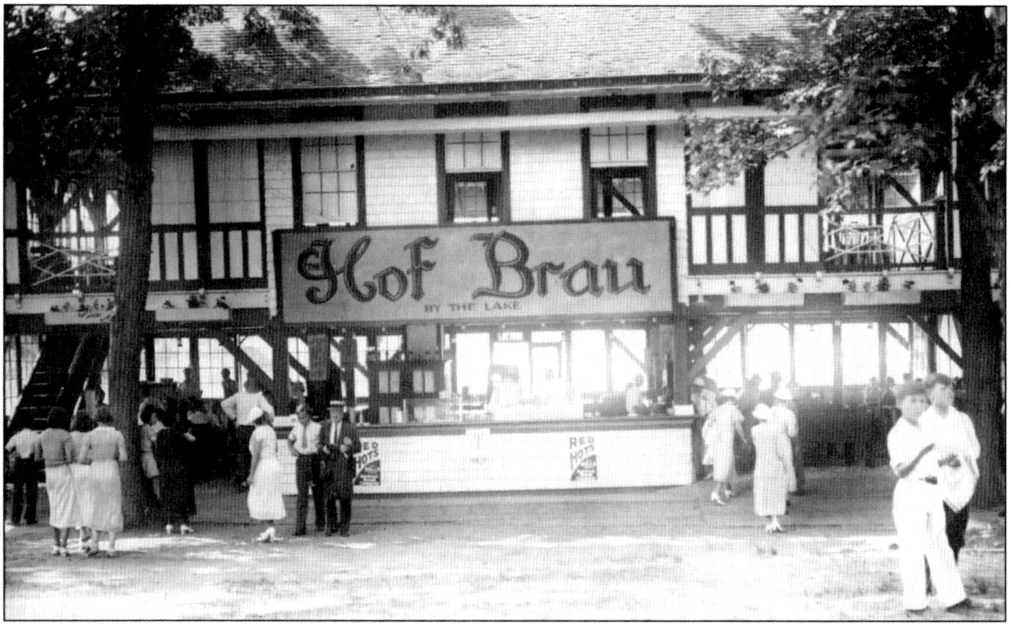

The Hof Brau offered cold drinks and light fare to park goers. Only nonalcoholic beverages could be sold or brought into the park, a regulation by its owners to make sure the park retained its reputation as a family destination. (Courtesy of Sharon Nichols Formato.)

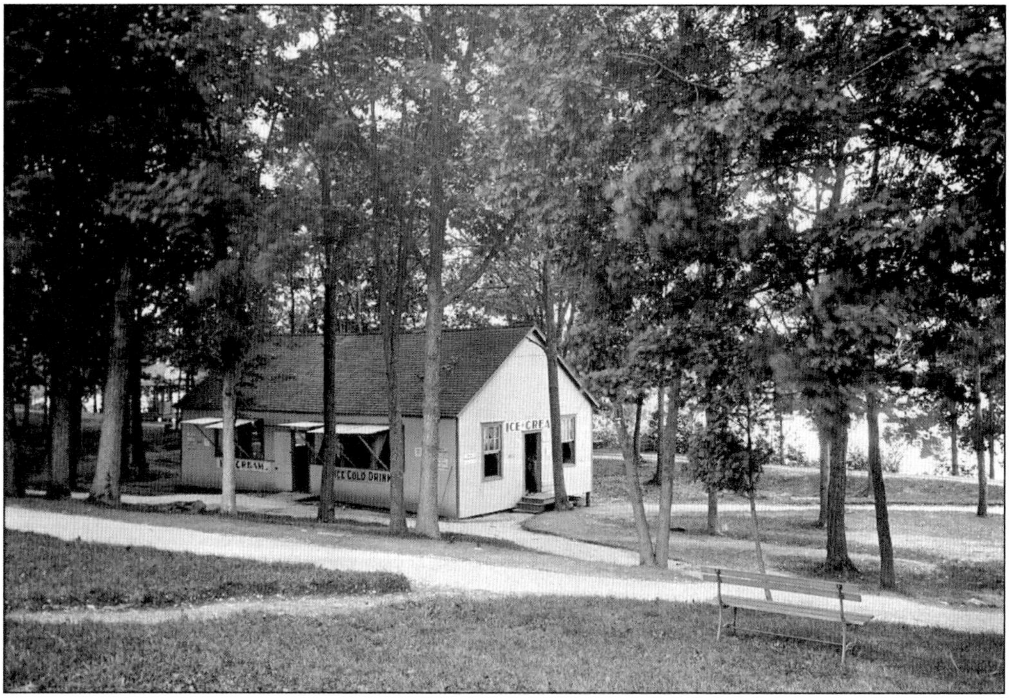

The ice-cream and cold drinks concession was one of the busiest places in the park. Children of all ages consumed hundreds of gallons of ice cream in a day. Carbonated beverages and ice-cream sodas were also big hits. So why is there no one at the stand? The picture was taken before the park opened. (Courtesy of Sharon Nichols Formato.)

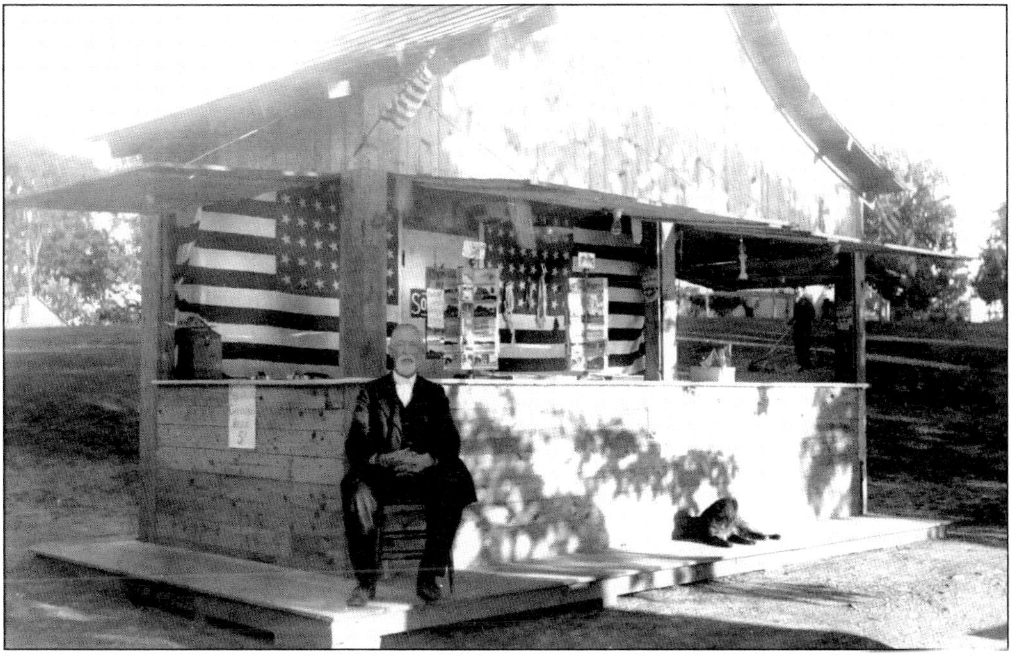

James Sarvis was superintendent of the park for many years. He also operated the souvenir shop on the grounds. It was from this shop that thousands of postcards were sold each week, providing many collectors the basis for their collections today. Sarvis also operated a parcel service that, for a small fee, allowed park goers to check packages in and pick them up at the end of the day. (Courtesy of Sharon Nichols Formato.)

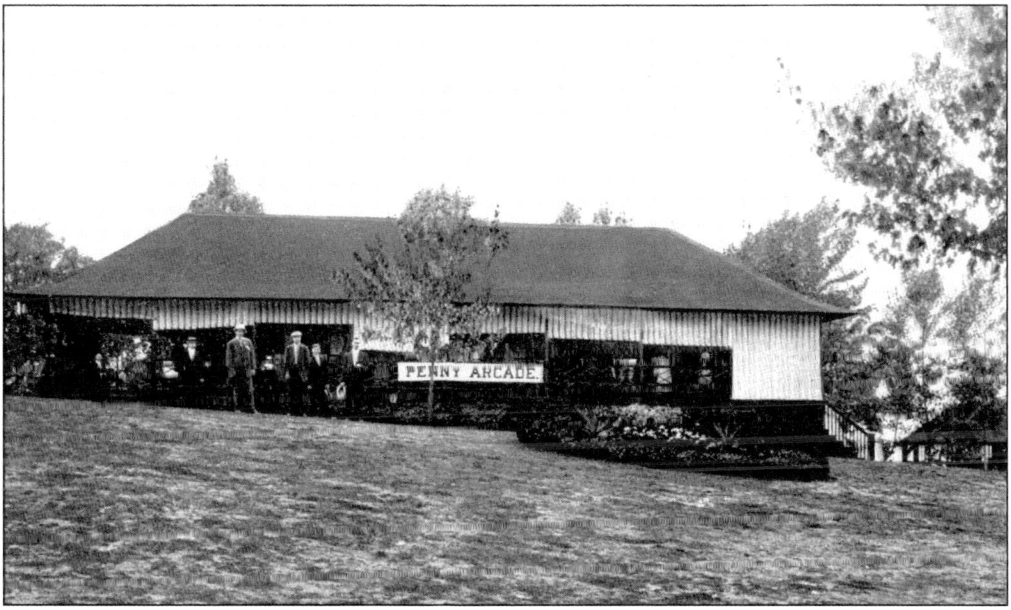

The Kamp and Conway Company operated the arcade at Orange Lake Amusement Park and the one at Kingston Point Park. It advertised its arcades were "better than a circus" and boasted that its laughing galleries let "you see yourself as others see you, you laugh, you scream." (Courtesy of Robert Goodbread.)

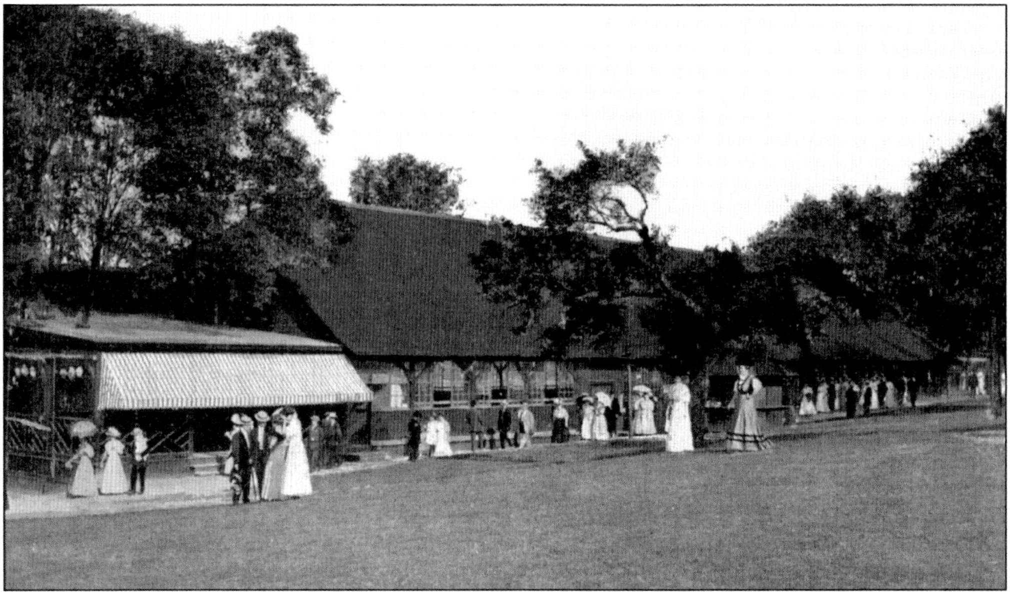

The Japanese tea garden is at the left of this postcard view, and the roller rink is on the right. In 1930, the rink was open daily from 2:00 p.m. to 5:00 p.m. in the afternoon and 6:00 p.m. to 11:00 p.m. each evening. Admission was 25¢ for each session in 1933. (Courtesy of Robert Goodbread.)

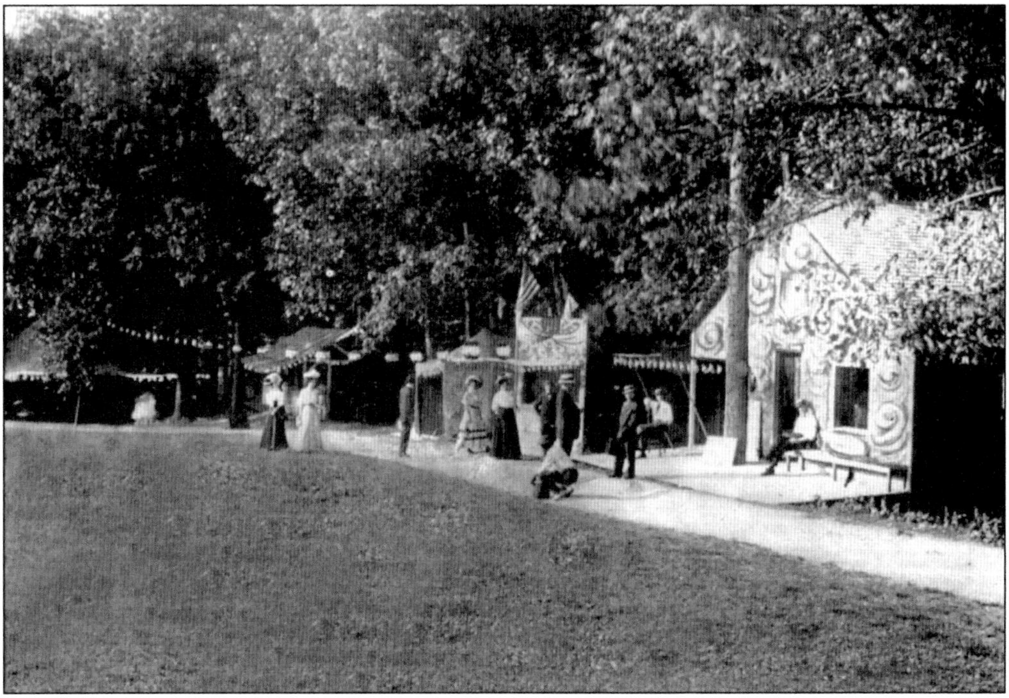

In the mid-1920s, during park renovations, a new attraction called the Monkey House was added to the midway. It was one of the favorite places for children to gather. There monkey families would perform on a trapeze and then hang on the links of the cage waiting to be fed treats by the crowd. (Author's collection.)

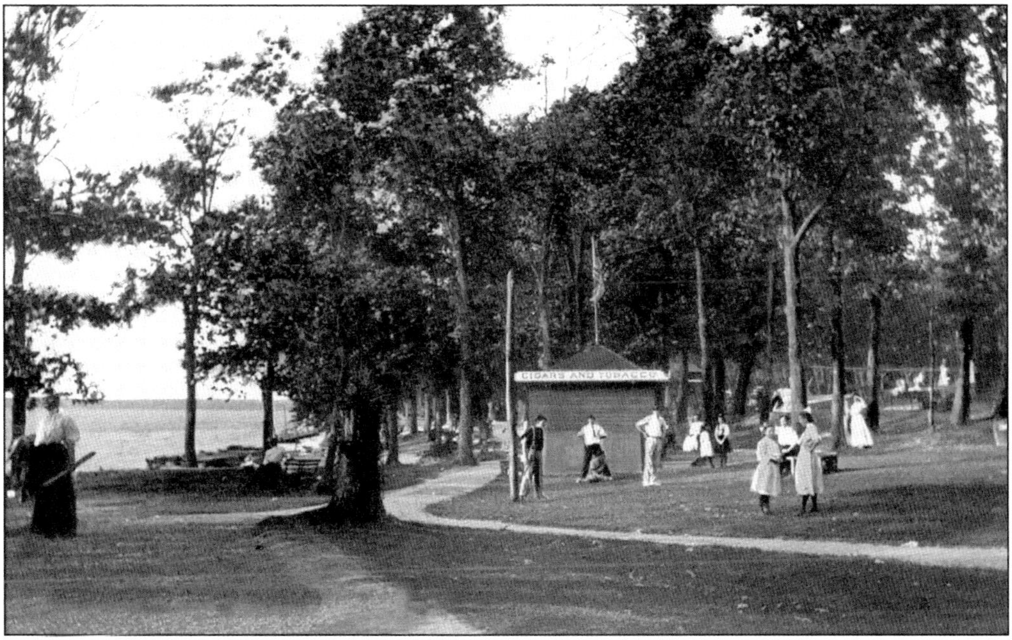

According to the information printed on the back of this postcard, this vacant walkway was called Flirtation Walk. Apparently on the day the photograph was shot, people in the park were too busy to be flirtatious. (Author's collection.)

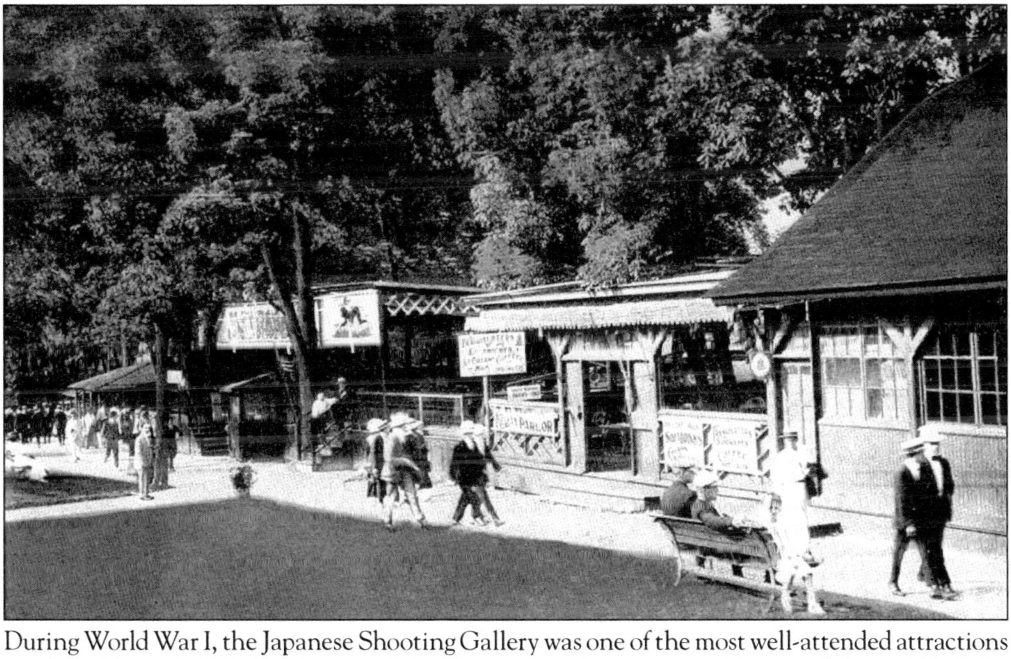

During World War I, the Japanese Shooting Gallery was one of the most well-attended attractions on the midway. A 1917 brochure explains the reason why. It states, "One good shot will kill the Kaiser and good shots win you cigarettes." (Author's collection.)

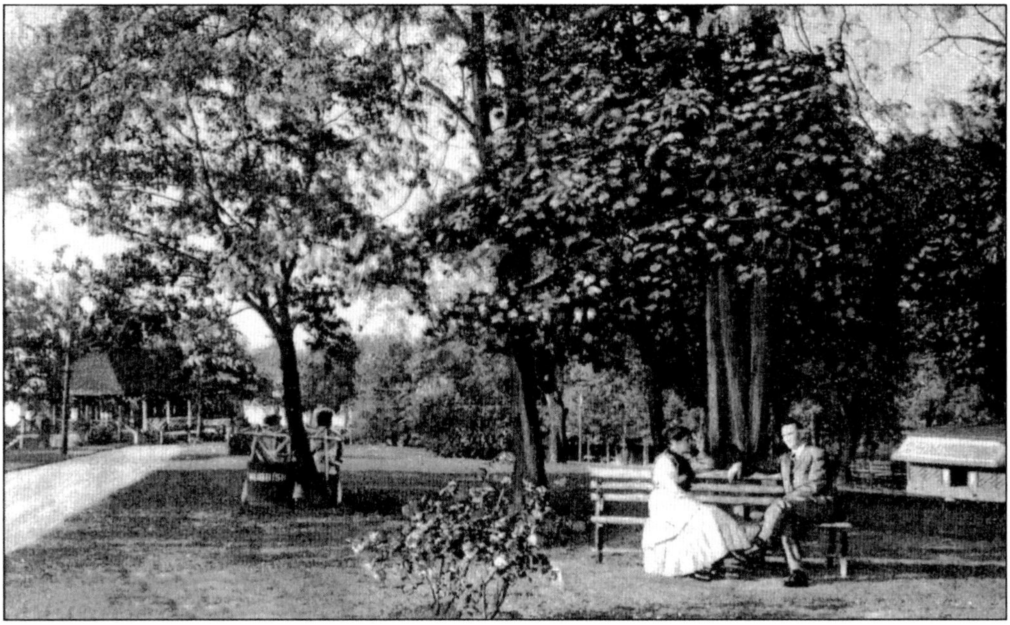

A young man and woman chat on one of the many rustic benches in the park during the 1911 season. The sender of the postcard must have had a very good time there because she tells her friend in the written message on the back, "You should spend your vacation here!" (Courtesy of Marguerite Harris McDermott.)

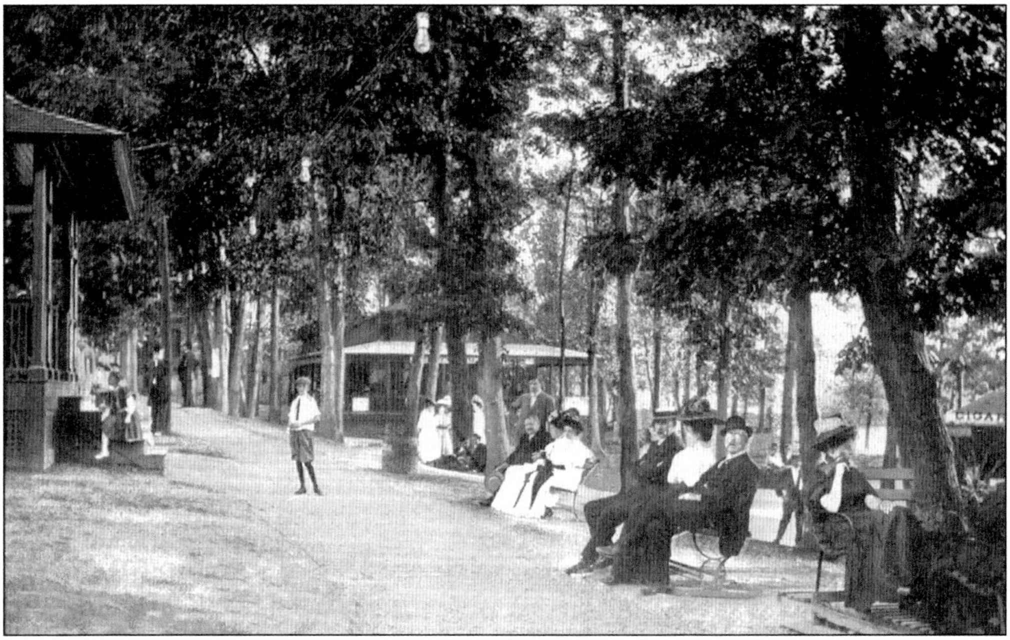

Scenic walkways lined with comfortable benches snaked through the park. In the early 20th century, workweeks were long with most people working six days a week. In nearby Newburgh, most people were employed in factories, and the park provided a healthy respite at an affordable price. (Author's collection.)

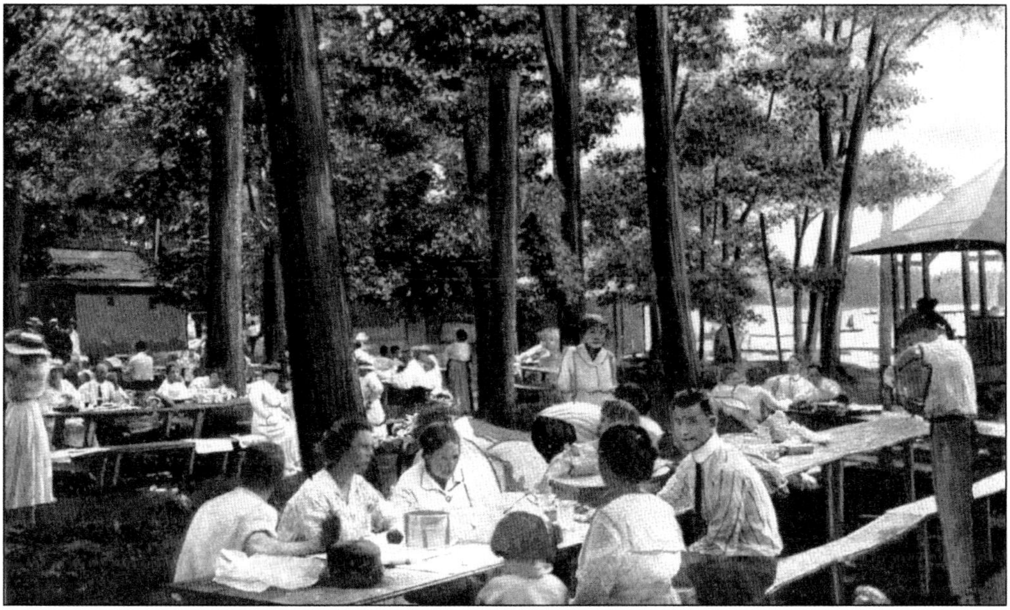

The picnic party was another popular event at the park that attracted hundreds each weekend. Close to the picnic area were a baseball field and an athletic field where baseball, softball, or other athletic contests could take place. In 1903, an advertisement for the park stated that "the Park is especially adapted for Sunday School and society picnic parties." (Courtesy of Robert Goodbread.)

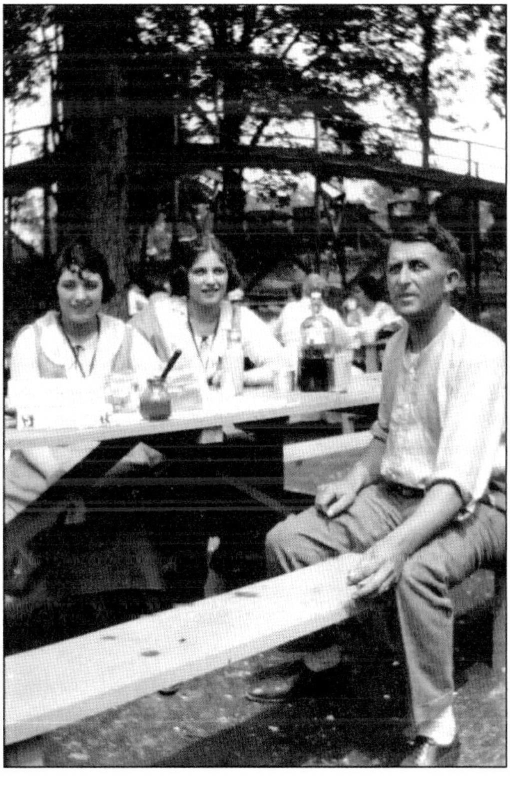

George Cranse, seated at the front of the picnic table; his girlfriend Charlotte Mitzner, back bench far left; and an unidentified friend take a break from their picnic to have their photograph taken in this 1920s scene at the park. Charlotte and George eventually married, but the marriage was cut short by George's untimely death. (Courtesy of Paul Yablonsky.)

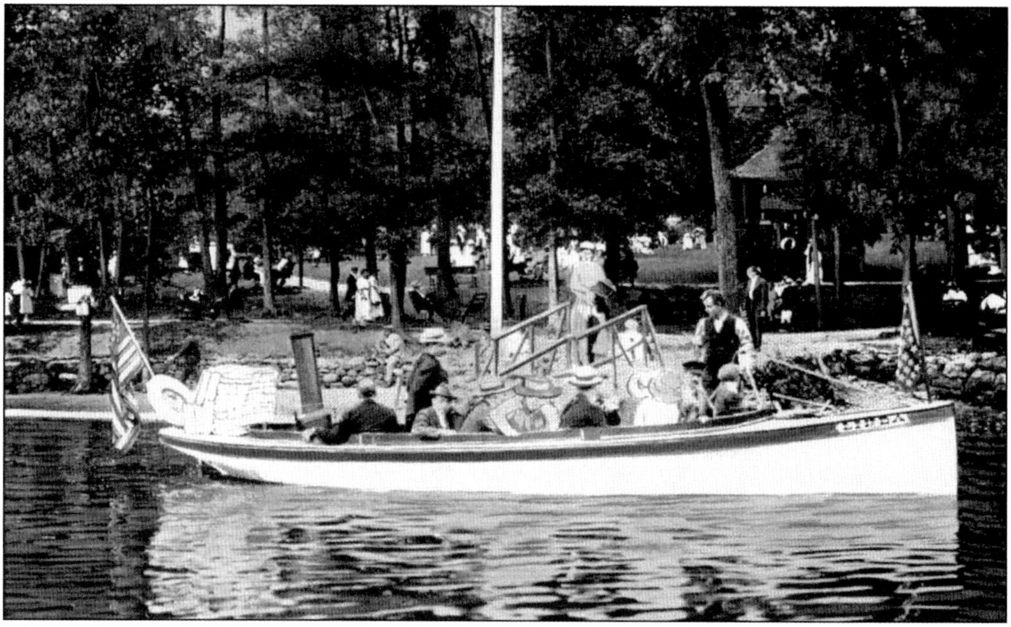

The *Linda* was a naphtha-powered launch that made "half hour trips around the borders of the Lake and to and from Orange Lake Park." It also ran to and from cottages and hotels at the north end of lake for patrons' convenience. On days when the sun was not strong, the awning was removed, providing a more open-air experience. (Author's collection.)

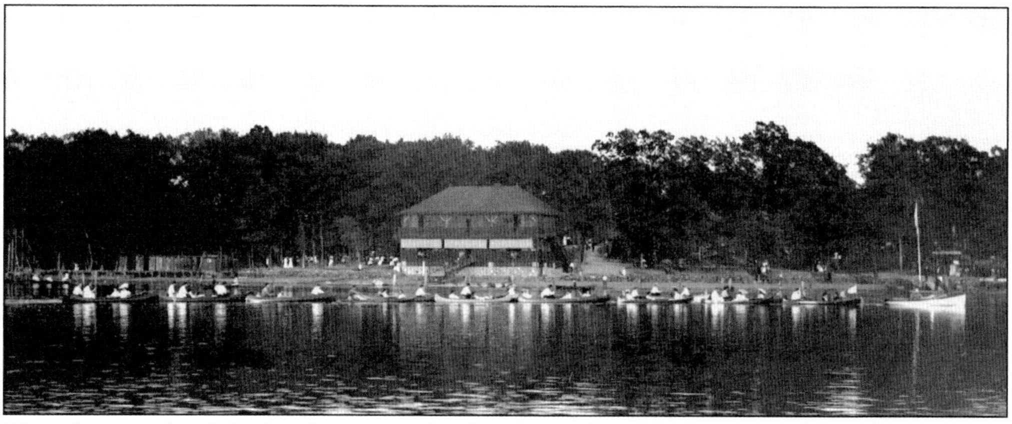

This photograph of the boathouse on the day the park opened in 1909 shows the extent to which people used the rental boats at the park. The boathouse was built in 1903, and the two large verandas allowed patrons "a magnificent panoramic view of the lake." (Courtesy of Sharon Nichols Formato.)

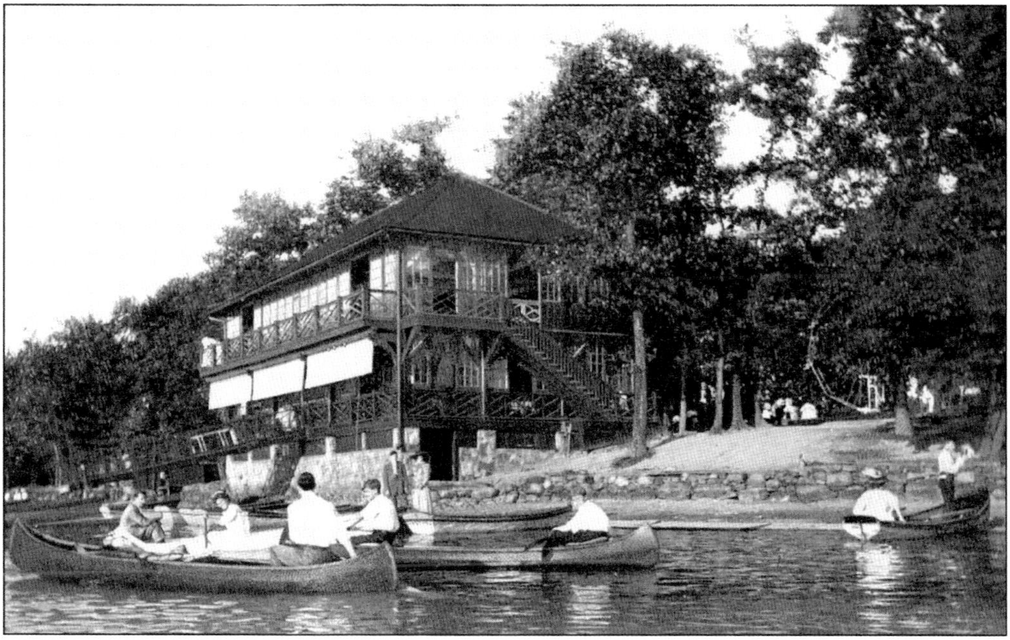

The lower floor of the boathouse was used to store boats, oars, cushions, and other seasonal equipment. The first floor had lockers for bathers. The two broad staircases on either side of the building led to the second floor where a restaurant and dancing area were located. (Author's collection.)

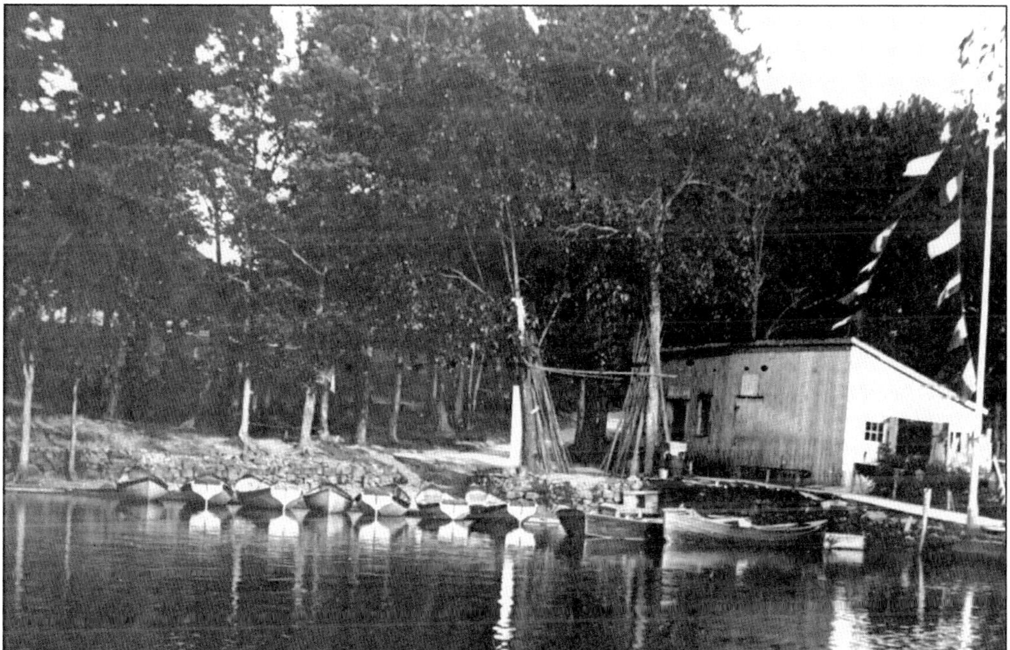

In addition to the park boathouse, many smaller entrepreneurs rented canoes and rowboats to summer visitors and local fishermen. This photograph is of one of those businesses, but the name of the owner and site is long forgotten. (Courtesy of Sharon Nichols Formato.)

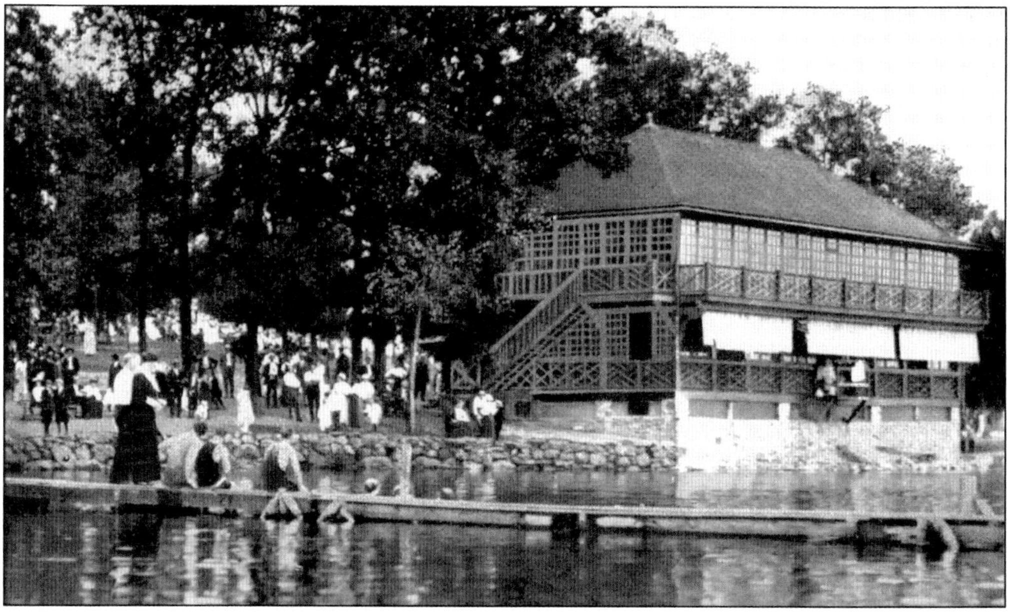

Bathing was another relaxing activity offered in the park. After changing in the boathouse, bathers and swimmers could walk out to the water or go on the narrow pier to sit. (Author's collection.)

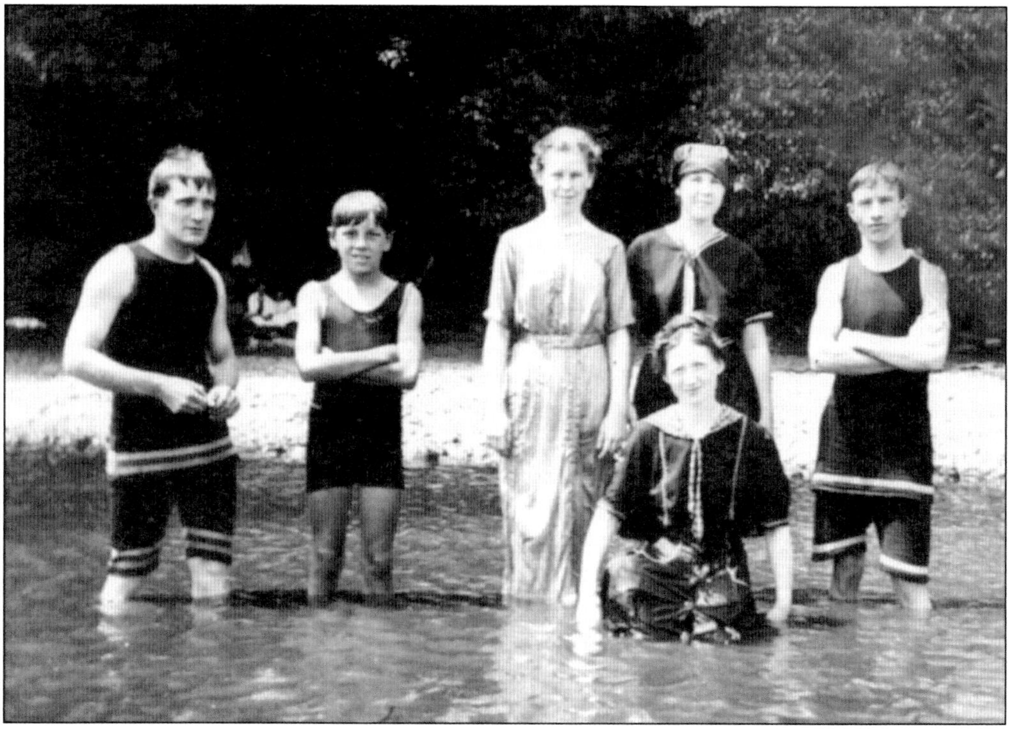

Not all people enjoyed swimming at the lake. This group of young people is unidentified except for Agnes Gillispie, who is in the light-colored dress in the center. A longtime lake resident, she was "frightened to death by the water," according to her granddaughter. (Courtesy of Janice Ruggiero.)

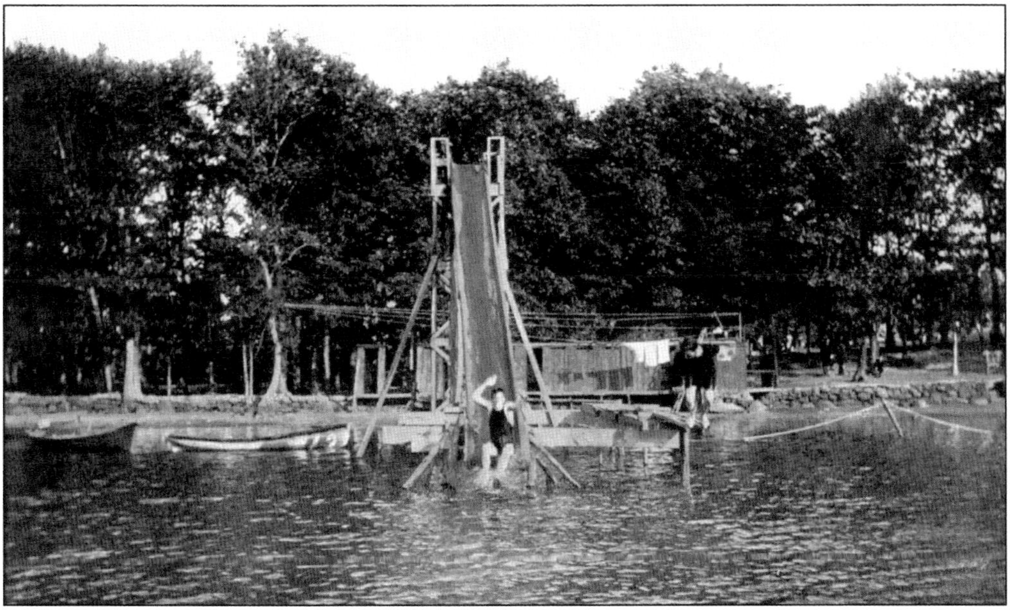

The Shute the Chute was similar to many of today's waterslides. The slide was about 18 feet tall with the frame constructed of wood and the slide of a light metal. Changing rooms for the slide were in the small building at the rear of the slide. (Courtesy of Arlene Hughes.)

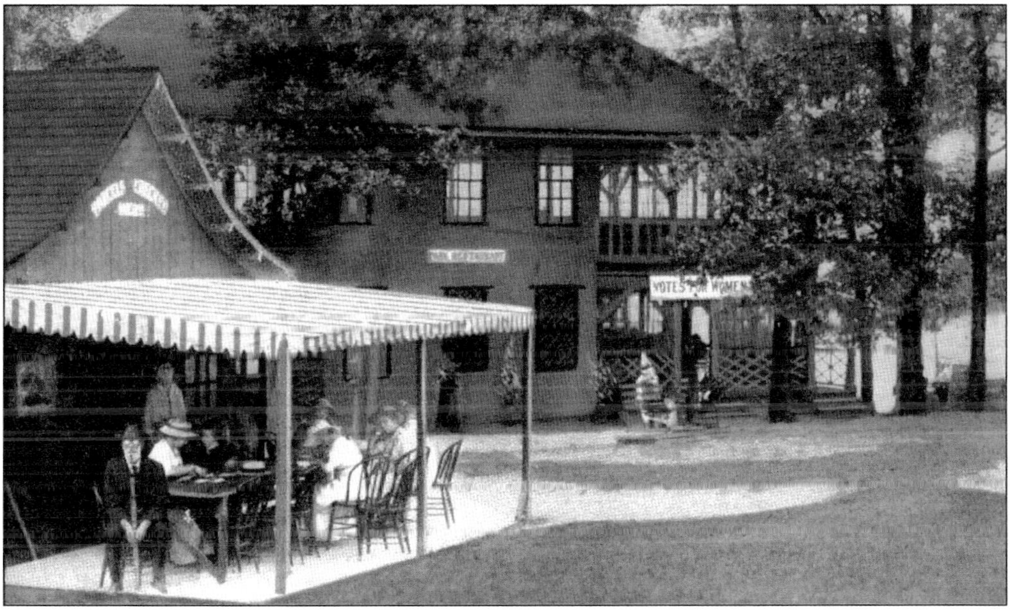

This postcard view of the souvenir stand on the right and the boathouse in the back is interesting because of the banner that can be seen over the entrance. The suffragette movement was very strong in the area, and the suffragettes hosted some events at the park. (Author's collection.)

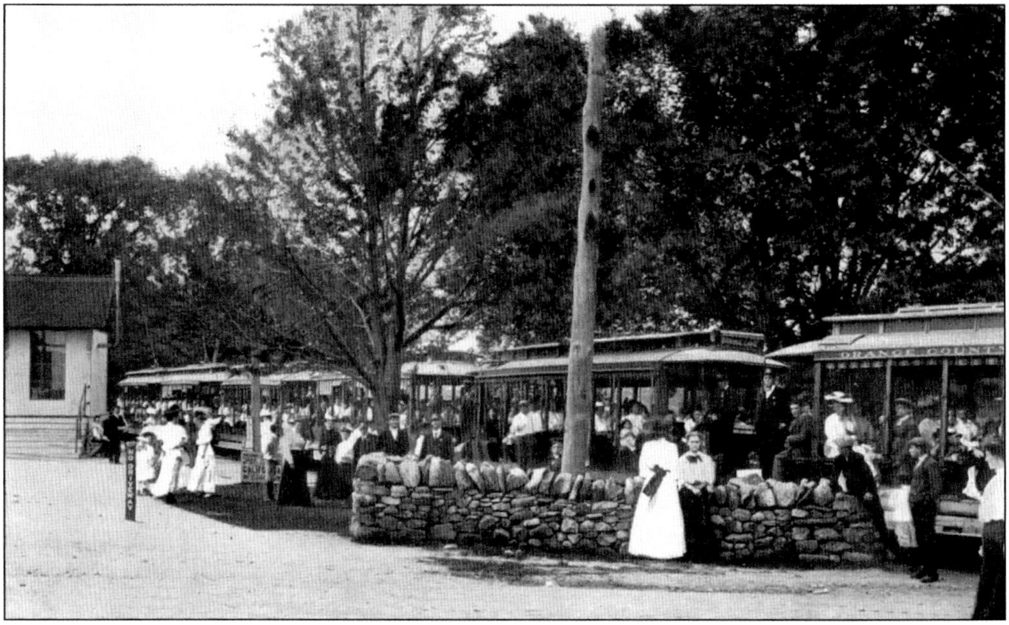

After a long day at the park, fun-seekers board the trolleys for the ride home. The last trolley from the park depended on the time of year. The park closed at dusk during the months from late May until the middle of September. (Courtesy of Robert Goodbread.)

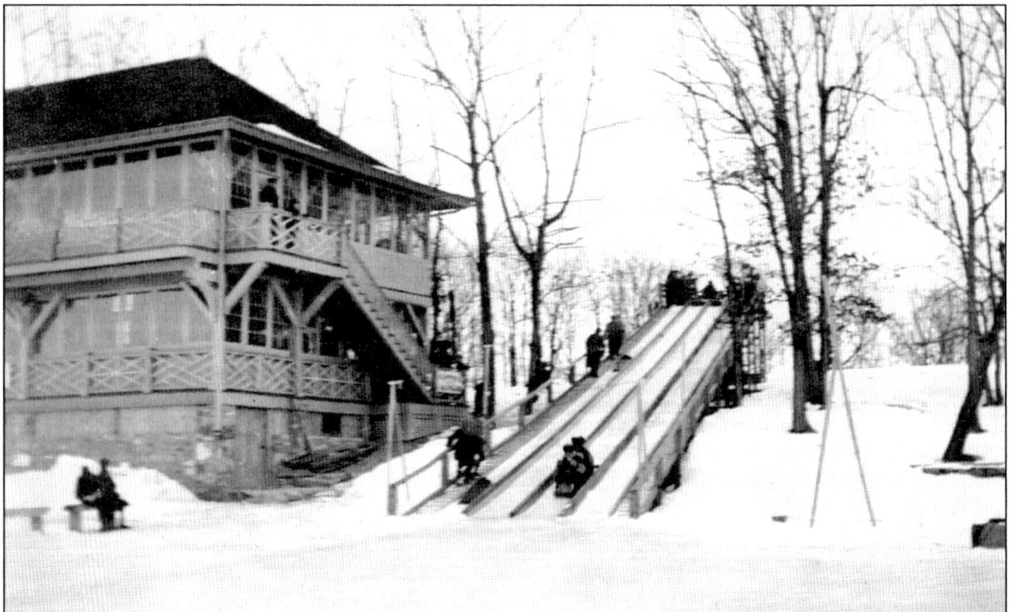

Sometime around 1928, a toboggan run was constructed alongside the boathouse. There is no record of whether a fee was collected to ride the run. It was in use even after the park closed, but lack of maintenance caused its demise. (Courtesy of Marguerite Harris McDermott.)

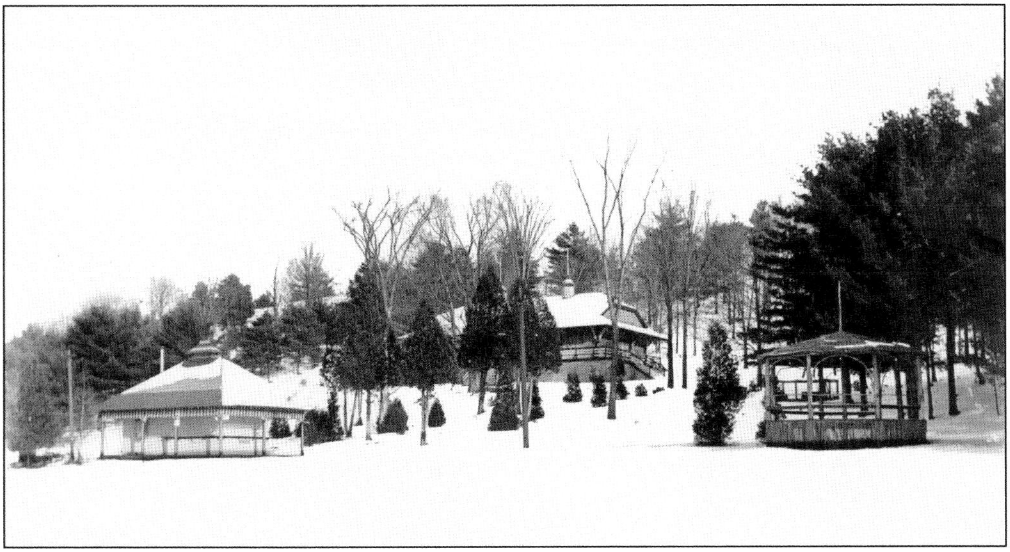

This is a very rare photograph of Orange Lake Amusement Park in winter. Attractions were boarded up each year at the end of the season. Only summerhouses like the one on the right were left to the elements the entire year. (Courtesy of Paul Yablonsky.)

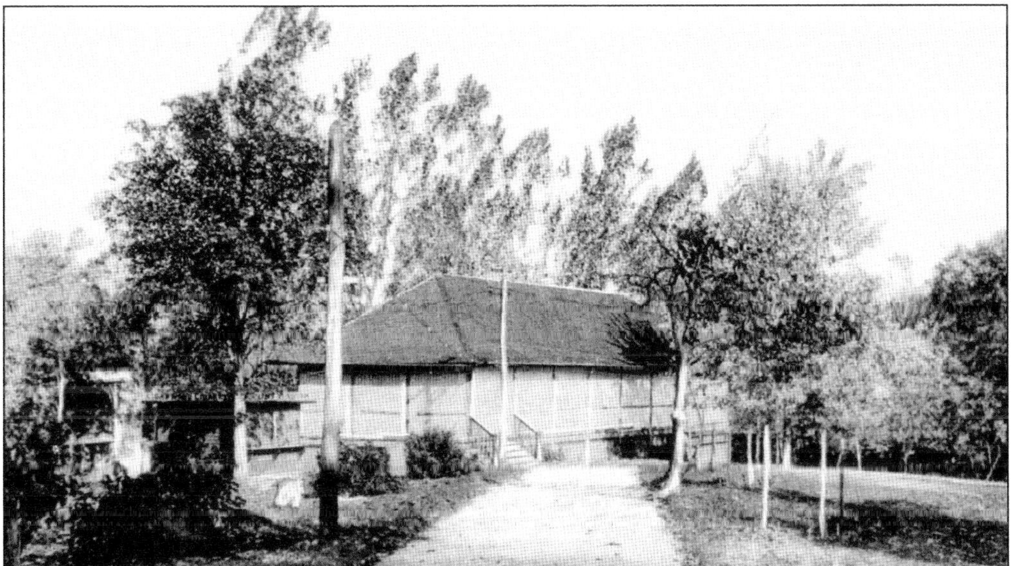

This early postcard depicts a boarded-up souvenir stand and penny arcade during the off-season. The card probably dates to the winter of 1904 or 1905. (Courtesy of Marguerite Harris McDermott.)

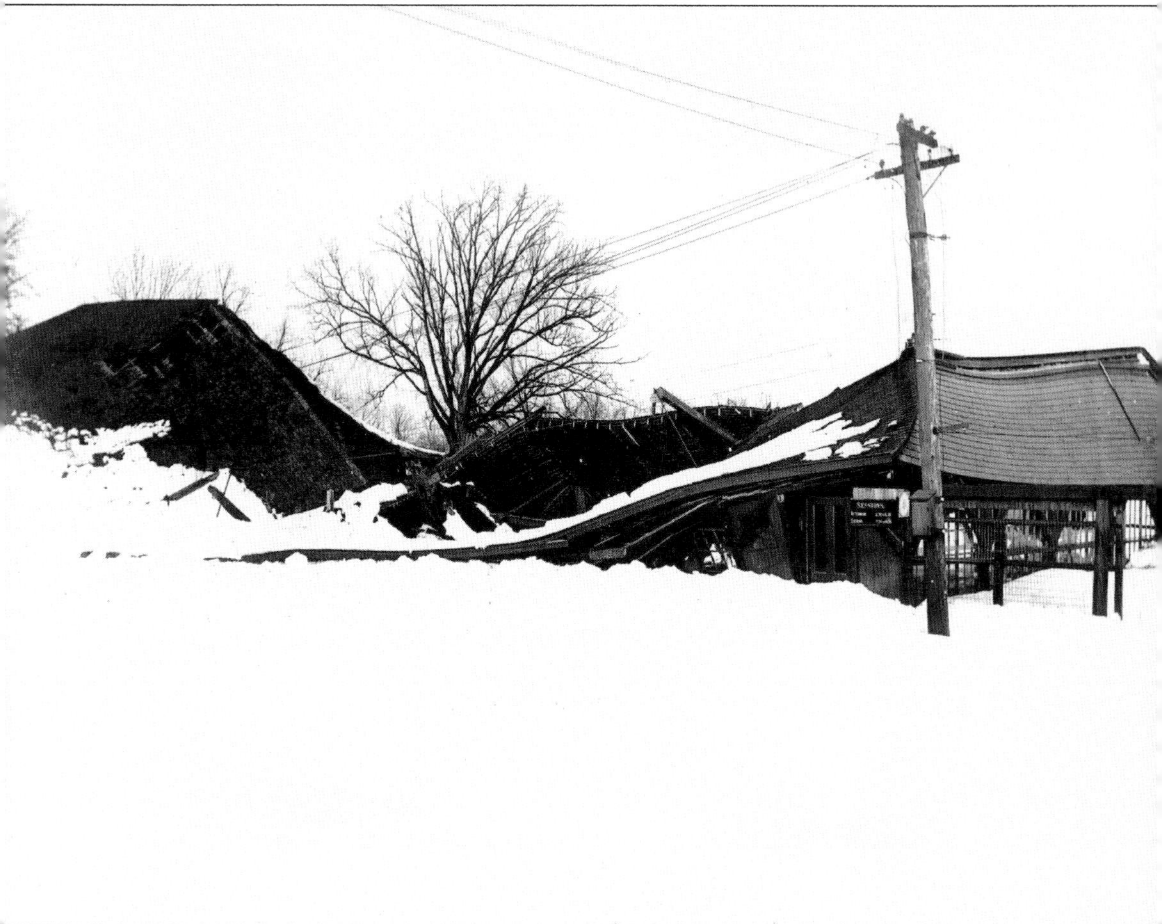

The roller rink, which once brought so much fun and excitement to skaters of all ages, collapsed under the weight of a heavy snowfall about 1941. The rink closed in 1937 and was one of the last buildings standing in the former park. (Courtesy of Marguerite Harris McDermott.)

Six

Early Cottages and Homes

Many early visitors came to experience the clean air, cool waters, and wooded surroundings. Most were city dwellers who lived in congested areas surrounded by factories and industrial complexes. The pace at the lake was very different from what these folks were used to on a daily basis. Time belonged to the cottage dwellers, thus there was no need to rush from place to place. Orange Lake was the ideal vacation spot for individuals and families to relax, enjoy boating and fishing, swim, or just enjoy the scenery.

Living conditions might seem harsh for bungalow and cottage residents by 21st-century standards. Kerosene was the primary source of heat and light until the late 1920s. There was no indoor plumbing, and potable water had to be hand carried from the many small wells around the lake. Water for washing came from the lake.

Residents of larger homes fared better, having better-constructed homes with larger stoves and early access to electricity. Two of the most substantial homes belonged to a Dr. Lempke, a New York City eyewear designer, and superintendent of the park James Sarvis.

Dr. Lempke was a very wealthy man who summered and spent occasional weekends at the lake. His stuccoed house was built on a large lakefront lot on Lakeside Road. He also owned property on the road opposite his home.

James Sarvis, a former police chief in the city of Newburgh, owned 80 acres of property around the shores of Orange Lake in the years preceding the amusement park. He operated a naphtha launch around the lake named the A.C. *Smith* and rented rowboats to early lake visitors. He also owned one of the first fine restaurants in the area, known as the Lakeside Palatine. He built his year-round electrified home at the south end of the lake above the trolley line in 1911.

Regardless of the structures they lived in, the people of the day considered Orange Lake a paradise, and anyone who could stay for a week, a month, or the season considered themselves very fortunate.

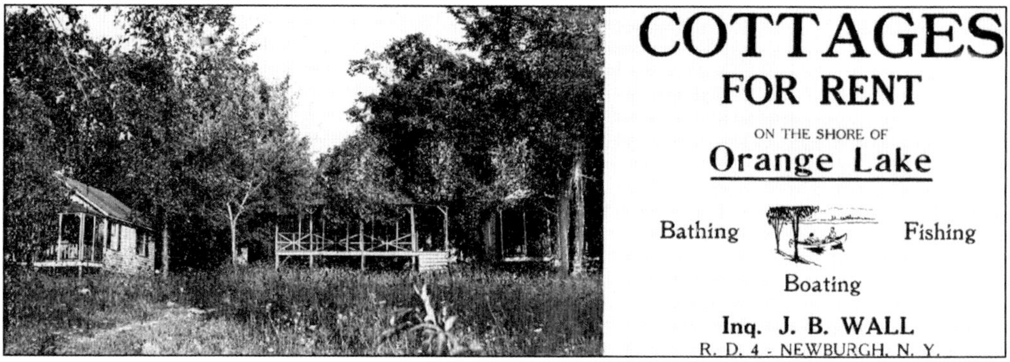

This frugal owner of early cottages at Orange Lake had his advertisements printed on heavy card stock so that they would last for more than one season. There is no mention of the amusement park in this advertisement, so it probably dates to the end of the 19th century. (Courtesy of Kathleen Martel Sileno.)

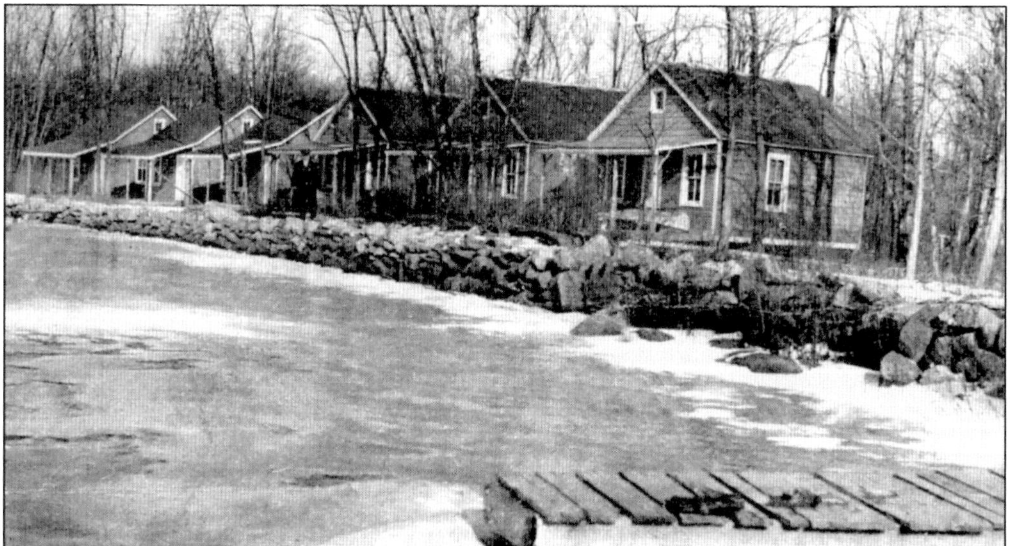

The cottages pictured are located near the northeast end of the lake and were originally known as Quinlan's Cottages. They were owned by a New York City police officer named Quinlan who rented them out each year. They were later owned by a man named Wolf who moved the cottages up from the lake because they flooded so often. (Author's collection.)

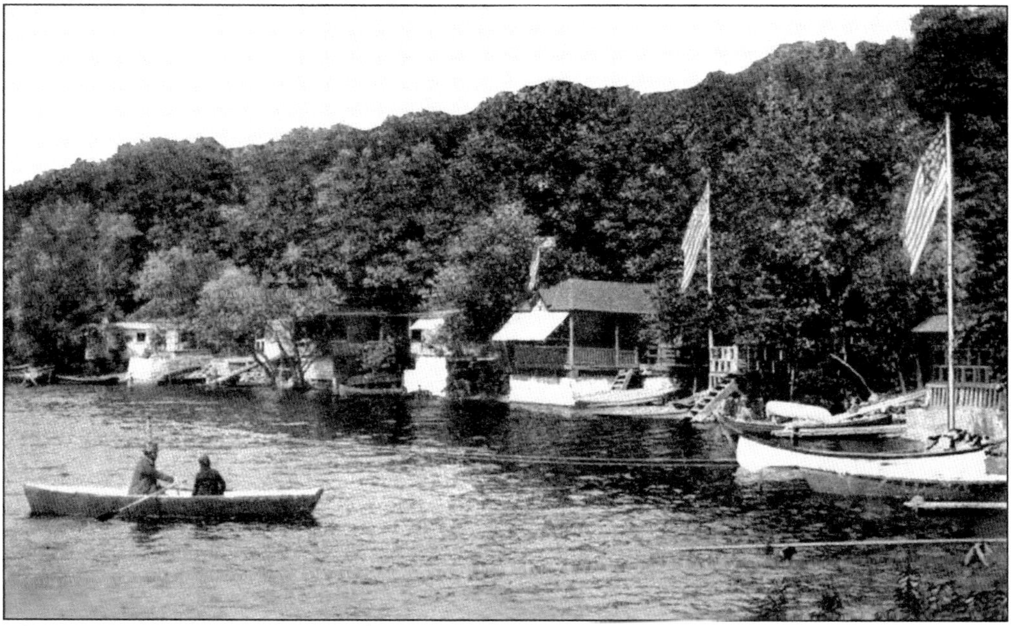

These cottages were located in the south cove on east side of the lake. To the left of the second flagpole is the outlet where the water level in the lake is controlled by a simple gate. (Author's collection.)

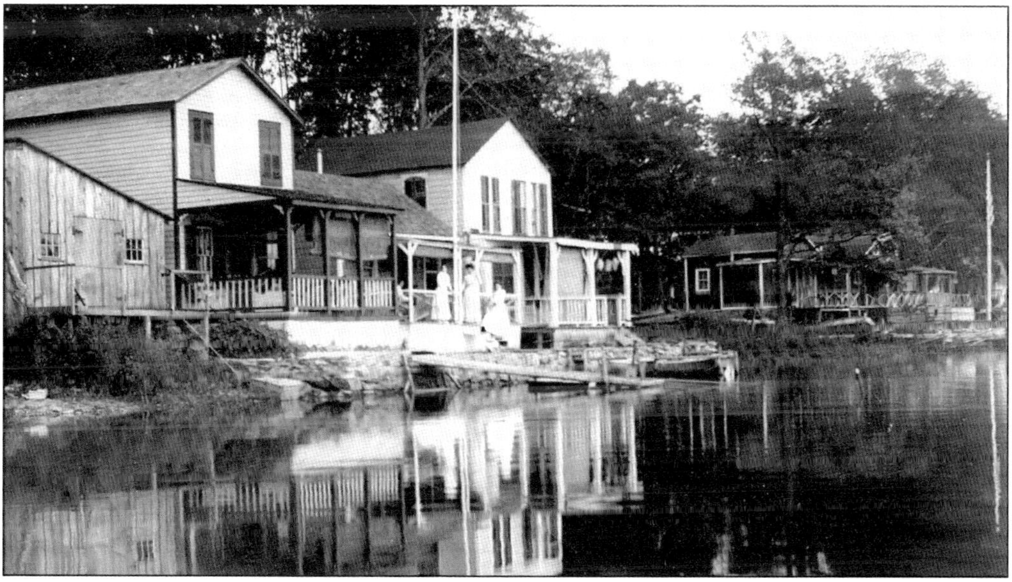

From the reflection in the lake and the dress of the women on the porch, it looks like a perfect day when this photograph was taken in 1915. This picture was taken at the northern end of the lake in the area of the present Lakeview House. (Courtesy of Sharon Nichols Formato.)

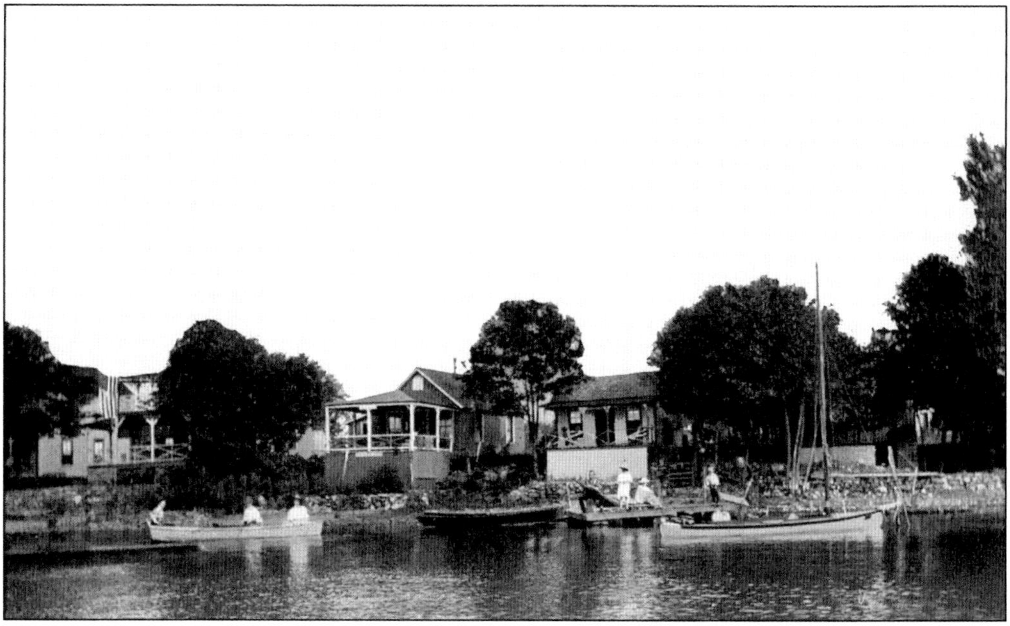

Fishing and pleasure boating were two of the early pastimes for cottage dwellers. The cottages were simple structures. They had no indoor running water, plumbing, or electricity, and most were only used for a few months each year. (Author's collection.)

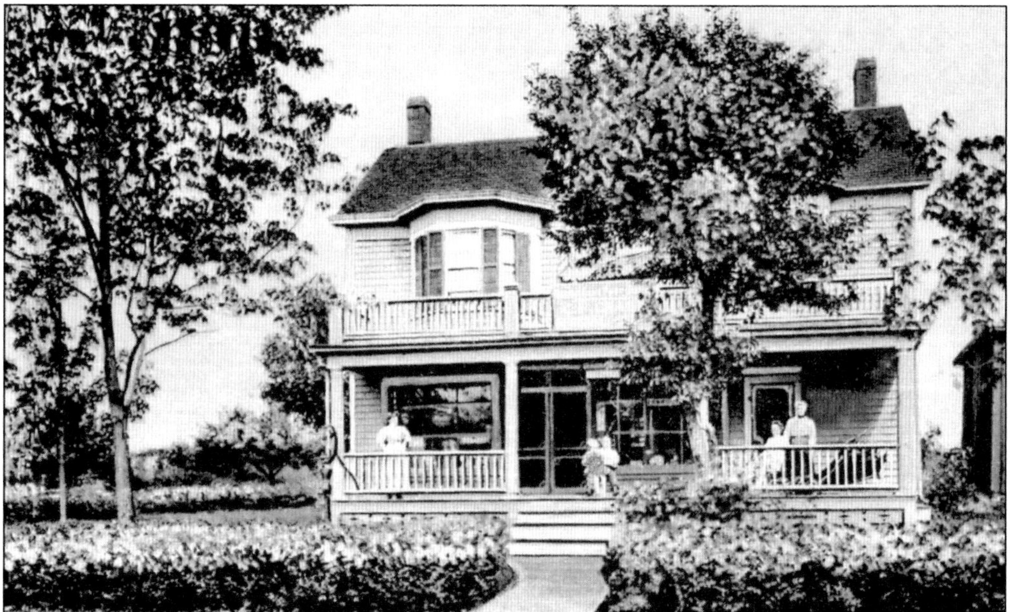

This is a picture of one of the post offices at the lake. It was located in a private home on the east side of Lakeside Road in the 1920s. Leghorn's Store was the site of another post office in the 1930s. (Author's collection.)

The gate mentioned on the top of page 79 is housed in this small structure at the south end of the lake. A simple gear mechanism is used to raise and lower a cypress wood gate that allows the water to leave the lake, thus controlling the water level. It is believed the house was constructed in the 1860s. (Courtesy of Arthur Nugent.)

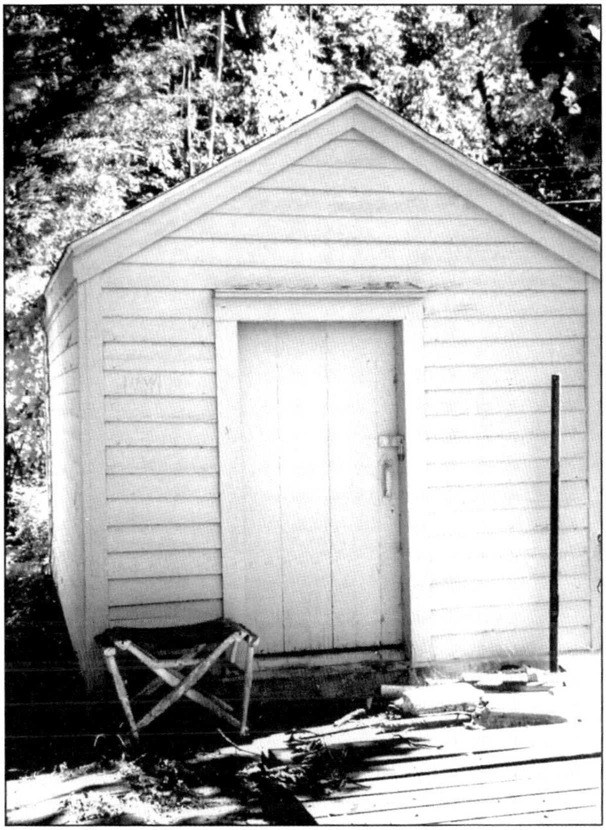

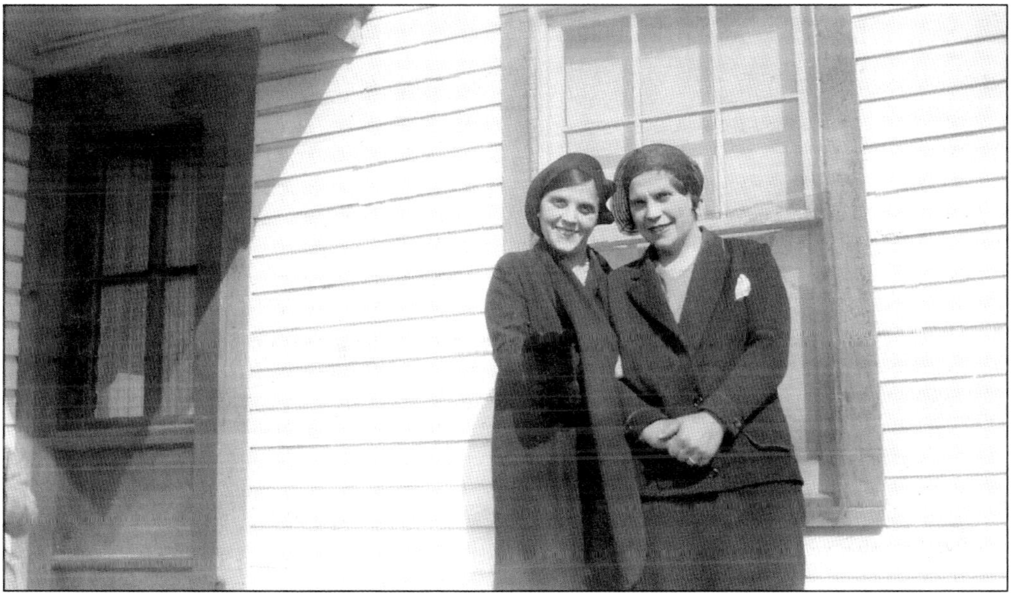

Lena Barclay (left) and her sister, June Grimley, stand in front of Frederick and June Grimley's cottage at Smith Street and First Street on the west side of the lake in this 1931 photograph. The Grimleys bought the cottage from a local cabinetmaker who built the small structure in 1929. (Courtesy of Jane Grimley McCaw.)

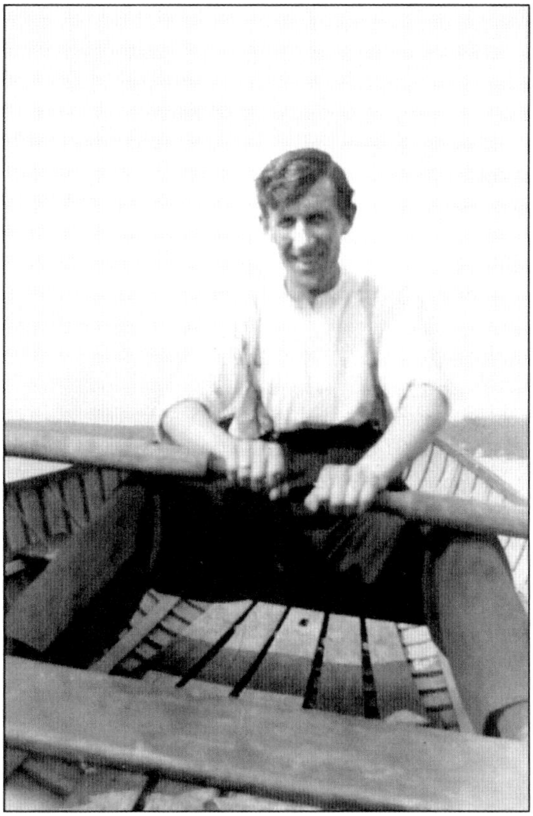

A lifelong resident of Orange Lake, William Gillispie rows his boat on the lake in 1913. His granddaughter still resides at the lake. (Courtesy of Janice Ruggiero.)

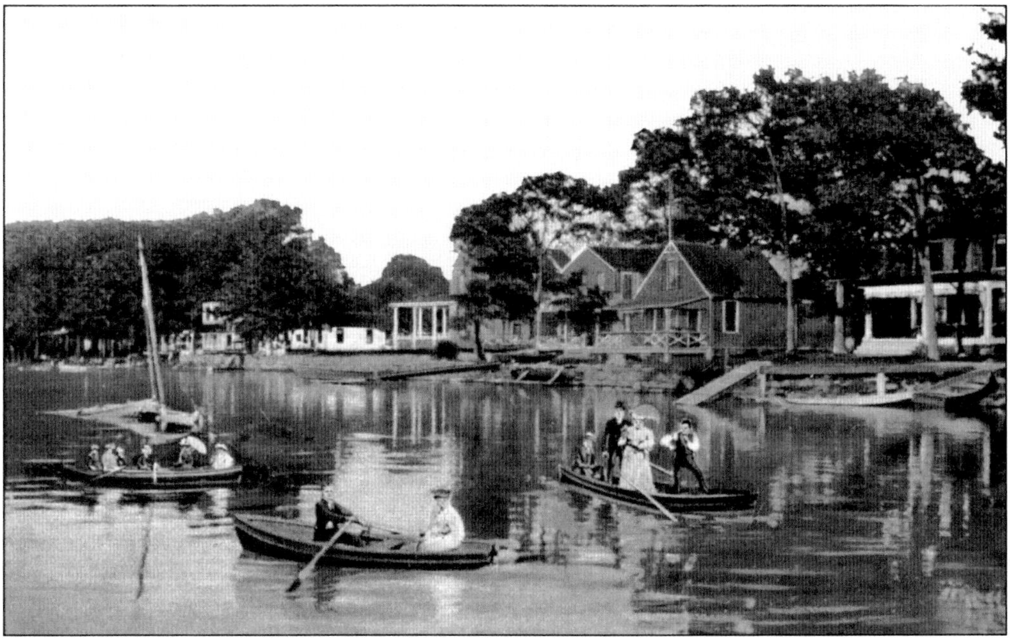

This is a postcard view of Miller's Cove. Families by the names of Applegate, Anderson, Kavanagh, Sneed, and Halstead owned some of these cabins over the years. (Author's collection.)

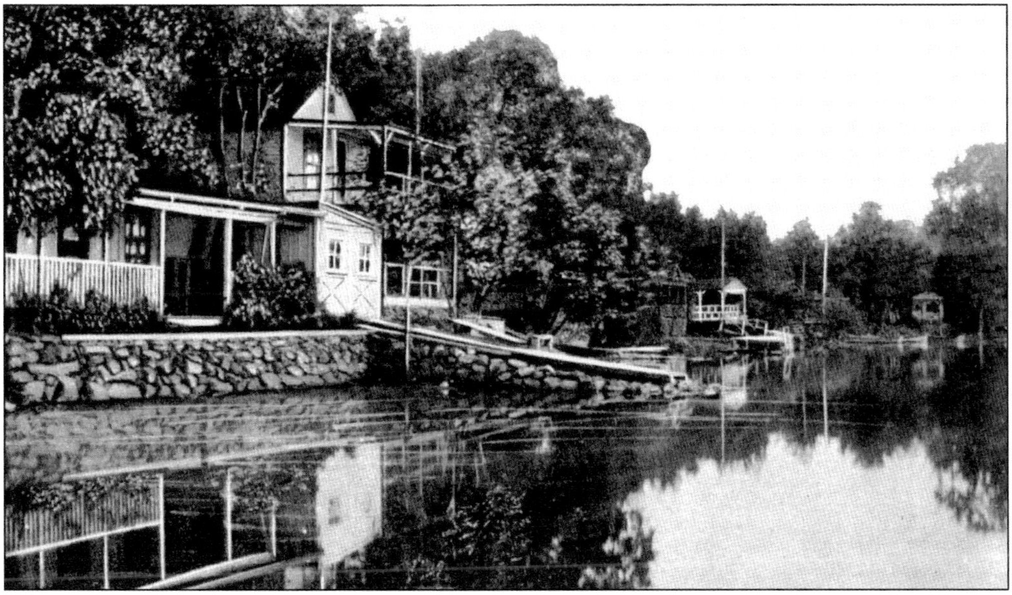

At Orange Lake, almost every section is known as a cove. This cove, located at the south end of the lake near Route 52, is known simply as the Cove. (Author's collection.)

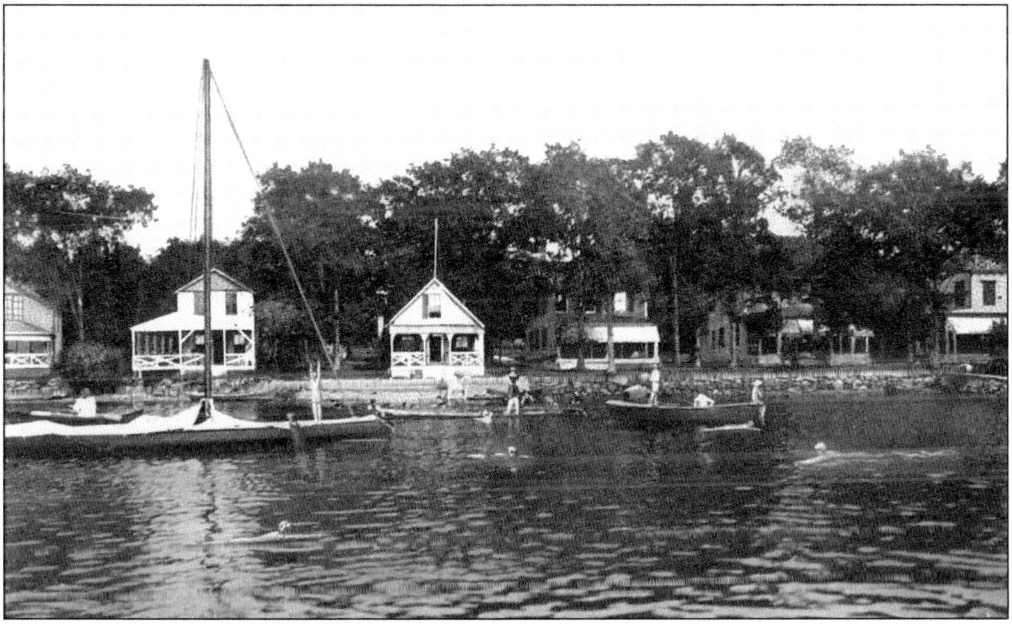

This postcard pictures some of the same cottages as the ones on the opposite page at the bottom. It was taken at a different time period and from a different angle. The proliferation of cottage cards is the reason it appears there were so many people living at the lake, when in fact there were probably less than 90 before 1909. (Author's collection.)

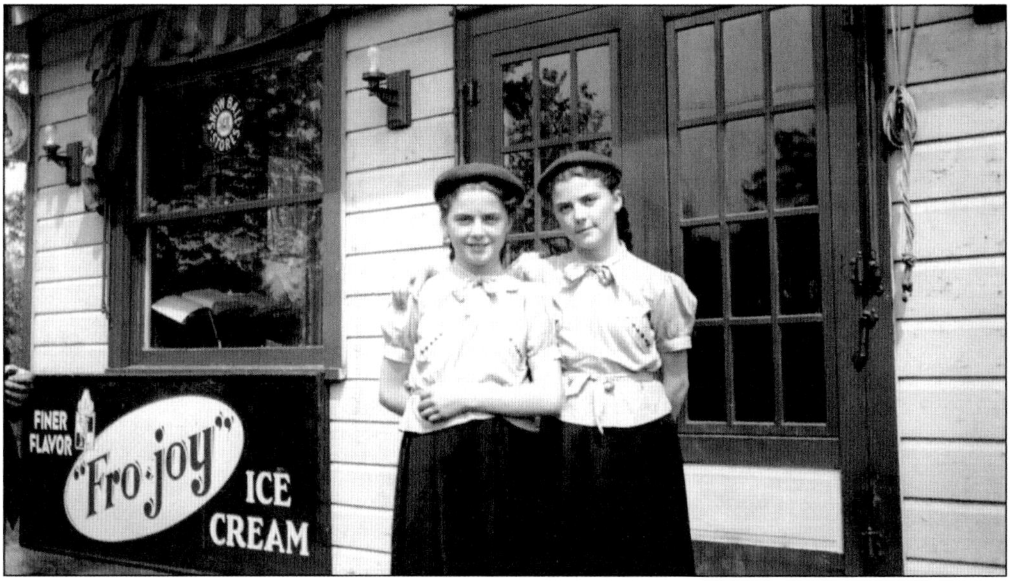

The Grimley twins, June (left) and Jane, stand in front of Leghorn's Store in 1932. The general store, located on the southeast corner of Lakeside Road and Route 52, provided all the essentials for lake residents and sold treats such as the Fro-joy ice cream, advertised on the sign on the building. (Courtesy of Jane Grimley McCaw.)

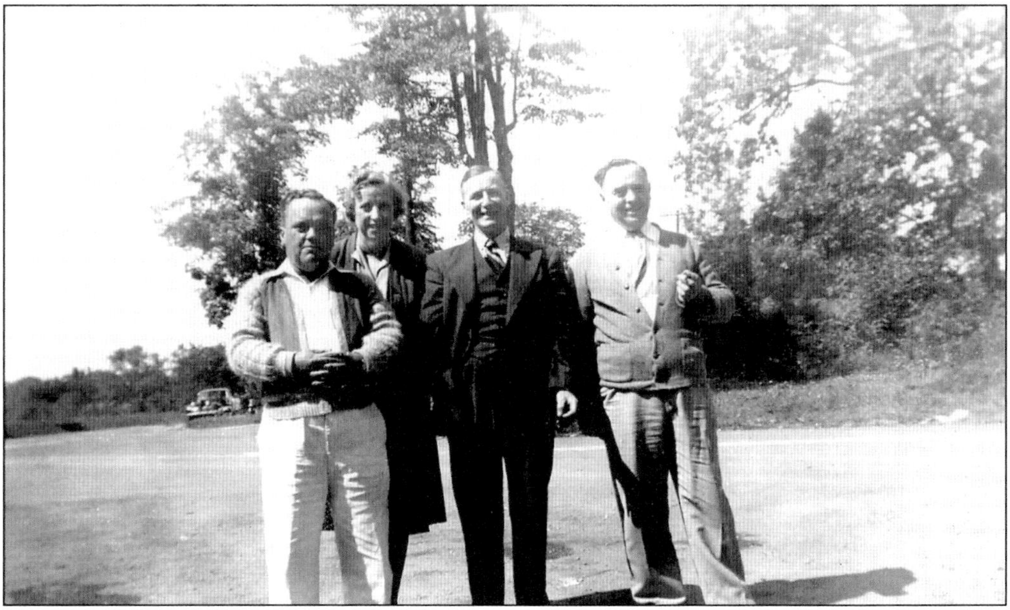

From left to right, William Knowlden, a Dupont employee; Emma Leghorn, co-owner of Leghorn's Store; Frederick Grimley, a foreman for the Hudson River Woolen Mills; and John Igo, cashier at the Columbus Trust Company, pose for a quick picture facing Leghorn's Store in the early 1930s. (Courtesy of Jane Grimley McCaw.)

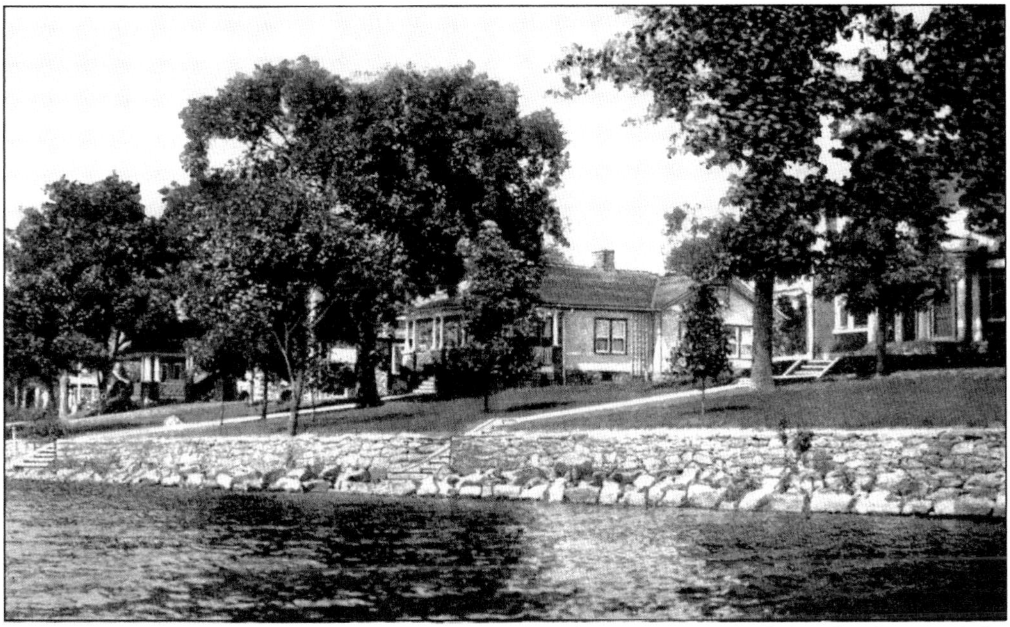

This postcard titled "Pretty Cottages on the Lake" shows cottages built by the Orange Lake Realty Company in the late 1920s. These summer homes had more amenities than the typical cottage and had electricity, which was brought to Lakeside Road in 1927. (Author's collection.)

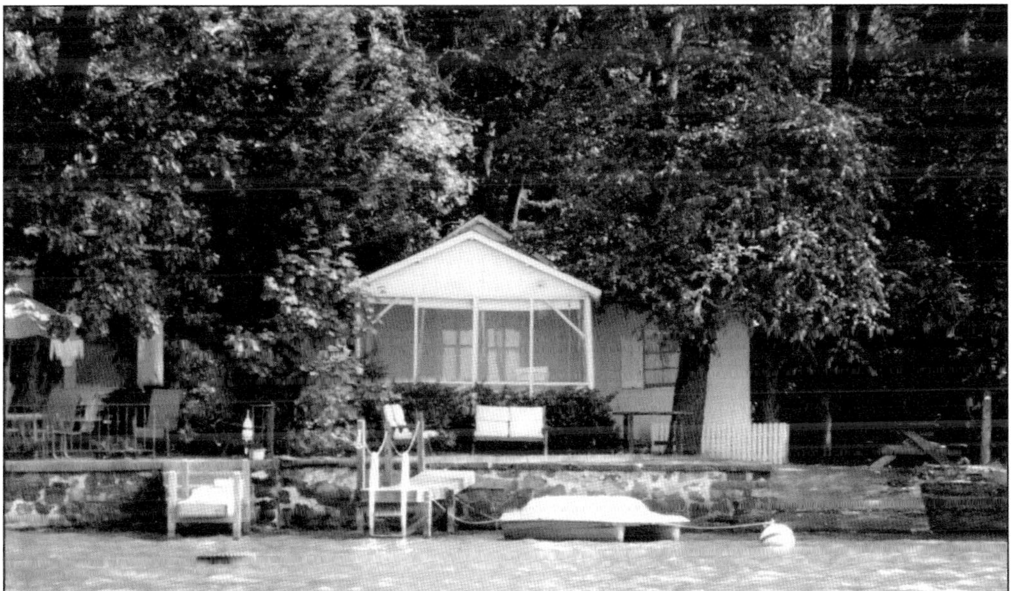

One of the few early cottages at the lake today that has experienced very few renovations is this one located by the outlet in South Cove. It has the look and feel of an original cottage and is only used seasonally. (Author's collection.)

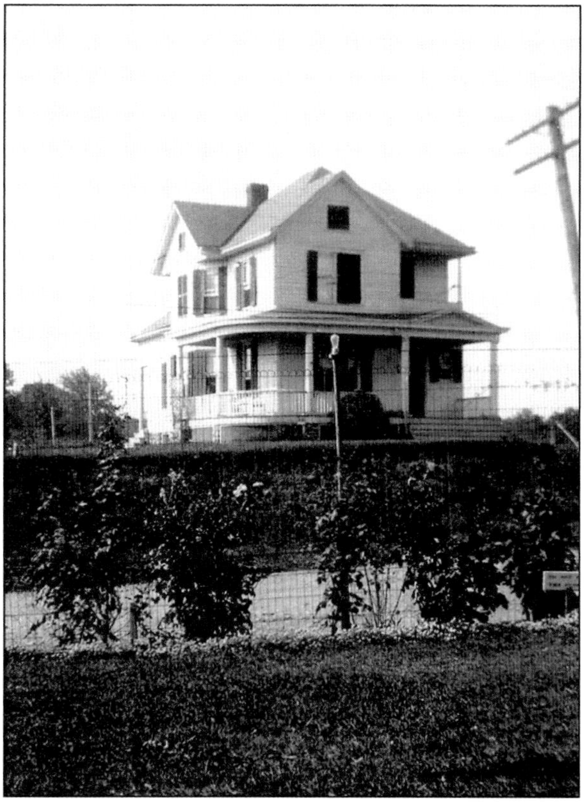

The superintendent of Orange Lake Amusement Park, James Sarvis, lived in this house overlooking the trolley station and amusement park. The house was built shortly before this 1911 photograph was taken. (Courtesy of Sharon Nichols Formato.)

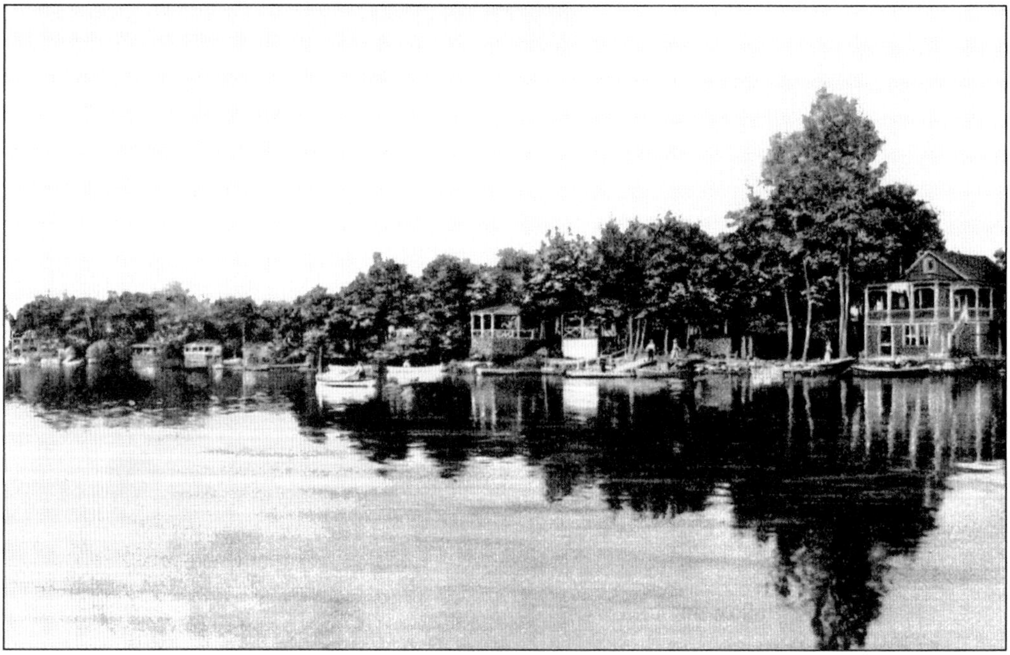

This is another postcard of cottages at the south end of the lake by the amusement park. The writer of the card, a man who calls himself "Unc," taunts the recipient, Betty, with the following message: "Don't you wish you were here at Orange Lake?" (Author's collection.)

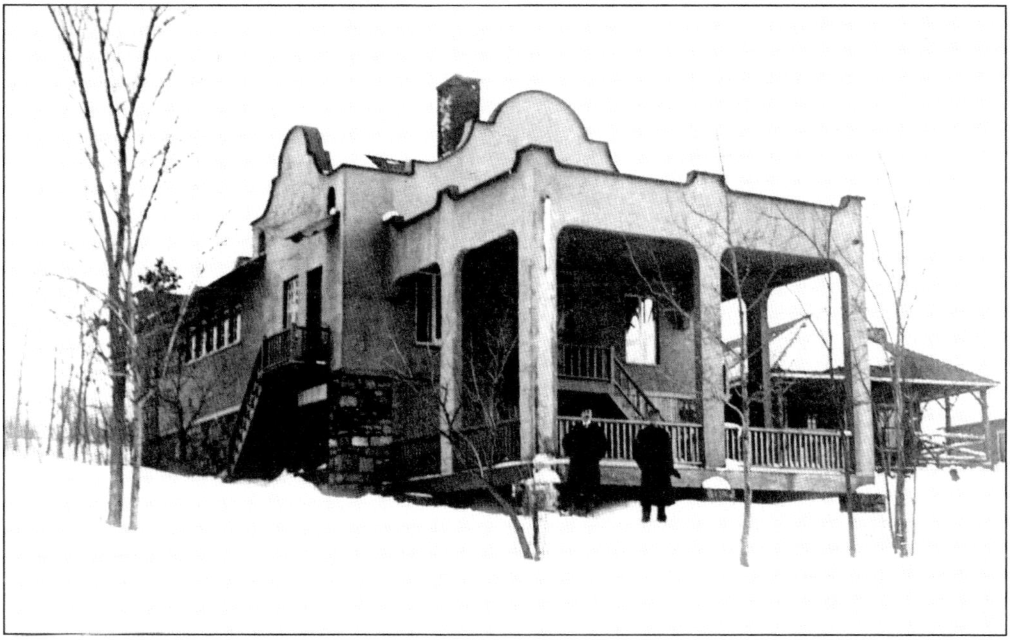

This is one of the larger early summer homes at the lake. It is believed that this 1910 photograph shows two members of Campbell family who owned the home then. In the 1920s, the Perrotts and then the O'Neils owned the home. In 1935, John and Tess Martel bought the house, and it remains in their family to this day. (Courtesy of Kathleen Martel Sileno.)

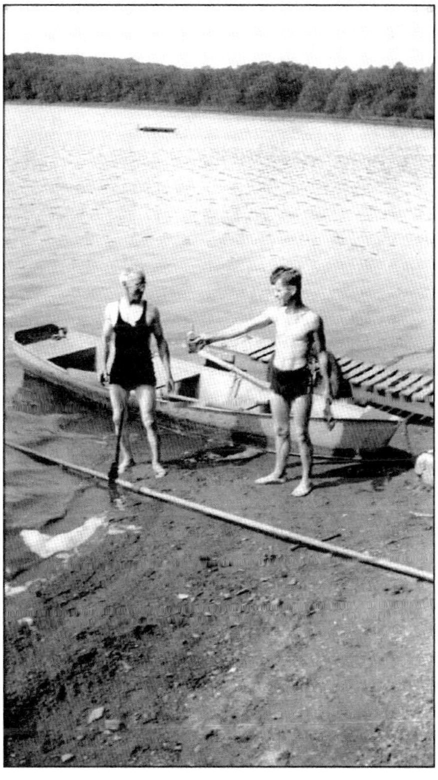

John Martel and his friend James Kahn share a cool beverage in front of the house after a swim in the lake in this 1937 picture. Note that the water level is low, a common occurrence over the years because of the mill owners' constant use of lake water. (Courtesy of Kathleen Martel Sileno.)

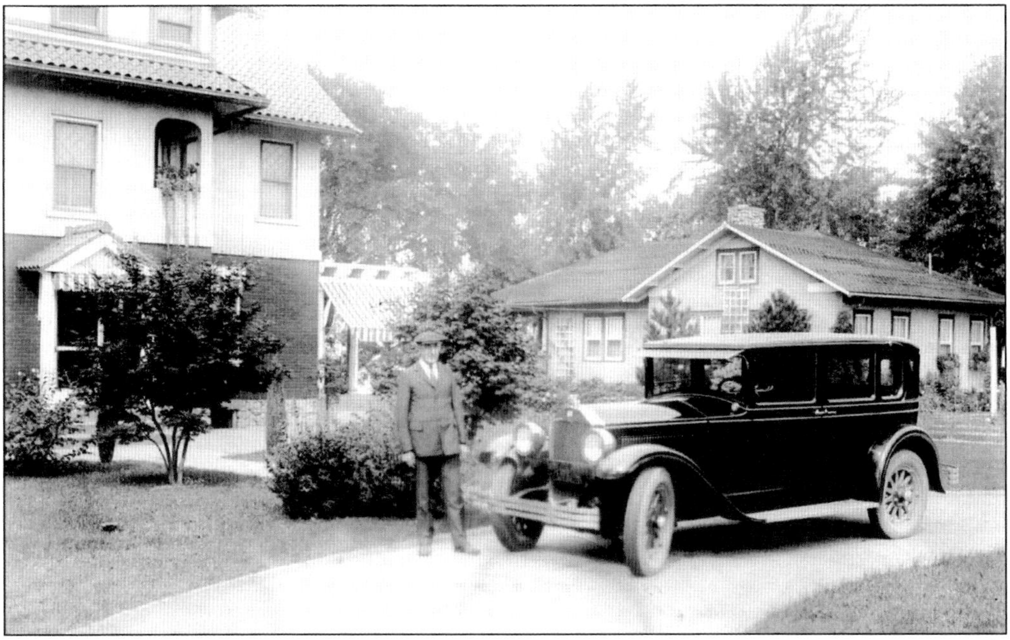

William Gillispie was caretaker and chauffeur to Dr. Lempke at his large home on the east side of the lake on Lakeside Road. Dr. Lempke was a seasonal resident who owned land on both sides of the road. When he died, he left a parcel of land across from his home to Gillispie. There Gillispie raised a family and led a very productive life, living into his 90s. (Courtesy of Janette Gillispie Sylvester.)

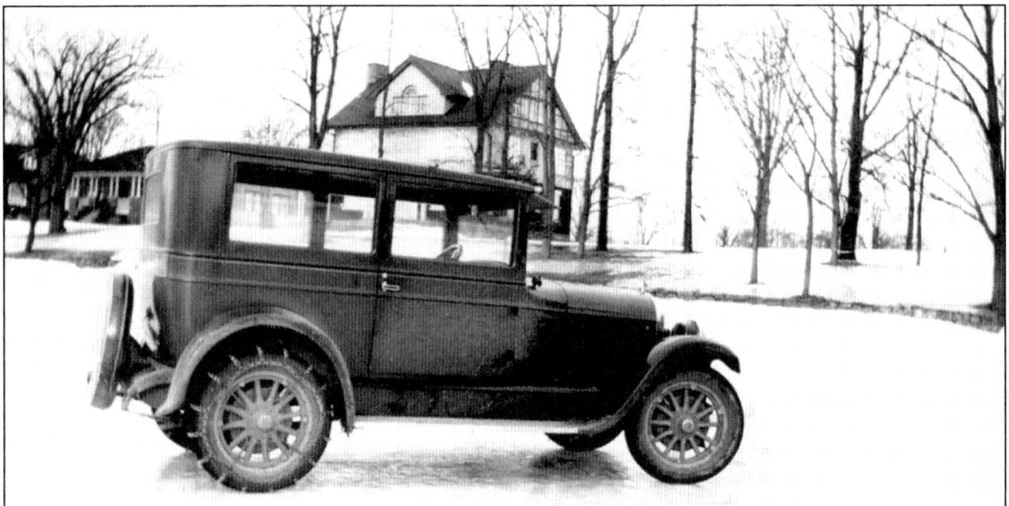

Gillispie had a sense of humor in addition to his other talents. In this picture Gillispie drove and parked Dr. Lempke's 1926 Chrysler on a frozen Orange Lake. This stunt was recalled with a smile for many years. (Courtesy of Janette Gillispie Sylvester.)

Seven

Camps, Events, Celebrations, and People

The land surrounding Orange Lake was ideal for camping. Game animals, fish, and local produce and dairy products provided a healthy diet for the campers. Hyde's general store provided all the other necessary gear and foodstuffs. Around their store, the Hydes built a series of platforms for tents, which they rented out to campers. The camp was known as Camp Hurrah.

Camp Baldhead on the Ramsdell property at the south end of Orange Lake was a first for the country. Sumner F. Dudley, a member of the Orange, New Jersey, YMCA, and George Sanford, a local YMCA official, took eight young men and their gear from Newburgh to the lake for a week of camping. The year was 1885. The group hunted, fished, hiked, swam, and did many of the same activities campers do today. The significance of this event was that up until that time camping was thought of as a rare occurrence. Camp Baldhead was so successful that the YMCA and other agencies soon scheduled camping into their regular programming.

The YWCA was bequeathed a large parcel of land toward the north end of the lake in the 1930s. One of the cabins from that camp can still be seen today.

The 4-H was very active at the lake, having many of its activities at the school or in private homes. Boys learned how to raise and care for animals, how to grow crops, and manual trades. Girls were taught how to cook, can, sew, and arrange flowers. The Orange Lake 4-H boys and girls were very skilled at winning prizes at county and state fairs.

The Patton farm was the site of another little-known fact. It hosted the New York State 156th Artillery of the National Guard on its farm in the 1930s.

Clambakes and community outings are part of the history of the lake and were special occasions. The lake also hosted a famous aviator and two homegrown celebrities, a poet and a folk hero who are profiled in this chapter.

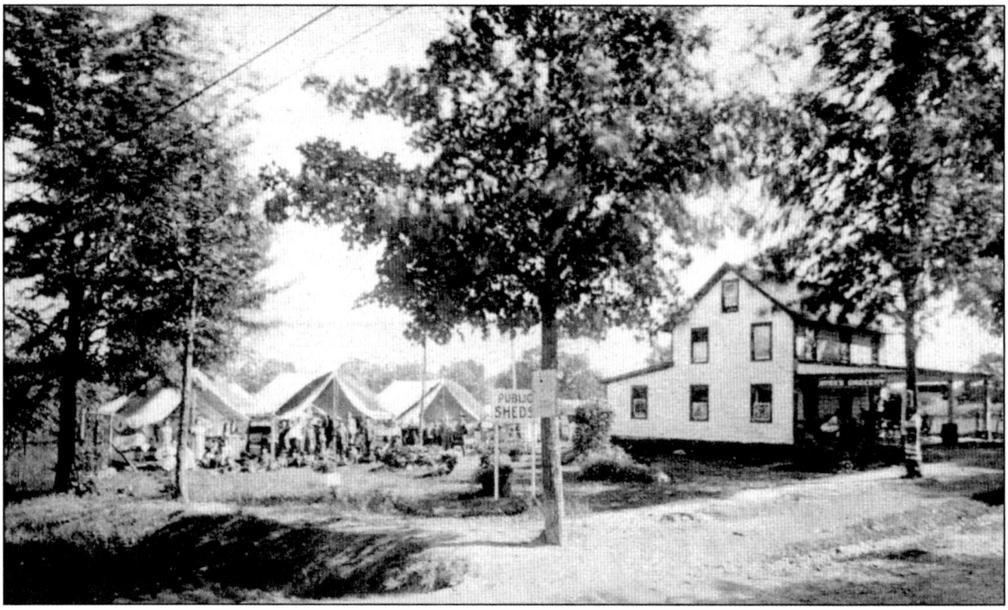

At the southeast corner of Lakeside Road and Route 52, Hyde's grocery store sold provisions for area residents and seasonal guests. In addition, it provided campsites for summer guests on a weekly, monthly, or full-season rate. The camp was known as Camp Hurrah. (Author's collection.)

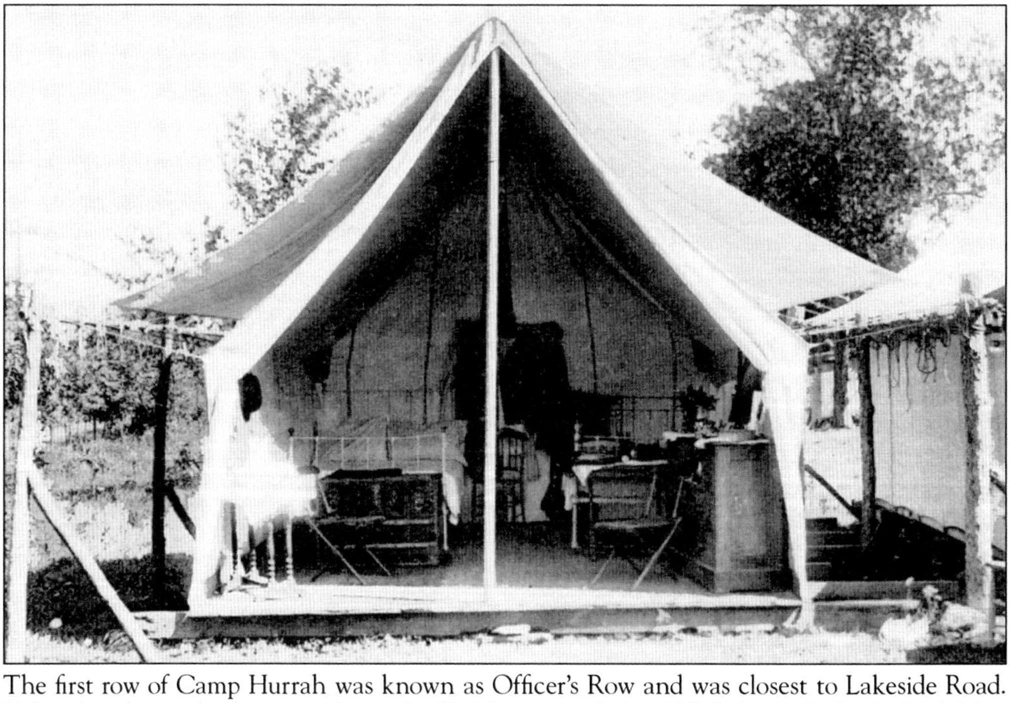

The first row of Camp Hurrah was known as Officer's Row and was closest to Lakeside Road. Other than being the first row of tents, it offered no special perks. This shows the basic furnishing of the tent: two cots, a bureau, and a chair. (Courtesy of Marguerite Harris McDermott.)

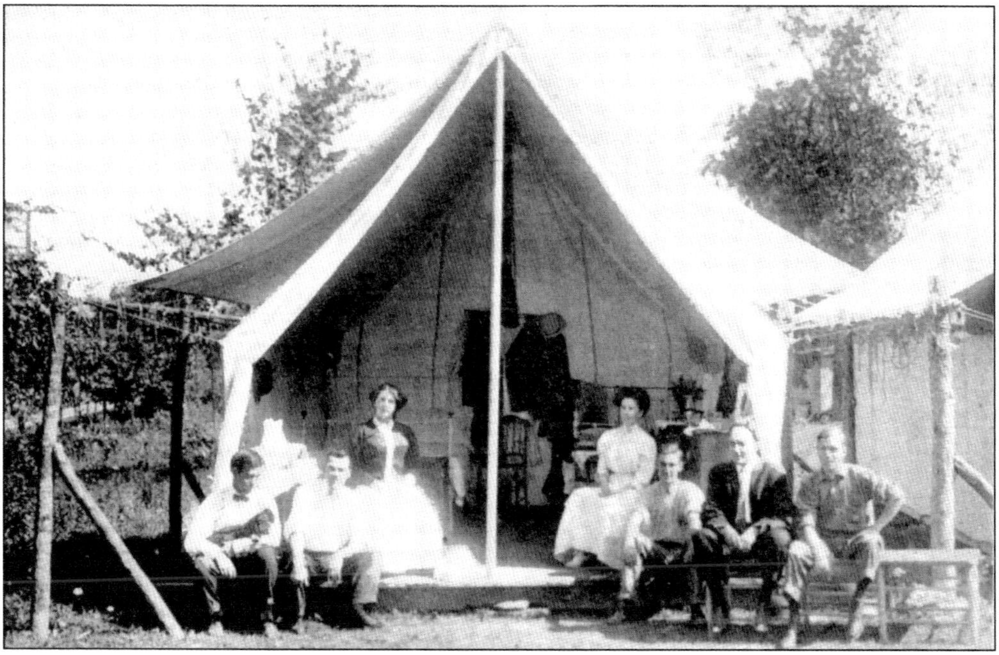

Families and friends often rented a group of tents for a specified time during the summer season. An unidentified group of friends poses in front of its tent in 1909. The tents were also called "sheds" at the time. (Courtesy of Marguerite Harris McDermott.)

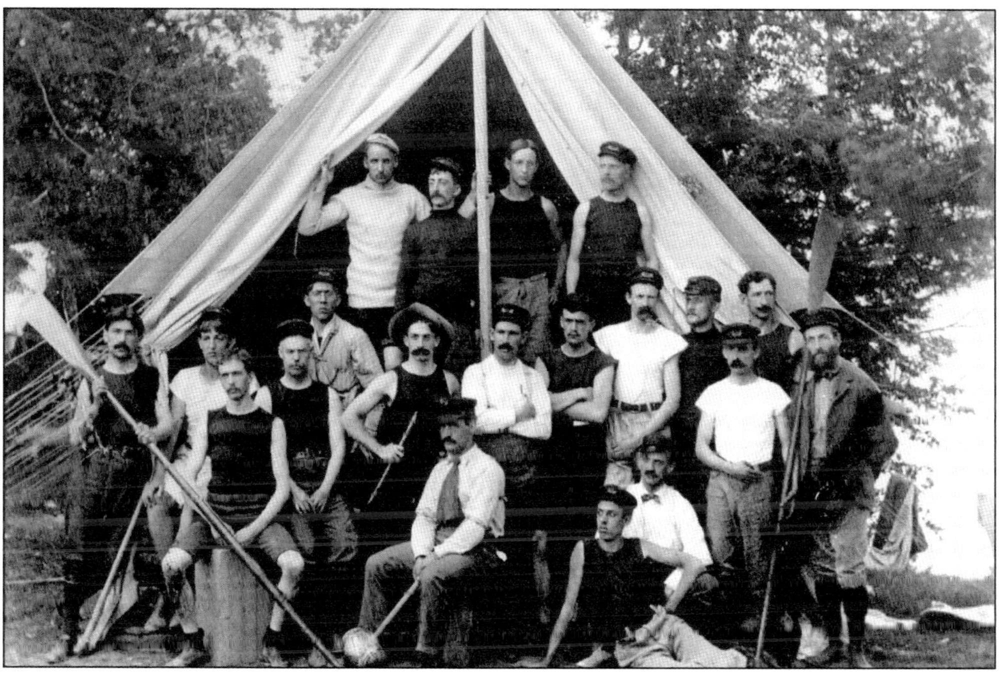

Sumner F. Dudley, seated in the front row, center, founded the first YMCA camp at Pine Point in 1895. He said the experience was "hearty, manly, fun." This outing was the first camp run by a youth agency in the United States and began the camping tradition that has become a part of so many similar agencies to this day. (Courtesy of the YMCA.)

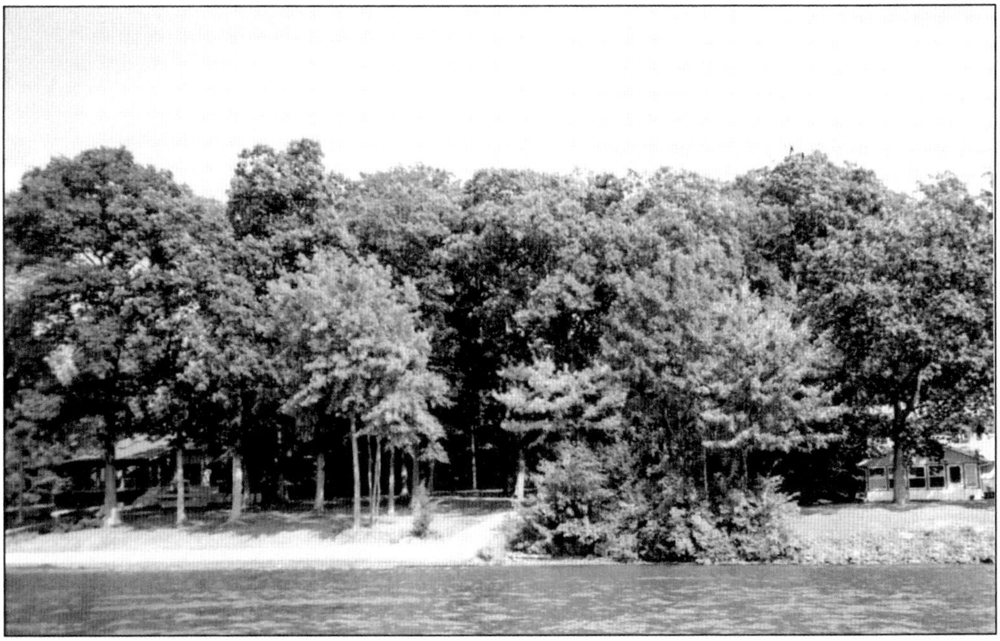

An Orange Lake resident, said to be a Mrs. Dougherty, left property in her will in the early 1930s for a YWCA camp for girls from New Jersey. The land was on the north end of the lake on Lakeside Road. When the camp closed, the land was sold and eventually smaller parcels became building lots. (Author's collection.)

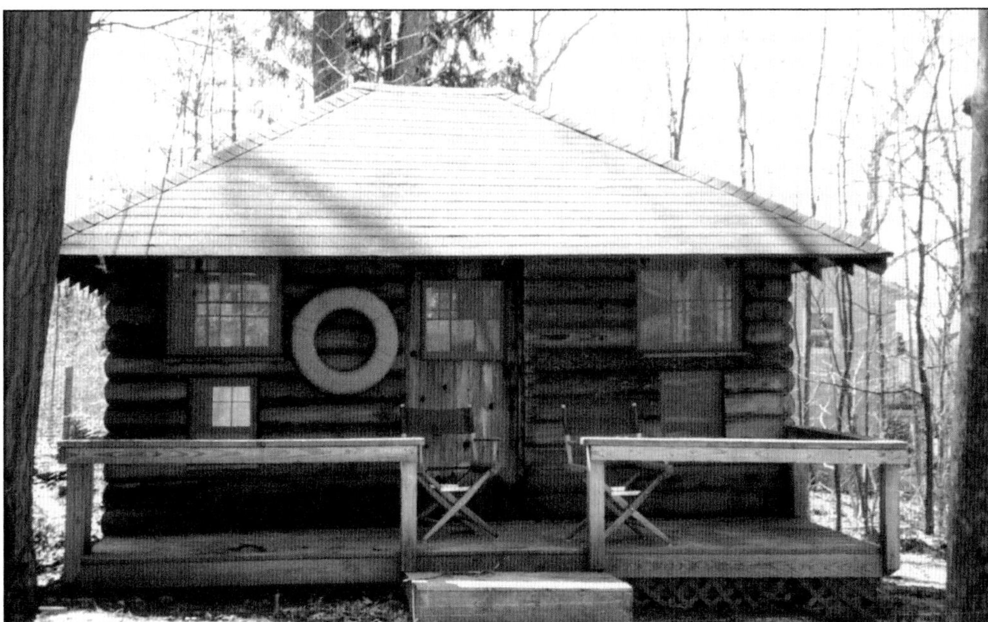

This is the only extant original cabin remaining from the YWCA camp at Orange Lake. The current owners of the property refurbished the cabin and made it into a playhouse for their grandchildren. (Author's collection.)

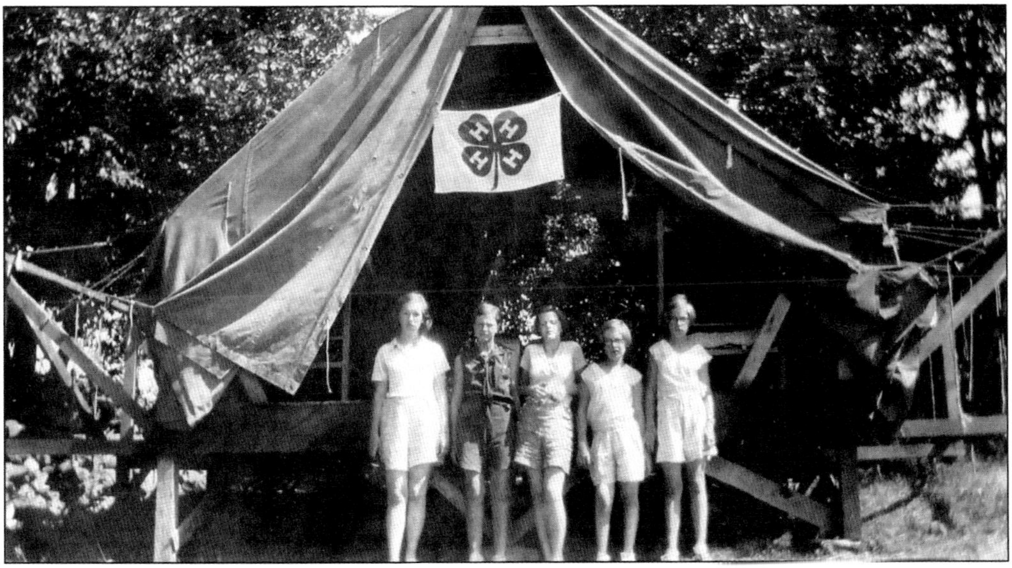

The 4-H clubs were very important to the children and young adults at Orange Lake. Above are, from left to right, Marguerite Harris, Ida Hazzard, Ruth Innis, Bernice Harris, and Evelyn Harris standing in front of their tent at a camp in the early 1930s. (Courtesy of Ilene Patton Siegman.)

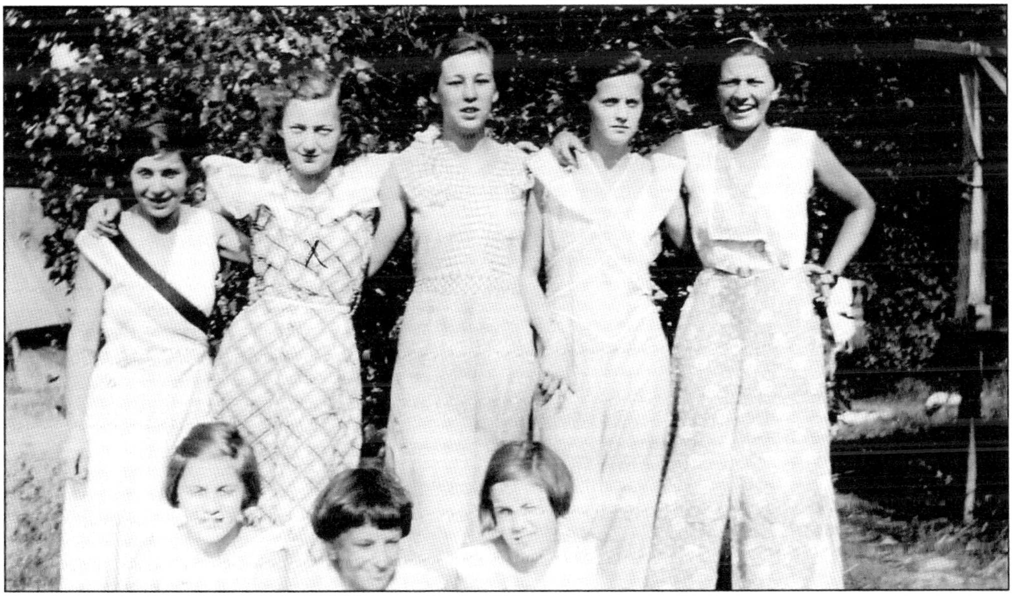

The 4-H clubs met at the Gardnertown Civic Center, the current American Legion building. In this 1935 photograph, some of the 4-H girls pose after a sewing competition. From left to right are (first row) Evelyn Harris, unidentified, and Bernice Harris; (second row) unidentified, Ilene Patton, Marguerite Harris, Ruth Innis, and Ida Hazzard. (Courtesy of Ilene Patton Siegman.)

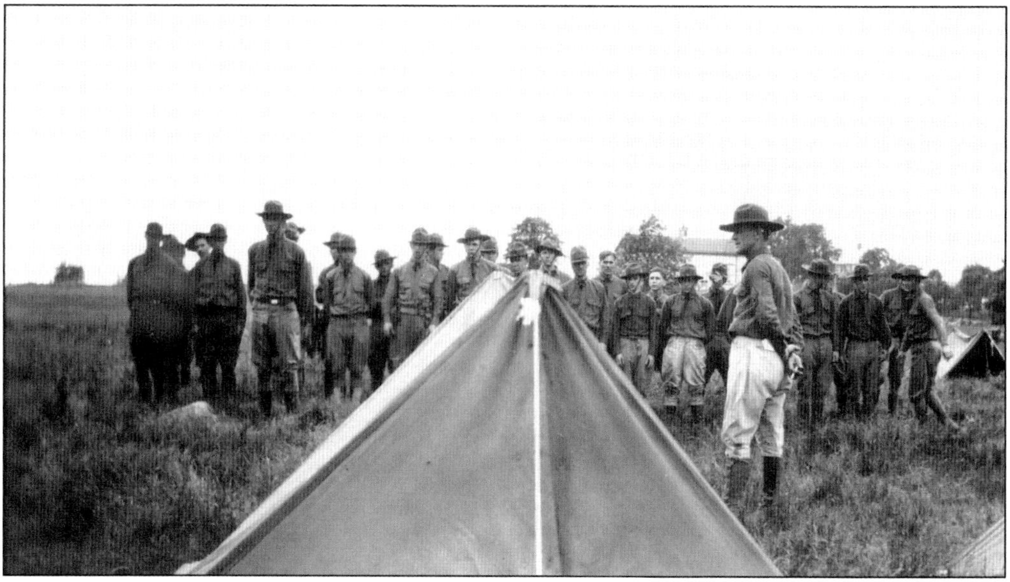

This is one camp that many area citizens took part in but has never been documented before. In the early 1930s, the New York National Guard 156th Artillery camped at the Patton farm. Some of the soldiers who took part in the exercise are lined up in front of a tent in this picture. In the background is the Patton barn. (Courtesy of Ilene Patton Siegman.)

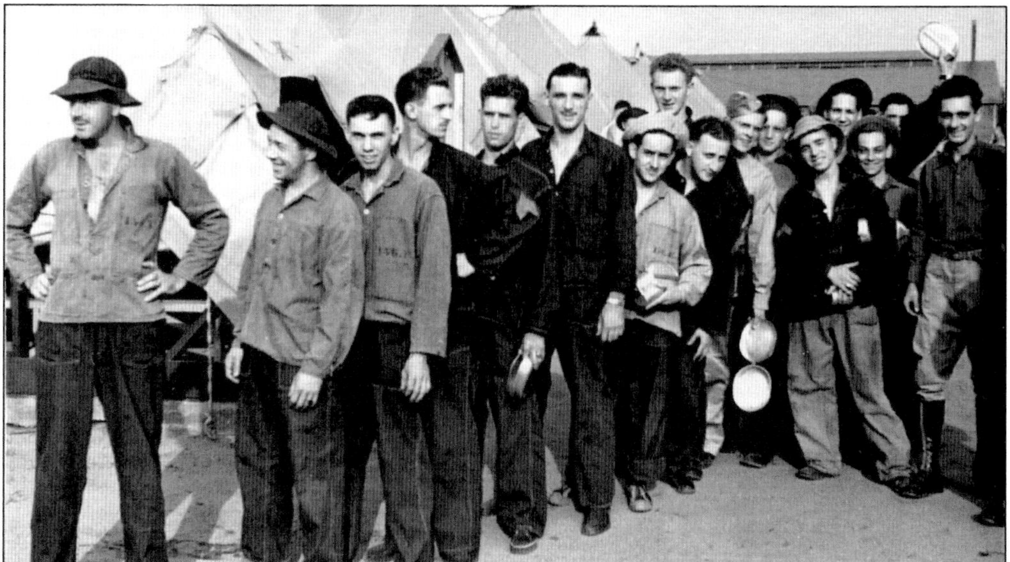

The guardsmen line up for chow in this picture. From left to right, they are unidentified, Albert Raab, William Robinson, Myron Randolph, Frederick Depew, Frederick Kratch, Anthony Franchini, Louis Gruberg, five unidentified, Elwood Eager, unidentified, and Andrew Koisch. (Courtesy of Ilene Patton Siegman.)

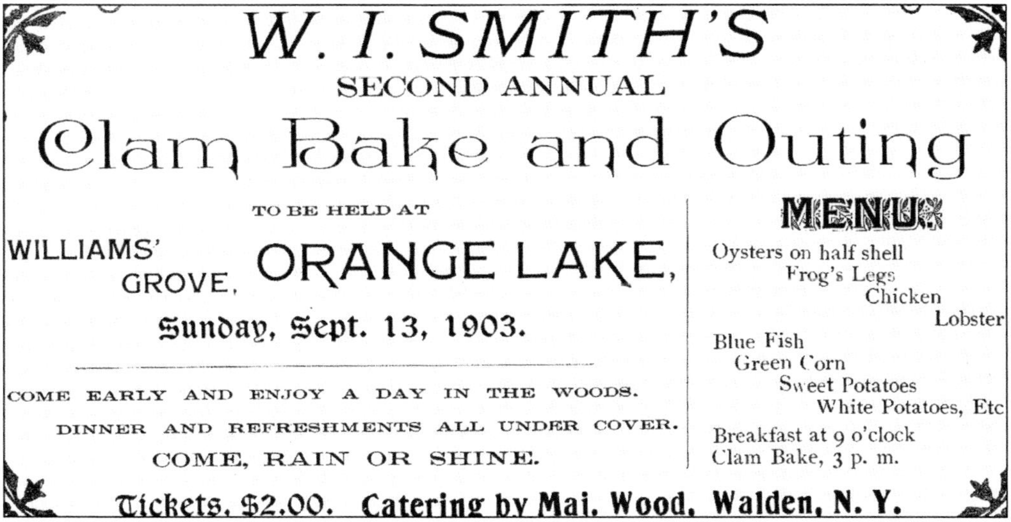

Williams' Grove, at the north end of the lake, was a popular picnic and clambake area. Clambakes were very common in the summertime at the lake and very well attended. Menus were extensive and featured many items that would not be considered picnic fare today, in this case frog legs. (Courtesy of Walter Whitehill.)

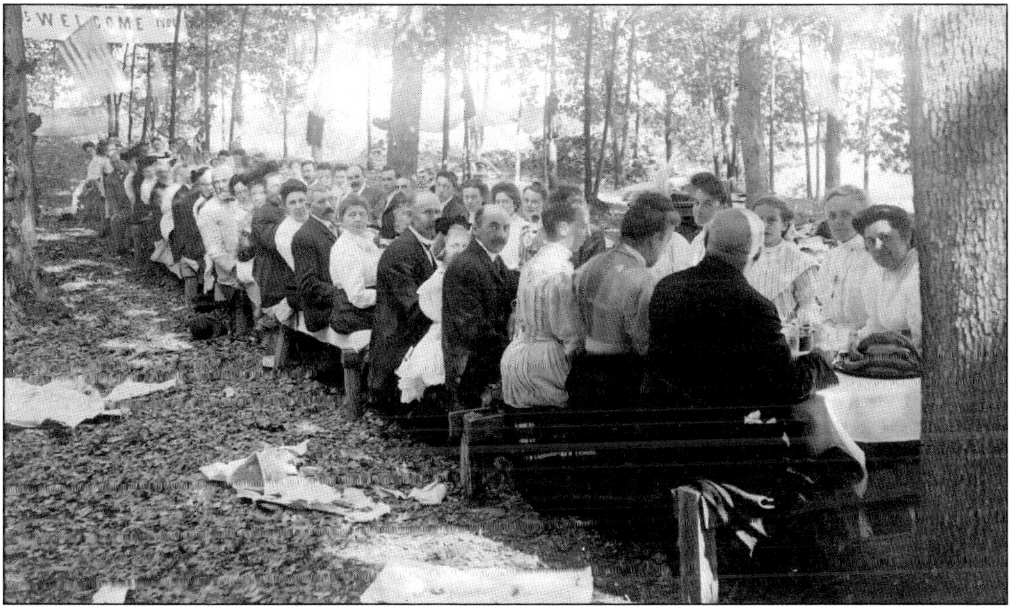

Newspapers, used as tablecloths, and napkins line the ground after one course at a church clambake. This crowd paused to have its photograph taken during a change of course, and unfortunately no one recorded the names of anyone in attendance. (Courtesy of Walter Whitehill.)

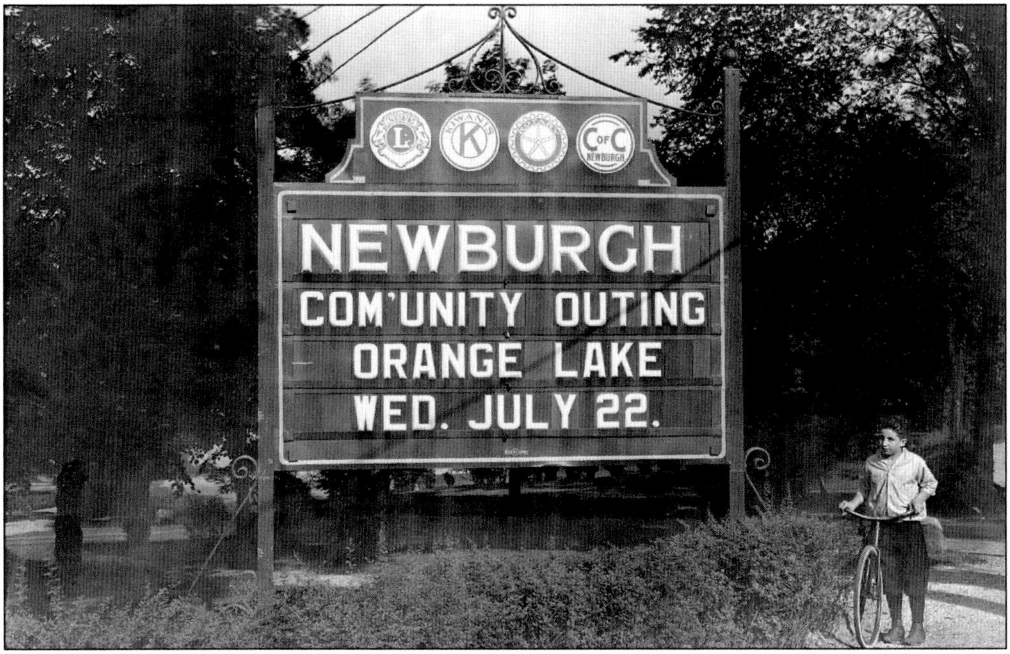

The Newburgh community day outing at the Orange Lake park, sponsored by the chamber of commerce and other service groups, was begun in 1917. It was an all-day event that attracted thousands of people each year for its contests, sports events, and special attractions. Here a boy in the early 1930s looks at one of the last advertisements for the event. (Courtesy of the Historical Society of Newburgh Bay and the Highlands.)

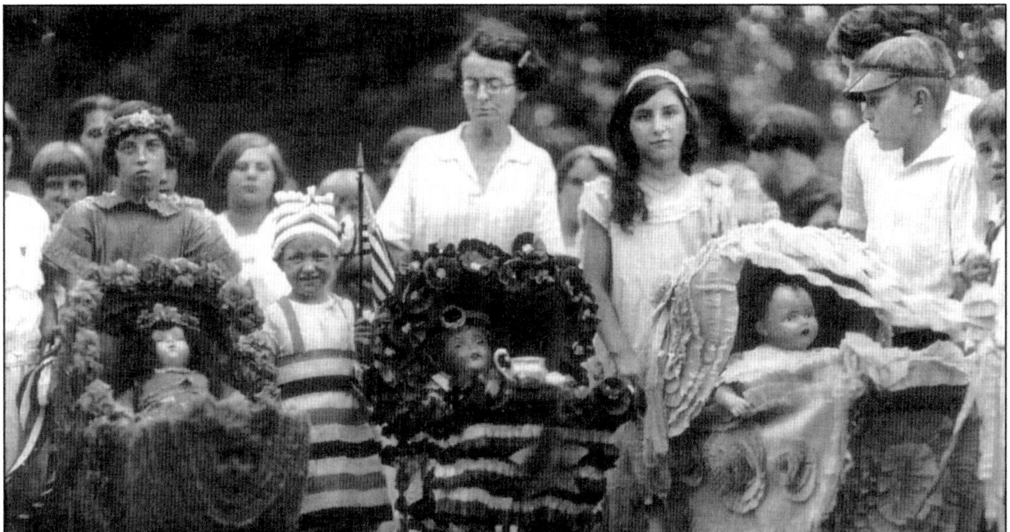
One of the most popular events sponsored by the early community day outing was the decorated doll parade contest. After parading around the grounds, the most beautifully decorated doll would be chosen. A silver cup was awarded to the winner. Apparently the doll in the center won, because she has the prized silver cup, although no one in the photograph looks particularly happy. (Courtesy of Stuart Berg.)

Located on the east side of Lakeside Road near the intersection of Lakeside Road and Union Avenue, the Stateside Airways was one of the many small airports in Orange County for the years from the 1930s through the early 1950s. It provided many services for residents, as can be seen in this poster, and was run by Gustave Jockers of Orange Lake. (Courtesy of Walter Whitehill.)

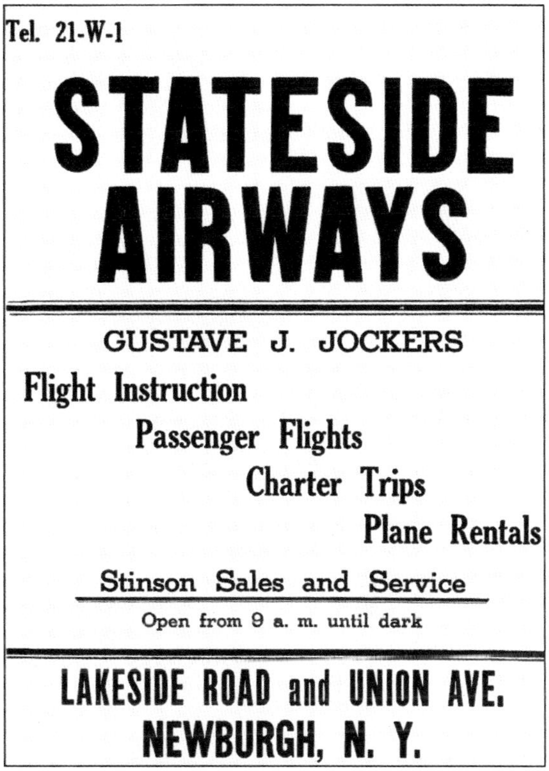

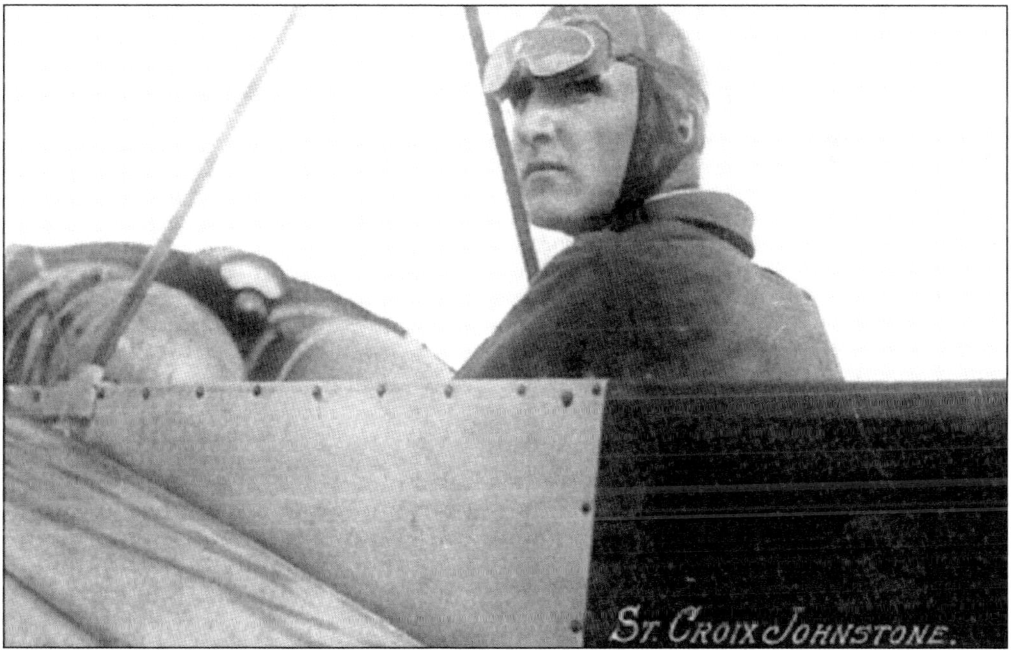

St. Croix Johnstone, an early aviator, was the major attraction at Orange Lake Amusement Park on opening day in 1911. According to newspaper accounts, over 15,000 people saw him that Memorial Day weekend. On his first attempt at flight he crash-landed in a farmer's field but was successful on his next two flights. (Courtesy of Roy Nagl.)

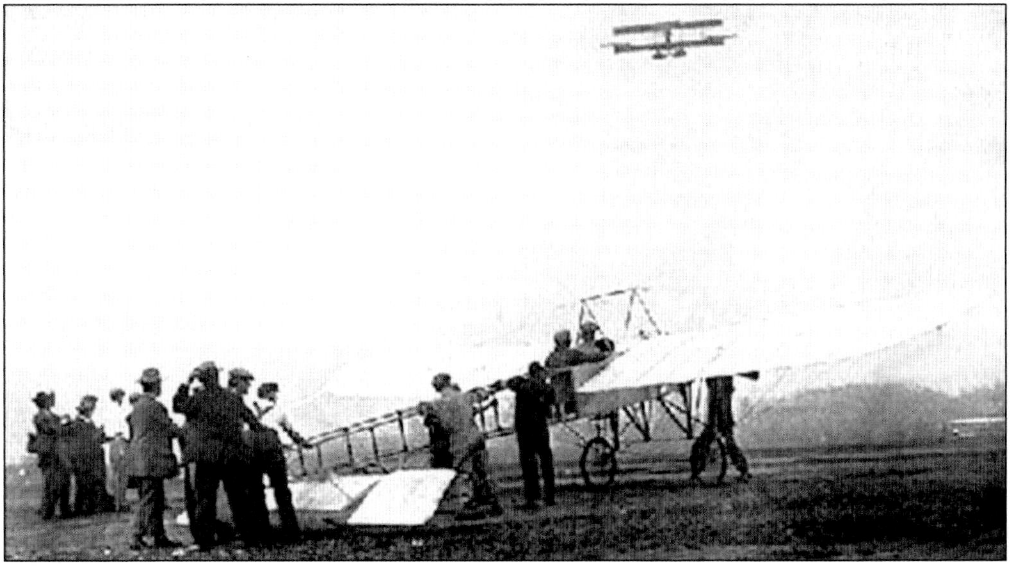

In July 1911, the popular St. Croix Johnstone, seen here taking off at Orange Lake, flew over Chicago, dropping hundreds of carnations on the population. After the flight, he warned the happy crowds that planes could also be used to drop more dangerous devices such as explosives on unsuspecting crowds. The visionary died in a crash over Lake Michigan in August 1911. (Courtesy of Roy Nagl.)

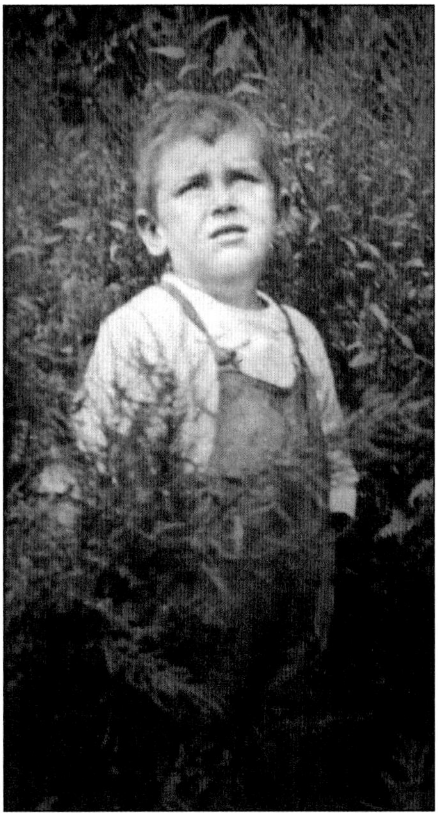

John Martel of Orange Lake told family members that this photograph of him was taken as he watched one of the first airplanes in the area fly over Orange Lake. He would have been three years old at the time of Johnstone's flight. Could he have been watching Johnstone? (Courtesy of Kathleen Martel Sileno.)

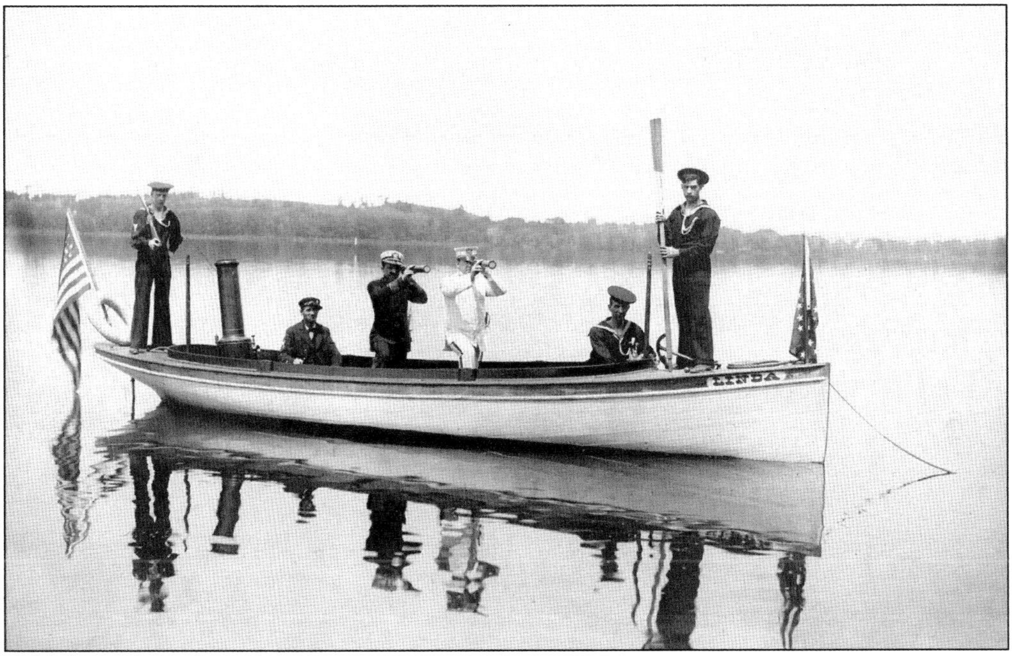
No one can recall why this posed photograph of sailors on the naphtha-powered *Linda* was taken in 1909. It could have been used in connection with festivities for the magnificent Hudson Fulton Celebration, which was held that year to honor Hudson's discovery of the river and Fulton's invention of the steamboat. (Courtesy of Sharon Nichols Formato.)

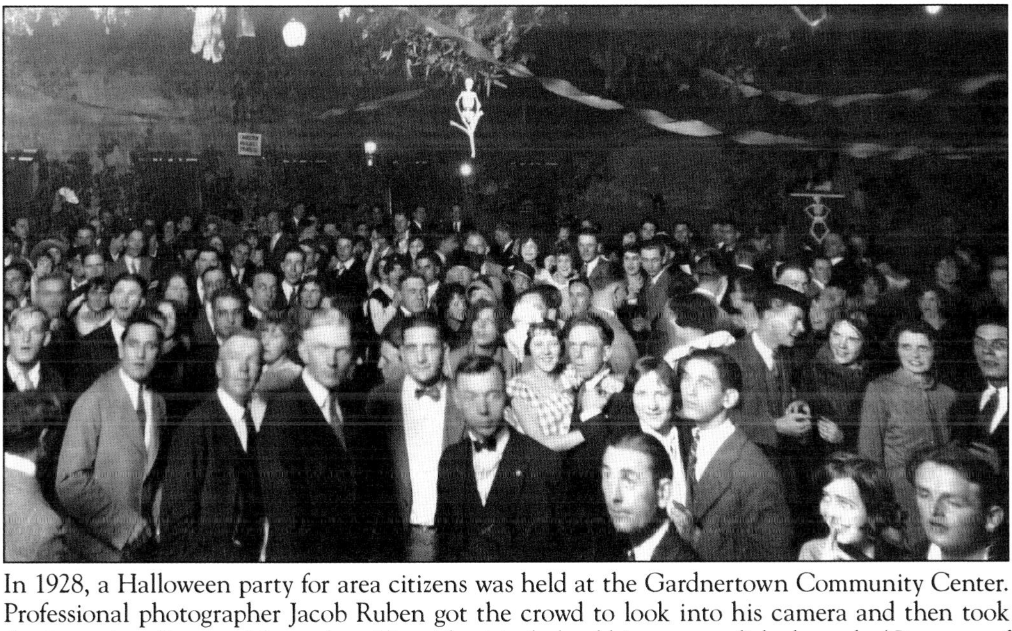
In 1928, a Halloween party for area citizens was held at the Gardnertown Community Center. Professional photographer Jacob Ruben got the crowd to look into his camera and then took the intentionally out of focus shot. He said spirits helped him accomplish the task. (Courtesy of Walter Whitehill.)

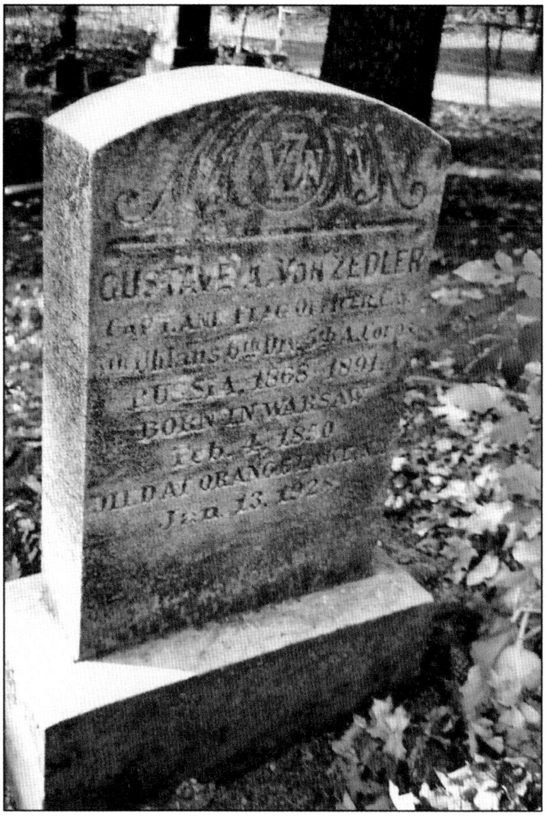

"Russian Gus" was an early folk hero at Orange Lake and was actually German. A tall man with a large moustache, he shot two men to protect two young women on the Bond farm. Acquitted of murder, he remained in the area doing odd jobs and spending time at the Lakeside House. (Author's collection.)

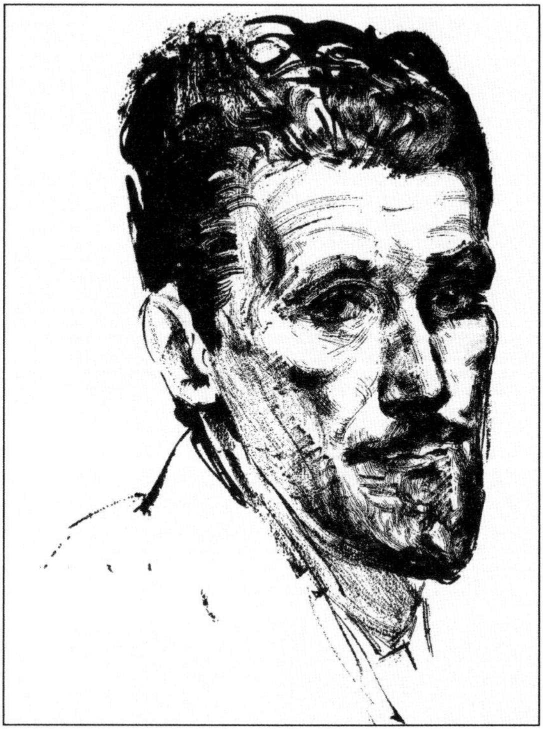

Francis Clough was an Orange Lake poet, publisher, and pacifist. A devotee of Mohandas Gandhi, Clough wrote to him for many years and received a bottle of water from the Ganges River from Gandhi shortly before he was assassinated. (Courtesy of Franz Clough.)

Eight

THE SPORTING LIFE

Orange Lake is a year-round mecca for sports. Iceboating, once the sport of well-to-do individuals, was more accessible to people. It is one of the most exciting sports to witness or experience. The Orange Lake Ice Yacht Club was first chartered in the 1880s by a group of local businessmen, including Henry C. Higginson and William H. Smith. It held regattas each year and had its own clubhouse. The shallow depth of the lake and the strong winds across it make the lake an excellent choice for iceboaters.

Although famous boats like the *Jack Frost* still populate the lake today, there are many smaller crafts.

Speed skating and ice-skating have also been part of the lake's history. The National Amateur Speed Skating Association's races took place there in the early 1900s. Pleasure skating and ice hockey are other common occurrences on the frozen water.

Canoeing has been popular on the lake since the days of the Native Americans. The Aetna Canoe Club was the first organized canoeing venture at the lake. Other pleasure craft and small motorboats have been used there for many years.

Orange Lake has also been a practice home to individuals and teams who enjoy sculling. The famous rowers Luke Grace Sr. and his son, Luke Jr., had a summer home on the west side of the lake and could often be seen rowing on the lake. The Newburgh Free Academy crew team used the lake in the early 1990s to practice.

Fishing for bass, wide-mouth bass, and pickerel has been a favored sport of lake dwellers and guardians of the lake. The Orange Lake Fish Protection Association, a forerunner of the Orange Lake Fish and Game Association, was established in 1885. In recent years, the present group has built a boat launch and parking lot, erected a pavilion, and continued its work of protecting the habitat of the lake for fish and fisherman alike.

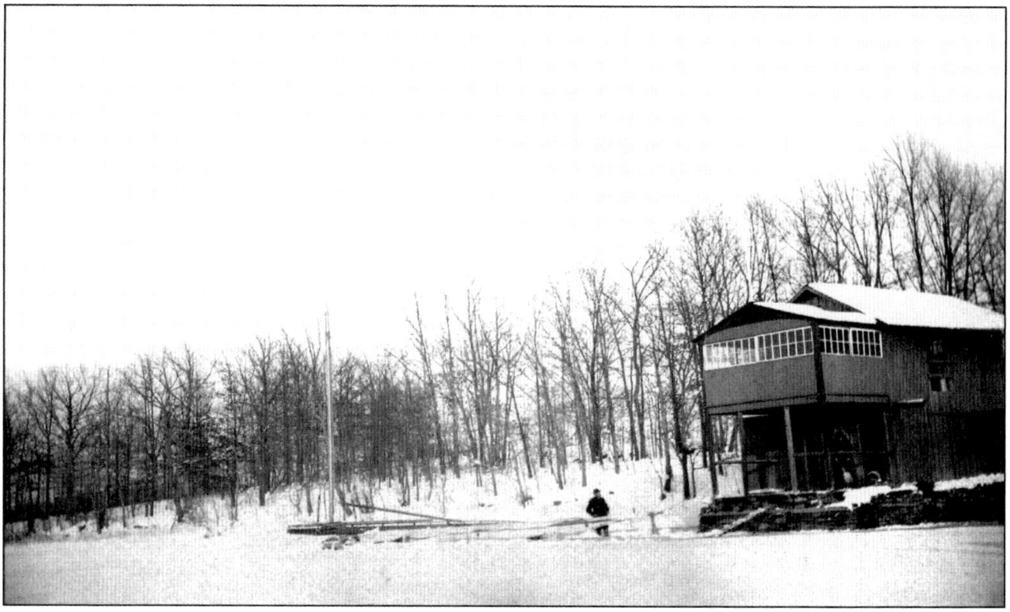

A man and his iceboat stand in front of the iceboat building near Ramsdell's Point at the north end of the lake. Another man who may be joining him sweeps snow off the porch in this early glass negative. (Courtesy of the Historical Society of Newburgh Bay and the Highlands.)

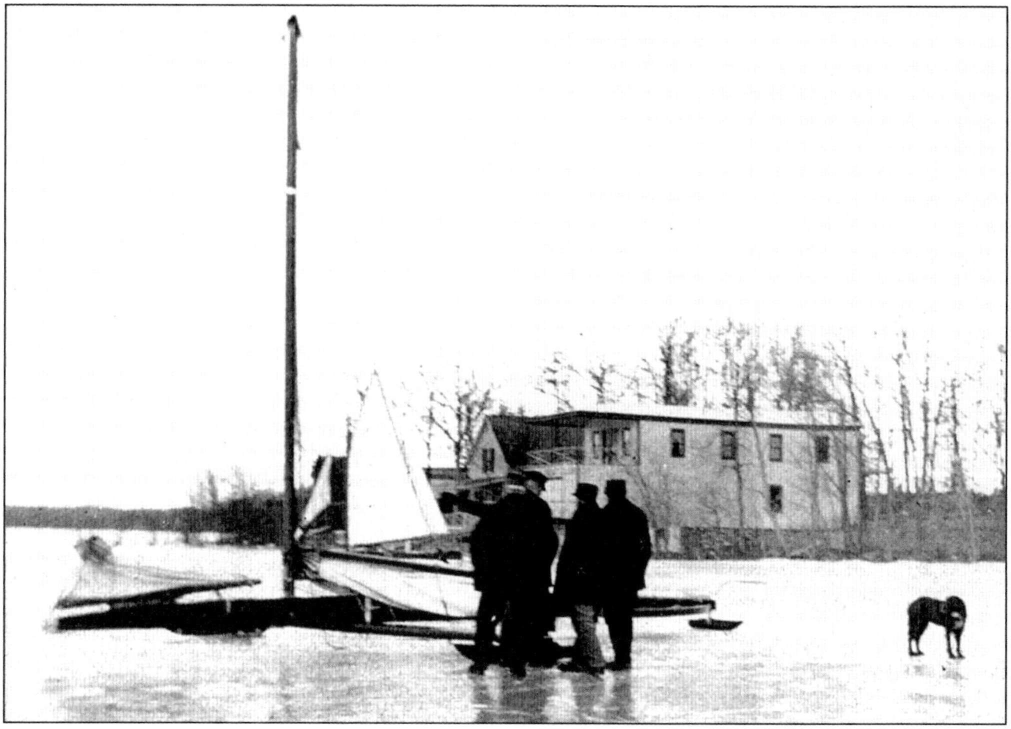

Four men work on a boat as a dog looks on in this old photograph taken at the north end of the lake on a frigid winter day. The shallowness of the water caused it to freeze early each season, making the lake a natural for iceboating. (Courtesy of Sharon Nichols Formato.)

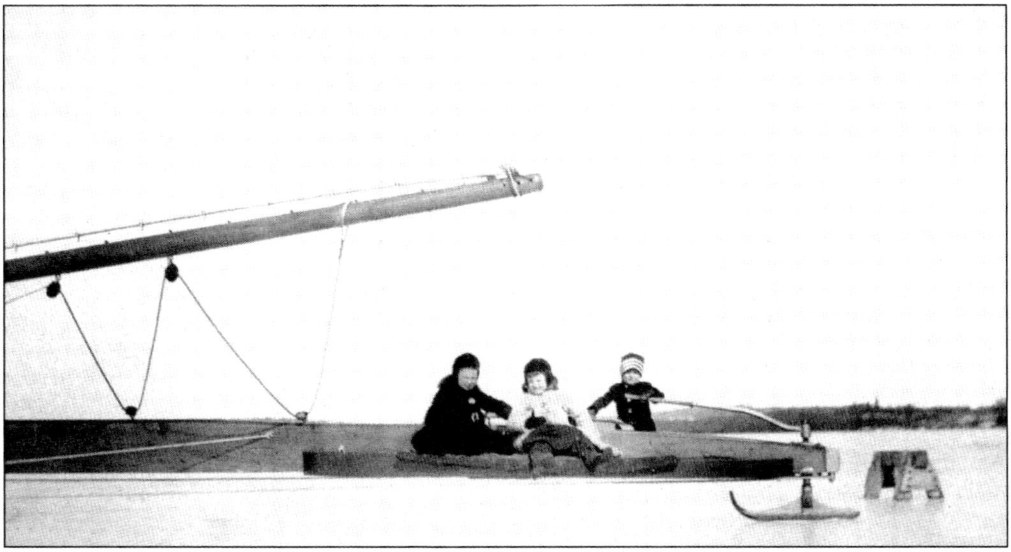

These children in this 1920s photograph are obviously too young to pilot an iceboat. However, their experience as passengers led many children to a lifelong interest in the sport. (Courtesy of the Historical Society of Newburgh Bay and the Highlands.)

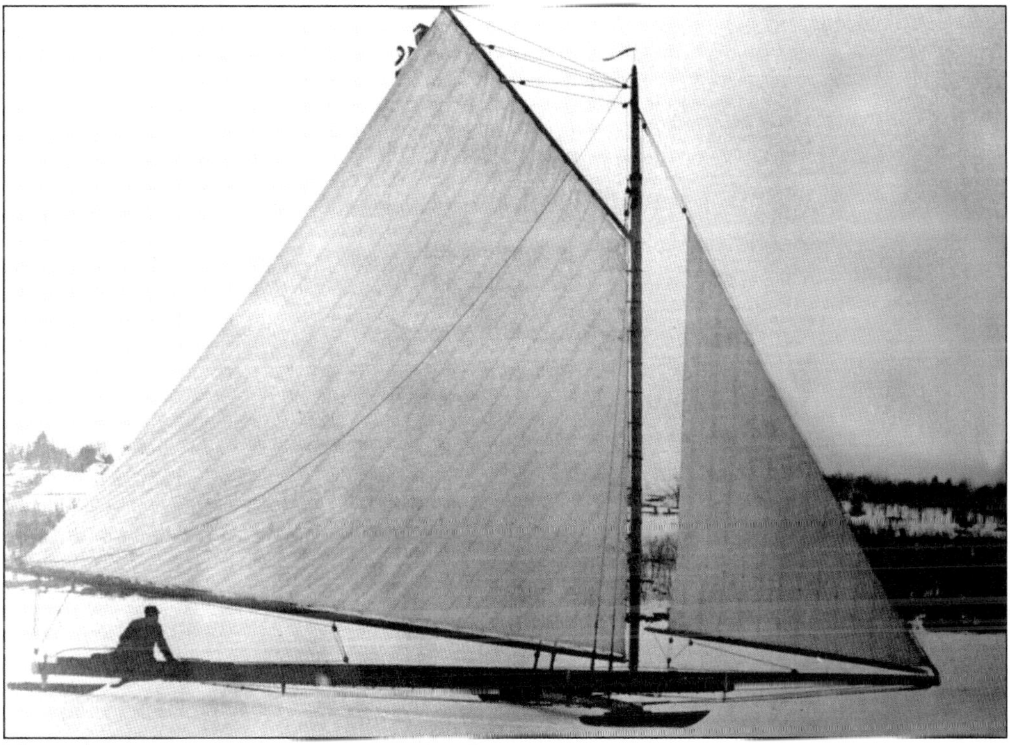

The iceboat *Jack Frost* was built in 1887 for Commodore Archibald Rogers of the Hudson River Ice Yacht Club in Hyde Park. It was rebuilt in 1972–1973 by the same club in Newburgh. To quote Robert Lawrence, owner of the boat and a lifelong iceboater, "A ride on the *Jack Frost* and any other boat is the difference between a Model T and a Rolls Royce." (Courtesy of the Historical Society of Newburgh Bay and the Highlands.)

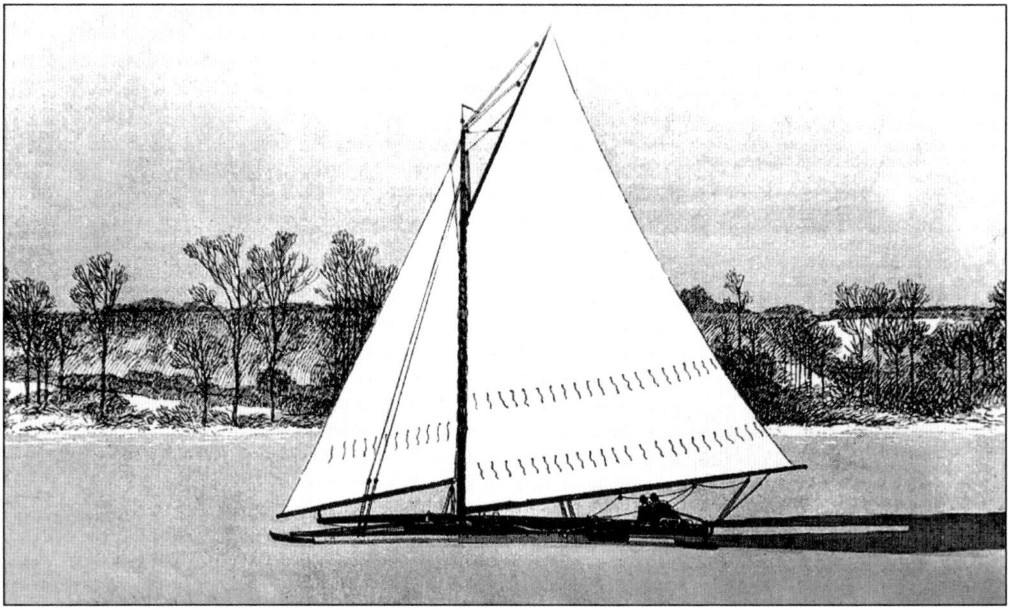

When the iceboating team from Red Bank, New Jersey, came to Orange Lake in 1891 to try and win the Challenge Ice Yacht Cup of America, the local residents were shocked to see something they had never seen before, an iceboat with cast-iron rudders. The rudders gave the *Scud* a speed advantage, and the cup went to Red Bank. (Courtesy of the Historical Society of Newburgh Bay and the Highlands.)

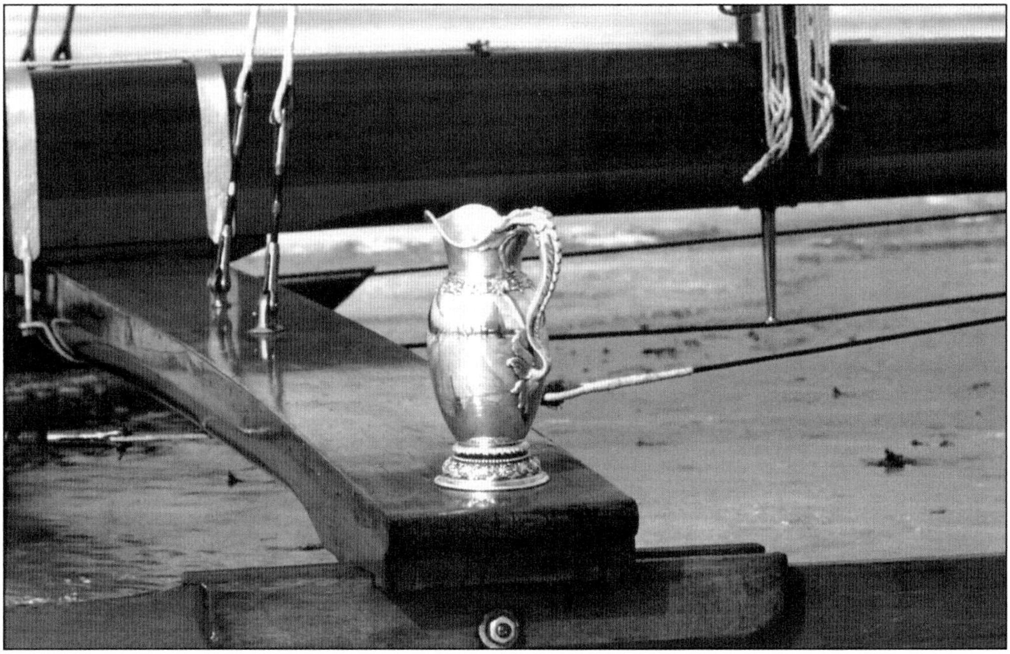

The Challenge Ice Yacht Cup of America, commonly called the Van Nostrand Cup after its donor, Gardiner Van Nostrand, who donated it in 1889, was to be a "perpetual cup for the friendly competition between ice yacht clubs of the country." It is pictured here on the *Jack Frost*. (Courtesy of Robert Lawrence.)

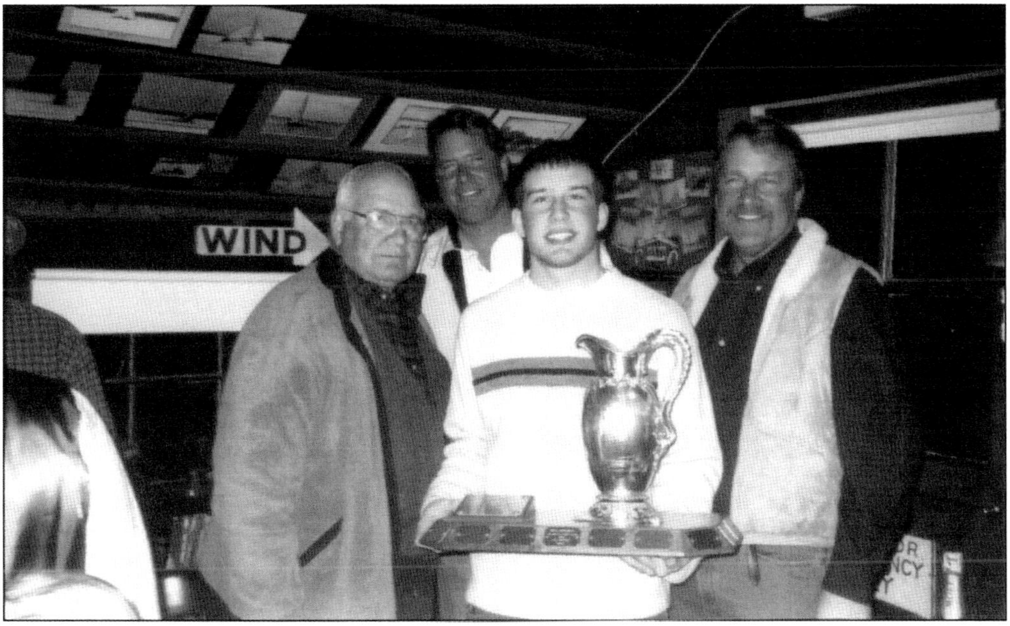

Three generations of the Lawrence family pose with the Van Nostrand Cup in the clubhouse of the Red Bank Ice Yacht Club after a challenge race in 2003. From left to right, they are Robert Lawrence, grandson Kevin, and son Richard. Son Daniel is in the second row. The trophy remains in Red Bank. (Courtesy of Robert Lawrence.)

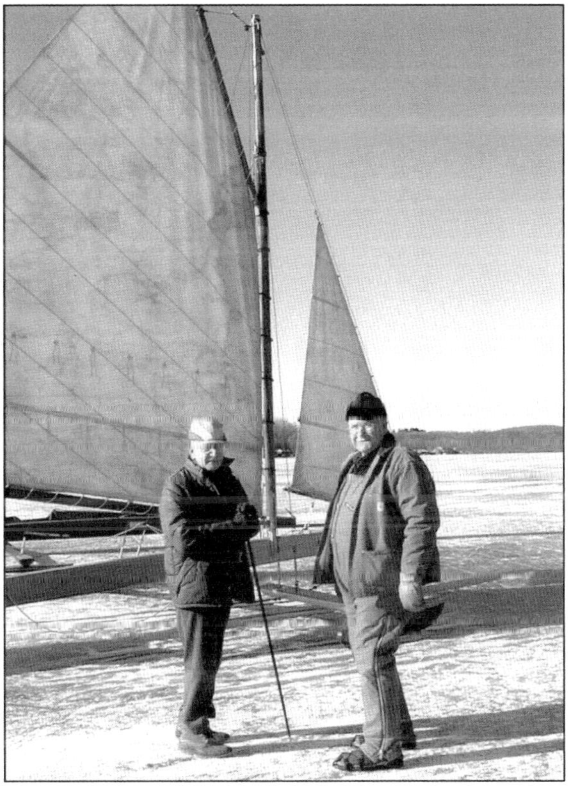

Gordon Anderson (left), a longtime Gardnertown resident and local historian, and his friend Robert Lawrence stand in front of another Lawrence family boat, the *Ice Queen*, on a sunny winter's day in this photograph taken in 2001. (Courtesy of Robert Lawrence.)

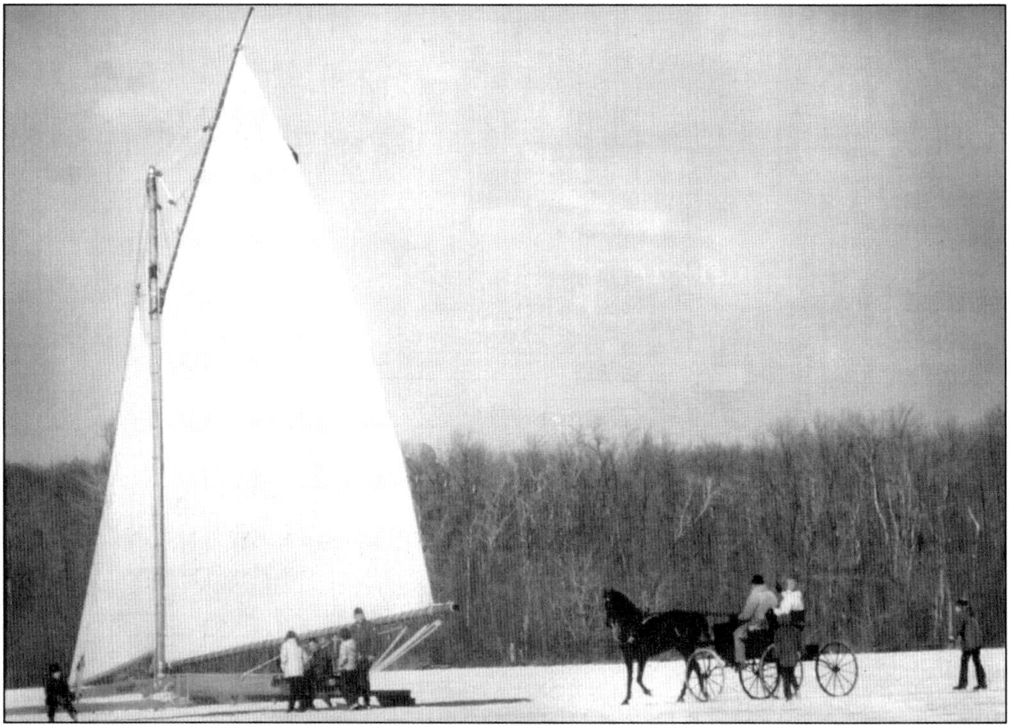

Stanton Hemmingway, a former high school teacher and coach, took great pleasure riding his horse and carriage around the Newburgh area. In the early 1970s, he took his carriage out on the ice to meet his friend Robert Lawrence and the crew of his boat. The photograph was later reproduced on canvas. (Courtesy of Marsha Tenny.)

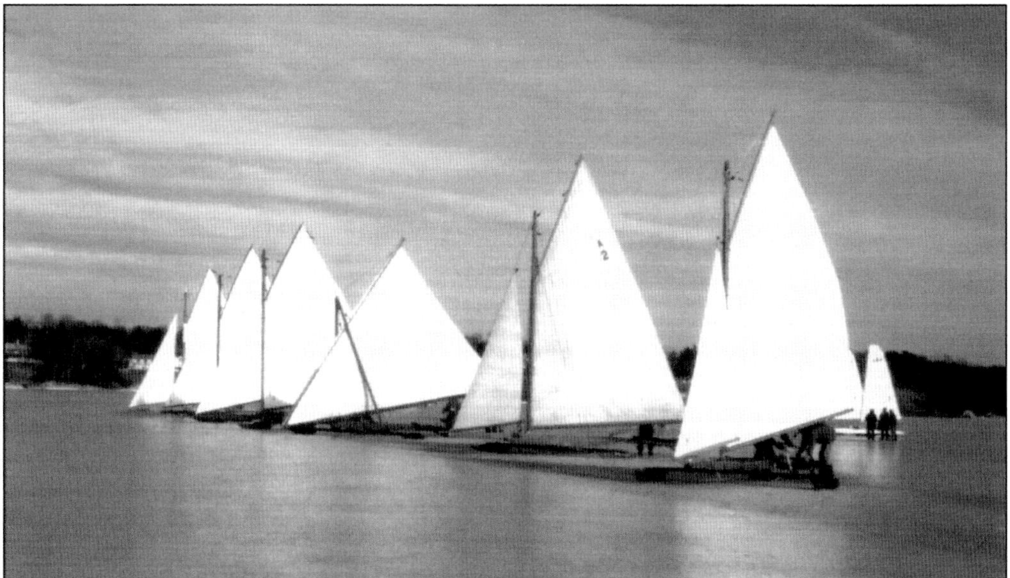

Iceboats line up for a race in a regatta on Orange Lake in this 1990s photograph. From left to right, they are the *Red Baron*, three unidentified, the *Vixen*, the *Northwest*, and the *Scout*. The *Vixen* was once owned by the Jova family of Newburgh. (Courtesy of Robert Lawrence.)

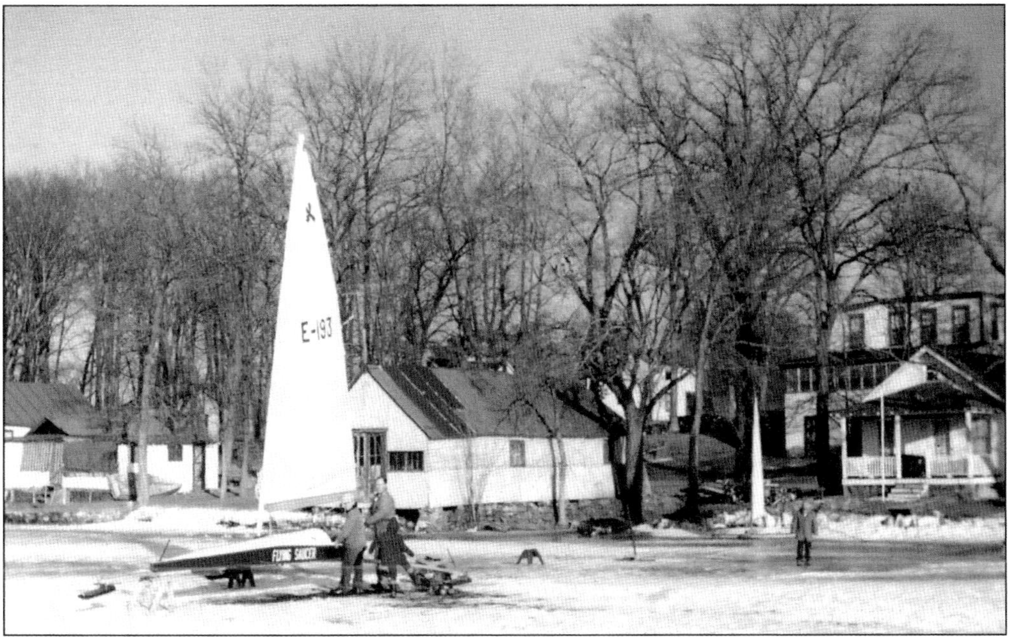

Paul Sbraccia, who was a primary mover in efforts to reincorporate the Orange Lake Ice Yacht Club in 1962, is seen launching his boat, the *Flying Sauce*, in front of O'Malley's in this 1980s photograph. O'Malley's was a popular place to launch iceboats because it offered easy and direct access to the lake. (Courtesy of Marsha Tenny.)

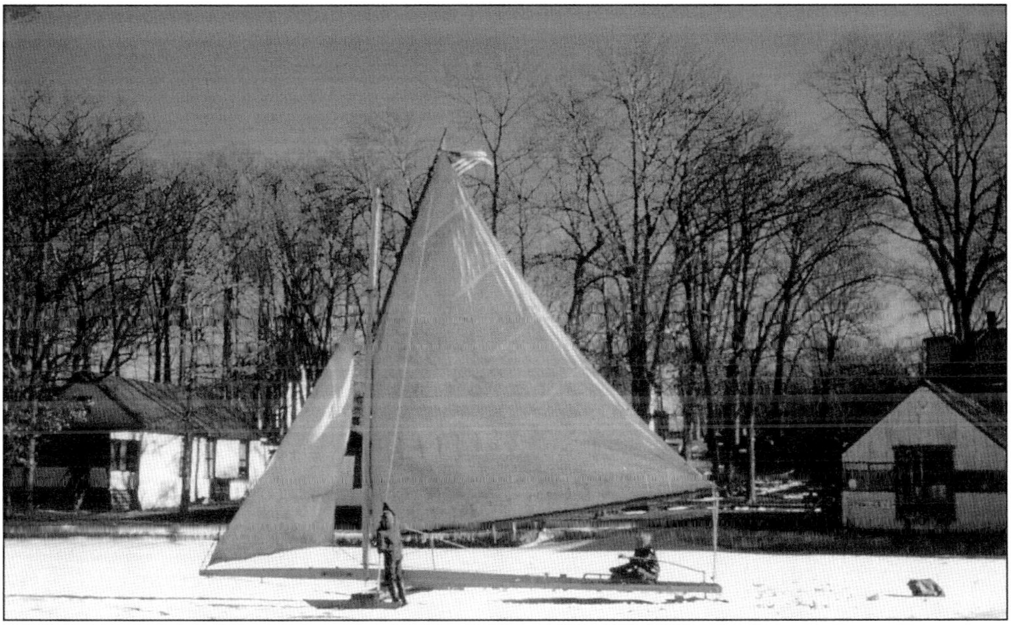

This is the *Arrow*, another old rebuilt iceboat, being readied for a trip in front of O'Malley's in 1958. The boat was owned by Raymond Innis. (Courtesy of Marsha Tenny.)

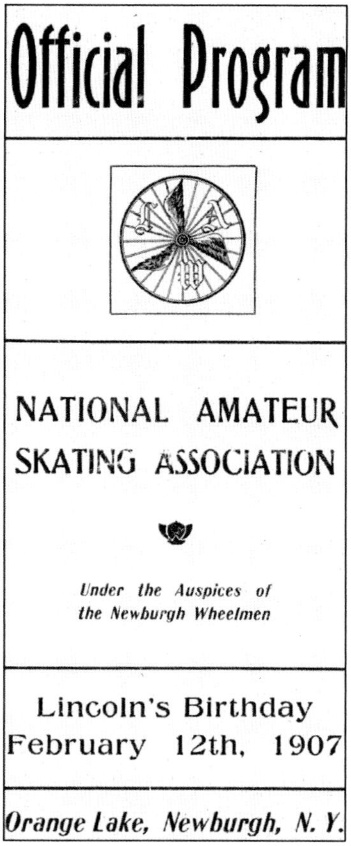

The Wheelmen, a popular Newburgh bicycle club, included some of the best athletes in the area. It sponsored many different sporting events, including the National Amateur Skating Association's speed skating races at Orange Lake in 1907. Participants came from Canada and the northeastern United States for the Lincoln's birthday event. (Courtesy of David McDermott.)

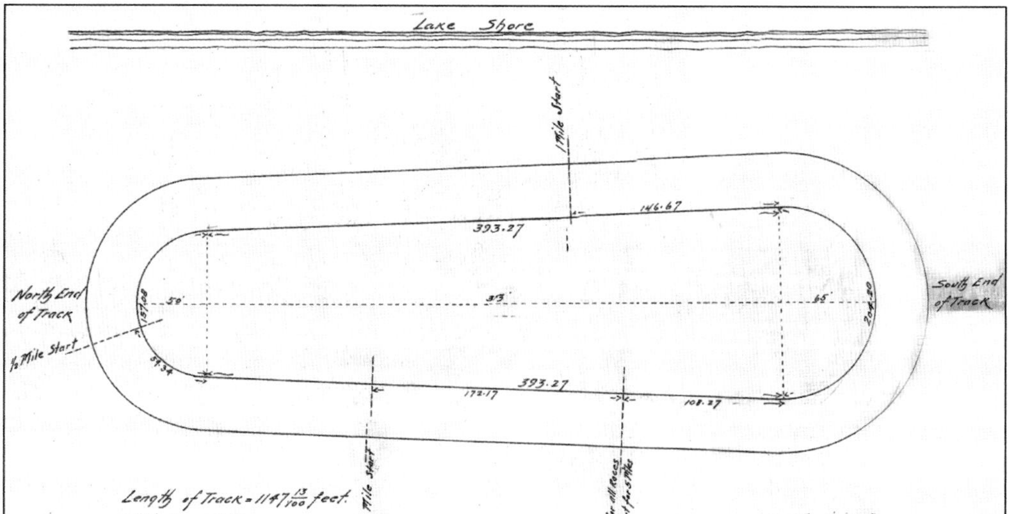

This drawing of the layout for the speed skating track for the race was found in the City of Newburgh archives. Medals were awarded to the first-, second-, and third-place finishers in five-mile, one-mile, half-mile, and quarter-mile races. There was also a one-mile novice race for younger skaters. (Courtesy of Elizabeth McKean, City of Newburgh Records Management Office.)

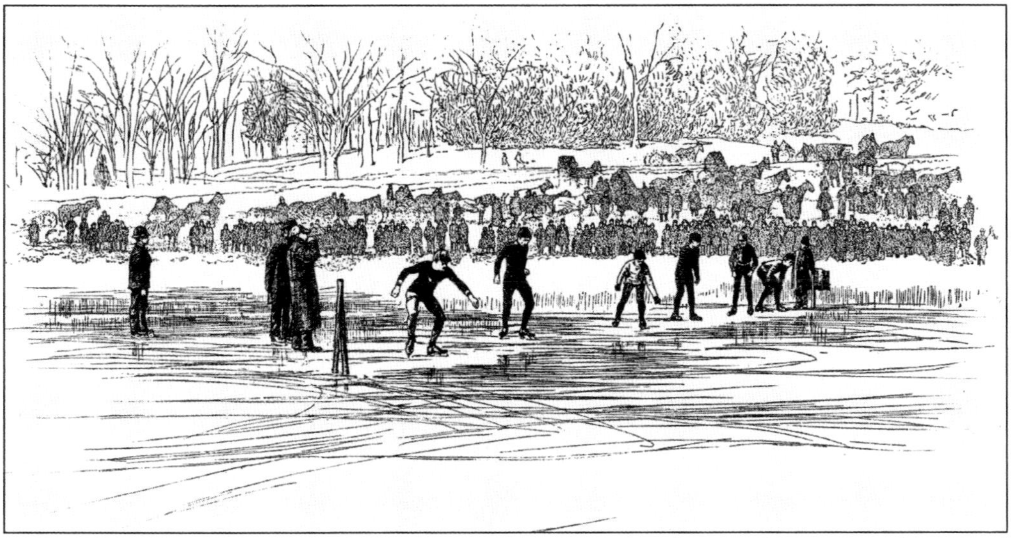

Speed skaters line up for one of the races held that day in this drawing that appeared in a local newspaper. It must have been a very cold day judging by the spectators and horses watching from the shore. (Courtesy of Russell Lange.)

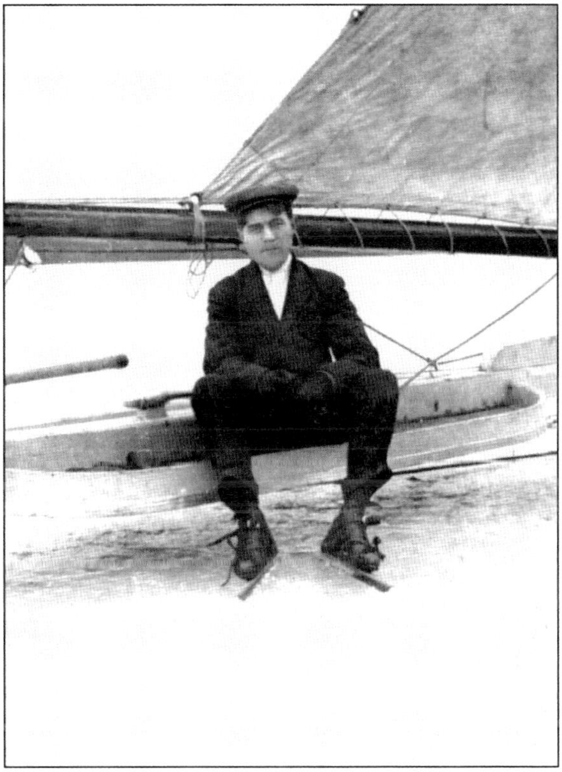

William Nichols rests on the side of an iceboat after a spin around the lake in this early-20th-century photograph. His skates are typical of the times. They were a single blade with a heel stop and straps that were buckled onto the skater's shoes. (Courtesy of Sharon Nichols Formato.)

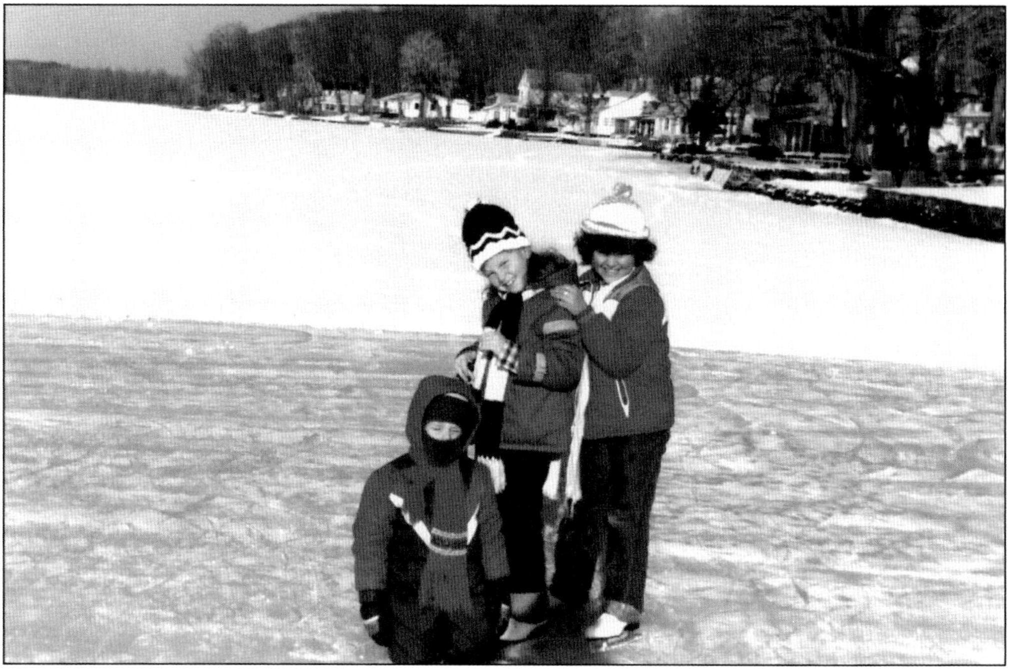

In order to ice-skate on Orange Lake, residents had to clear any snow from the ice in front of their homes. Above, from left to right, Ryan Nugent, Trisha Nugent, and Buffey Favata pose for a picture after their parents cleared an ice-skating area for them. (Courtesy of Sheila Gage Nugent.)

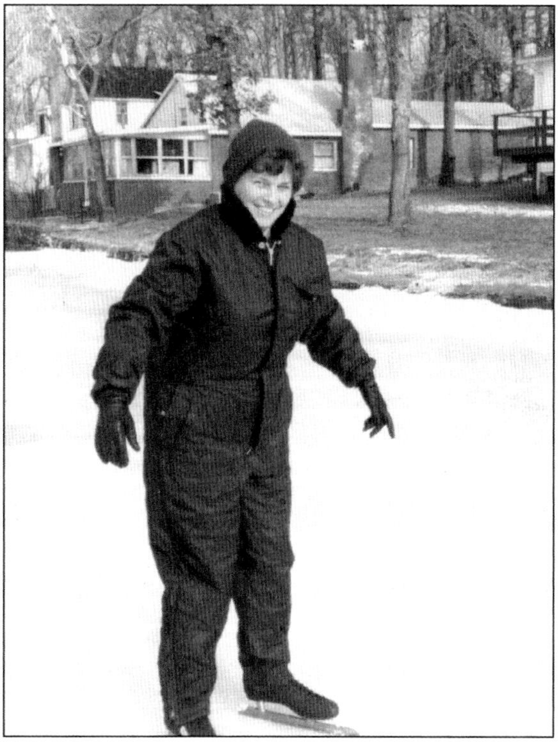

Dressed for warmth, Marsha Tenny takes to the ice wearing her racers, or pikes, the long-blade skates that competitors wore in speed skating races during much of the 20th century. (Courtesy of Marsha Tenny.)

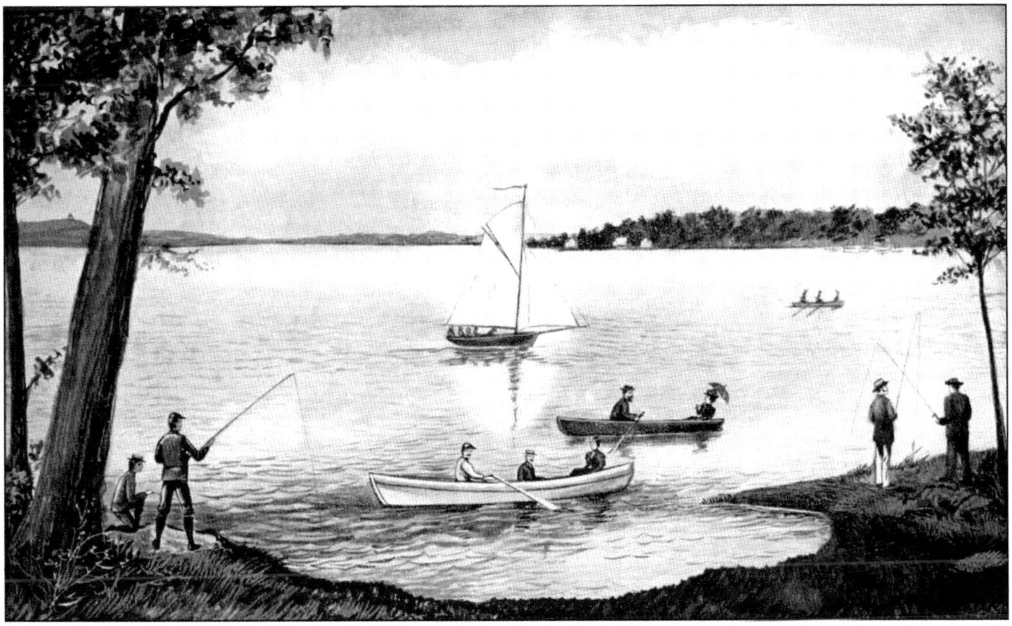

This idyllic scene from 1899 shows the many possibilities afforded a resident or visitor to Orange Lake. It includes fishing, rowing, and sailing. Sailing was never a successful sport on the lake because the lake is too shallow to support a vessel's keel. (Courtesy of the Historical Society of Newburgh Bay and the Highlands.)

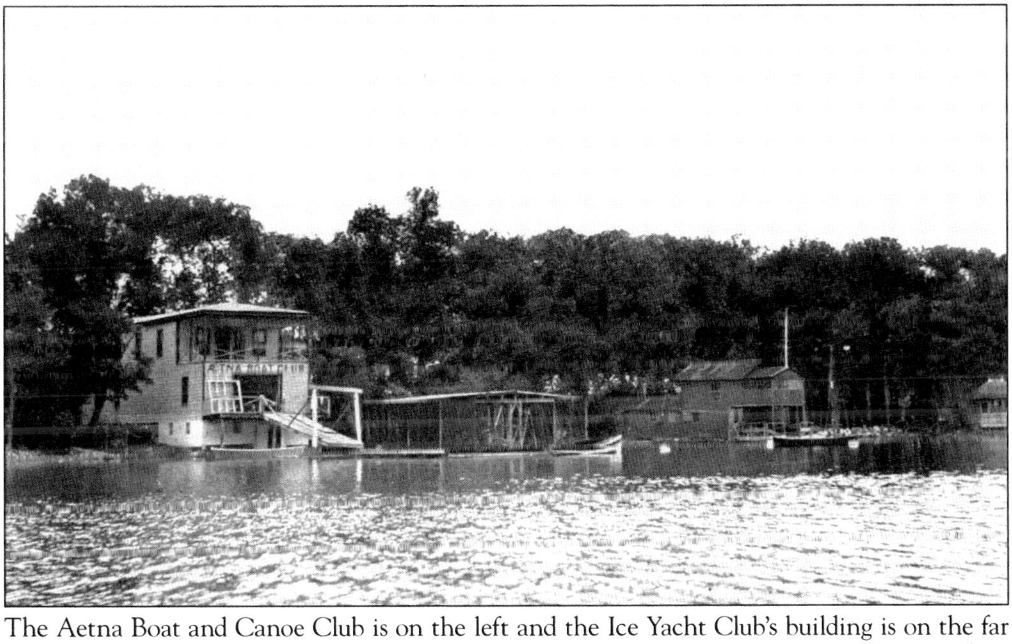

The Aetna Boat and Canoe Club is on the left and the Ice Yacht Club's building is on the far right in this early postcard view of the south end of the lake. Both clubs were very active in their many years of operation at the lake. (Author's collection.)

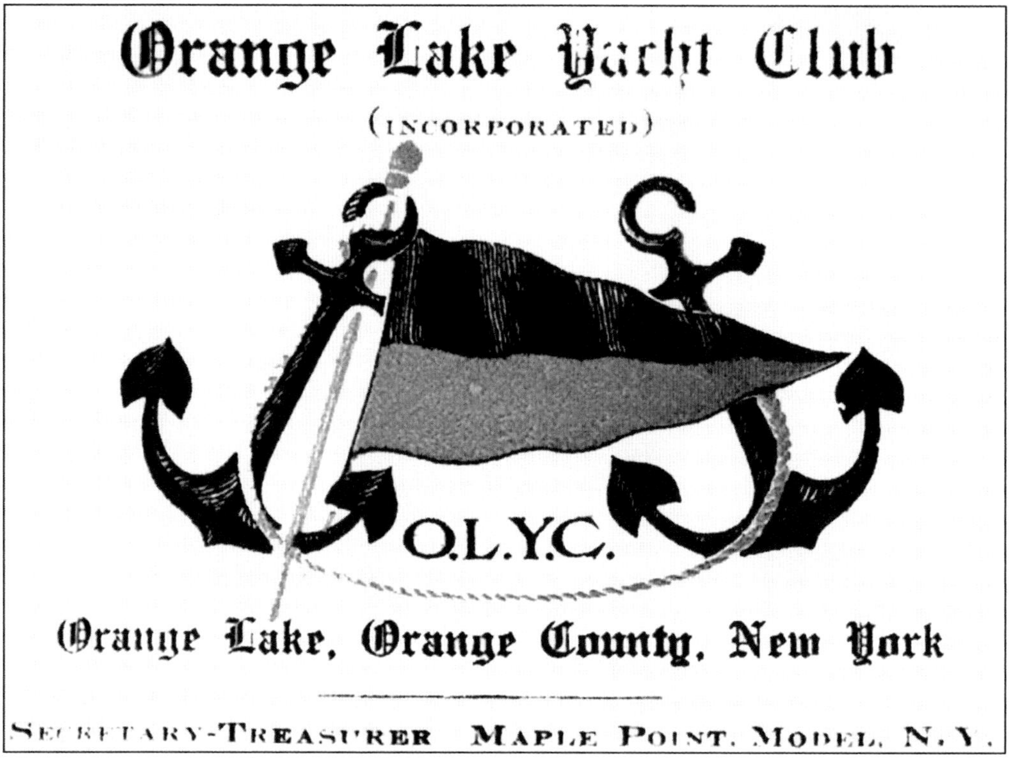

This is the insignia of the Orange Lake Yacht Club, which was incorporated in 1905. Members of the group owned "sloops, larks, cut-boats, launches, canoes, and motor boats." The club's address was Model, an area of New Windsor, because its secretary-treasurer's home was located there. (Courtesy of the Historical Society of Newburgh Bay and the Highlands.)

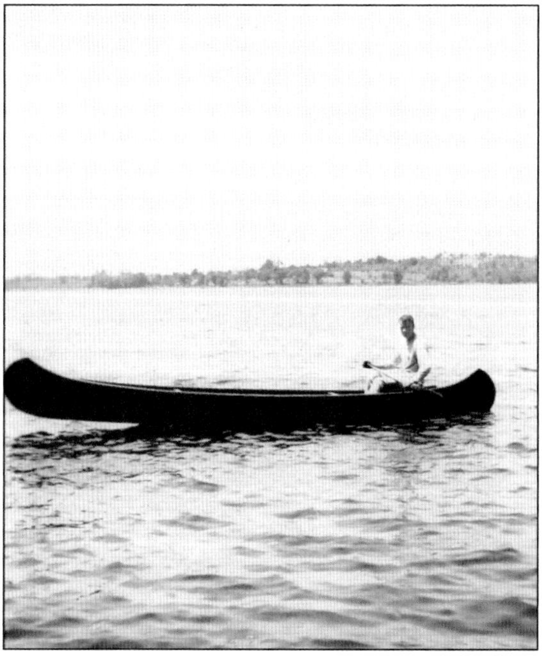
Evelyn and Arthur Petersen, relatives of the Martel family, spent many happy hours at the Martel family home at the lake. Here Arthur paddles his canoe past the home. (Courtesy of Kathleen Martel Sileno.)

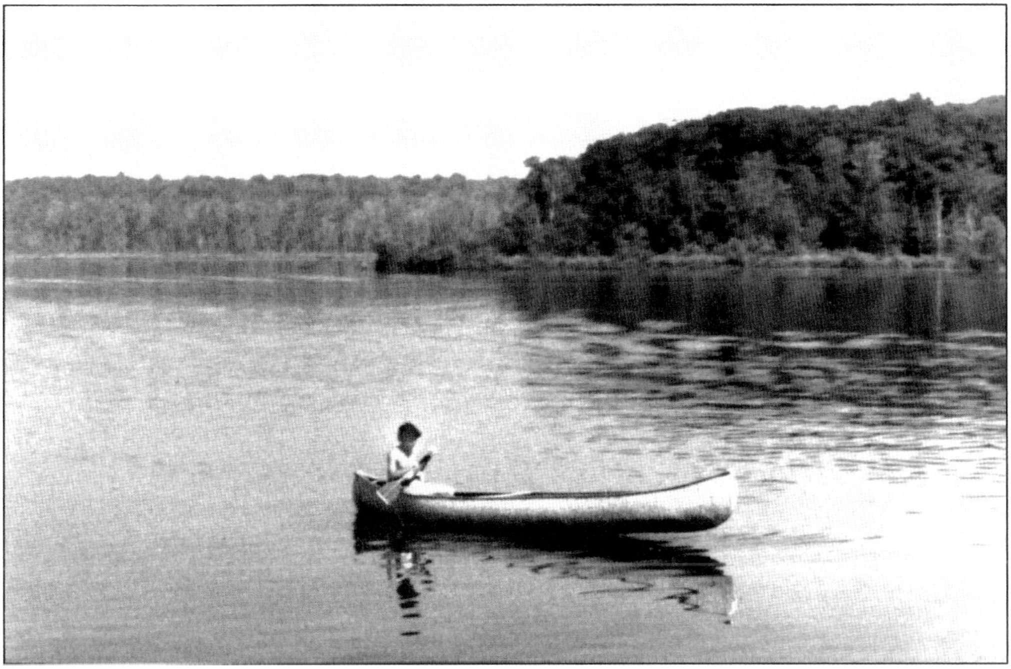

Some 40 years later, Arthur Petersen's grandnephew John Sileno paddles his canoe in almost the same location at the north end of the lake. The lake is ideal for canoeing and in the early years hosted many canoe regattas. (Courtesy of Kathleen Martel Sileno.)

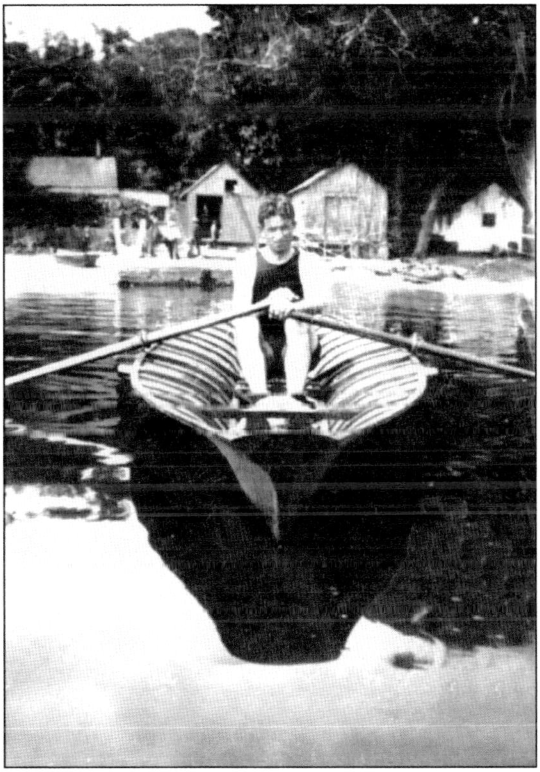

Luke Grace Sr. was a star athlete at Newburgh Free Academy in the 1920s who became a New York City policeman and summered at Orange Lake. He was a member of the New York Rowing Club. He is seen here in one of the family's sculls practicing on Orange Lake. (Courtesy of Sr. Mary Sheppard.)

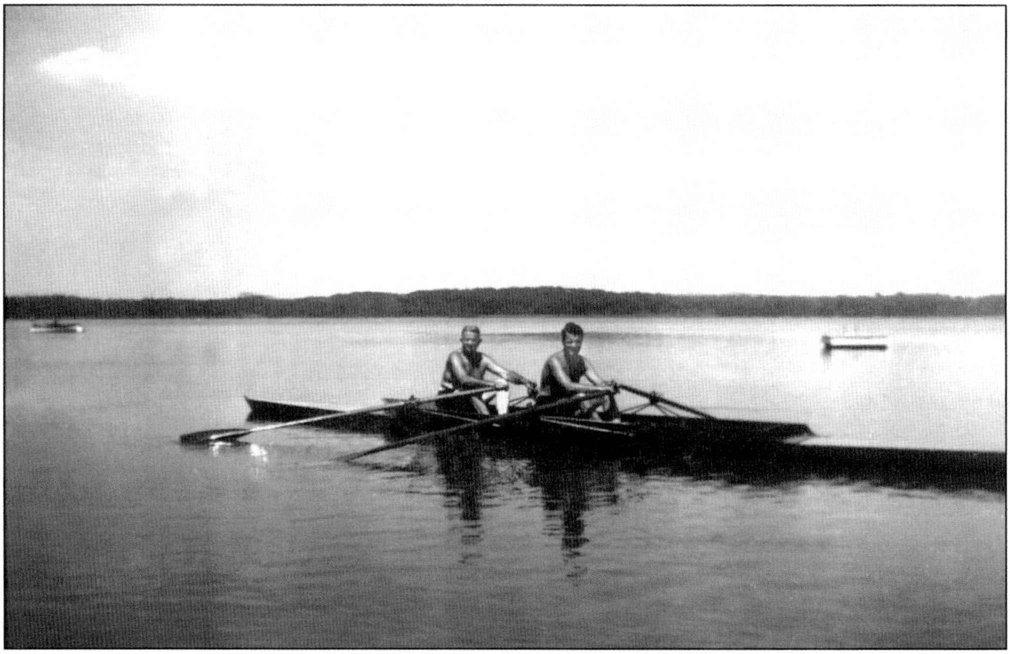

Luke Grace Jr. was also an accomplished athlete and a member of the Nonpareil Rowing Club located on the Harlem River. He spent his summers at Orange Lake, and he is seen here rowing with his father at the lake. (Courtesy of Sr. Mary Sheppard.)

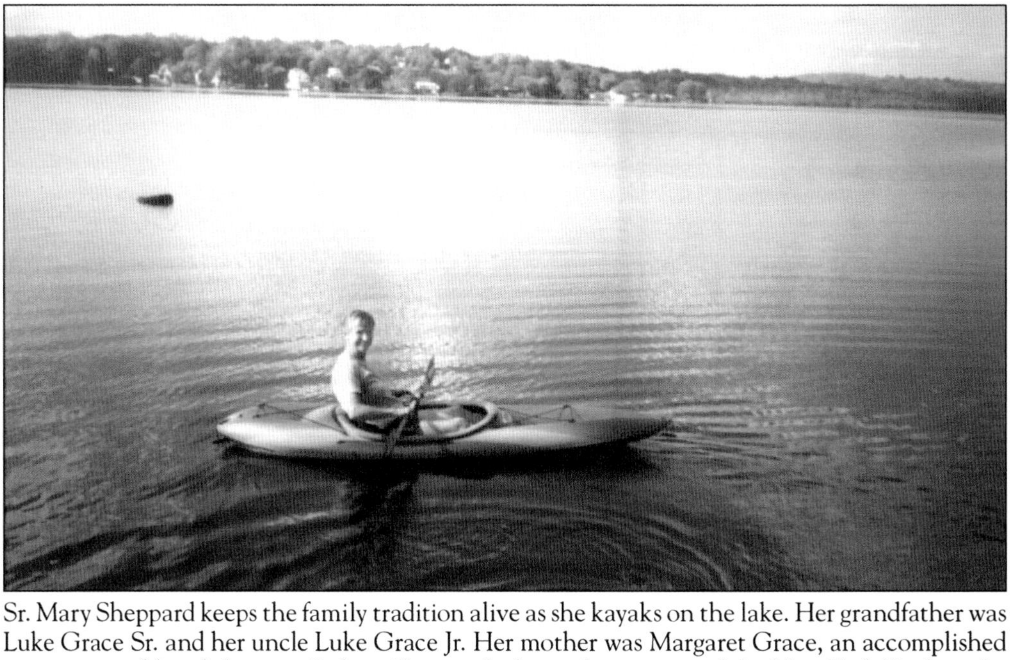

Sr. Mary Sheppard keeps the family tradition alive as she kayaks on the lake. Her grandfather was Luke Grace Sr. and her uncle Luke Grace Jr. Her mother was Margaret Grace, an accomplished swimmer, and her father was Robert Sheppard, the stadium voice of the New York Yankees for over 50 years. (Courtesy of Sr. Mary Sheppard.)

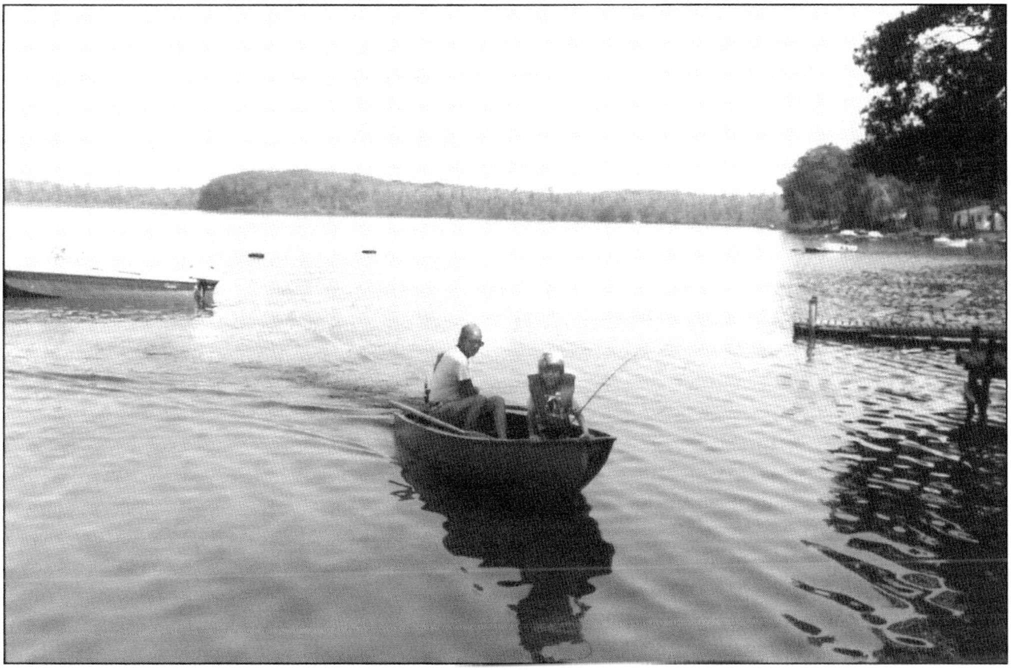

An avid fly fisherman, Snyder Gage could be seen fishing at the north end of the lake each evening. He taught many people his craft and is seen in this photograph with his grandson Ryan Nugent coming back to shore. (Courtesy of Sheila Gage Nugent.)

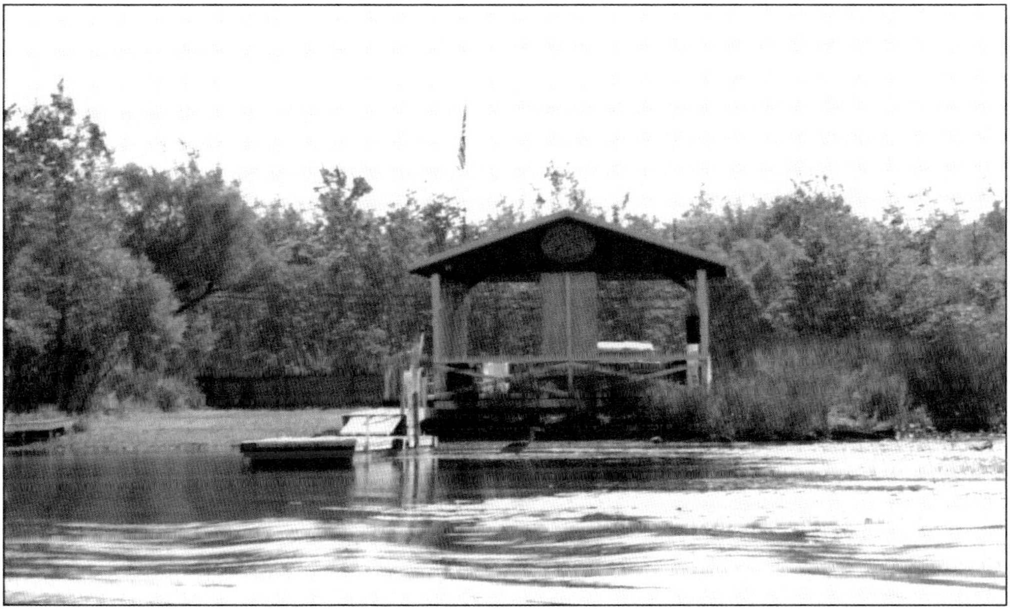

This structure is the pavilion of the Orange Lake Fish and Game Association. The private association was formed by a group of sportsmen and businessmen in 1914. These pioneers stocked the lake with fish and had control of the level of the lake with Thomas Chadwick, who owned the group's land until 1972. (Courtesy of Edward Stump.)

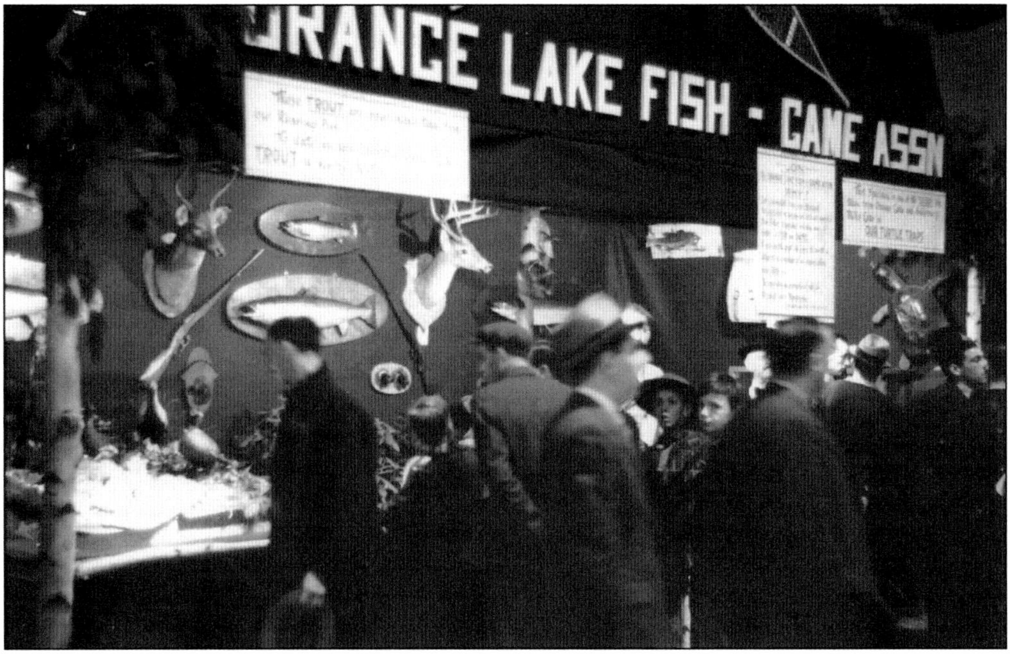

At an exhibition in Newburgh in 1938, the Orange Lake Fish and Game Association put up an impressive display of its outdoor activities. On exhibit were turtle traps, mounted fish and wildlife, and beaver dams. According to news accounts, the most popular part of the display was live pheasants. (Courtesy of the Historical Society of Newburgh Bay and the Highlands.)

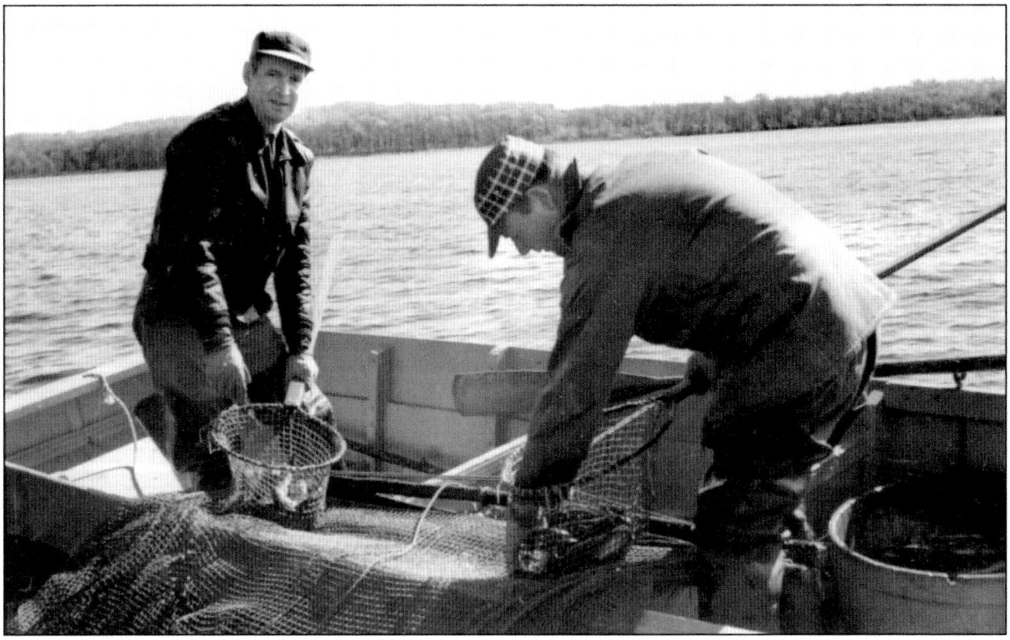

One of the most important works of the association was removing predator fish and restocking the lake with bass, pickerel, and big-mouth bass. This photograph shows some of the members at work in the 1950s. (Courtesy of Sheila Gage Nugent.)

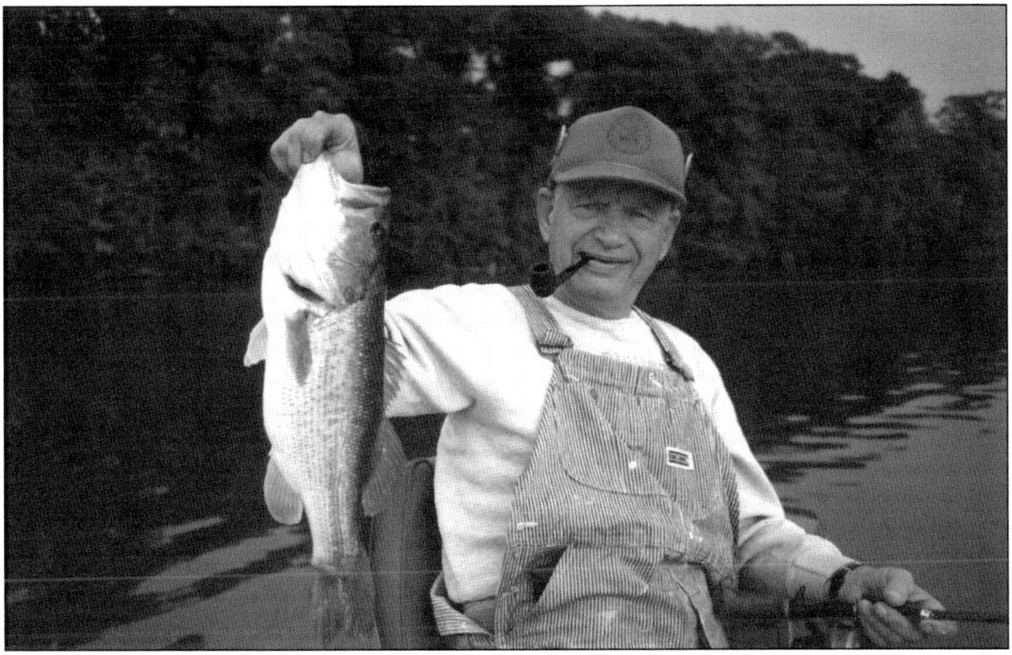

William "Heffie" Eckler, a senior member of the Orange Lake Fish and Game Association, shows off his prize-winning four-pound bass in this 1992 photograph. Eckler was club cook in his final years at the association's fishing tournaments, and it is said "he liked fishing and fisherman equally." (Courtesy of Edward Stump.)

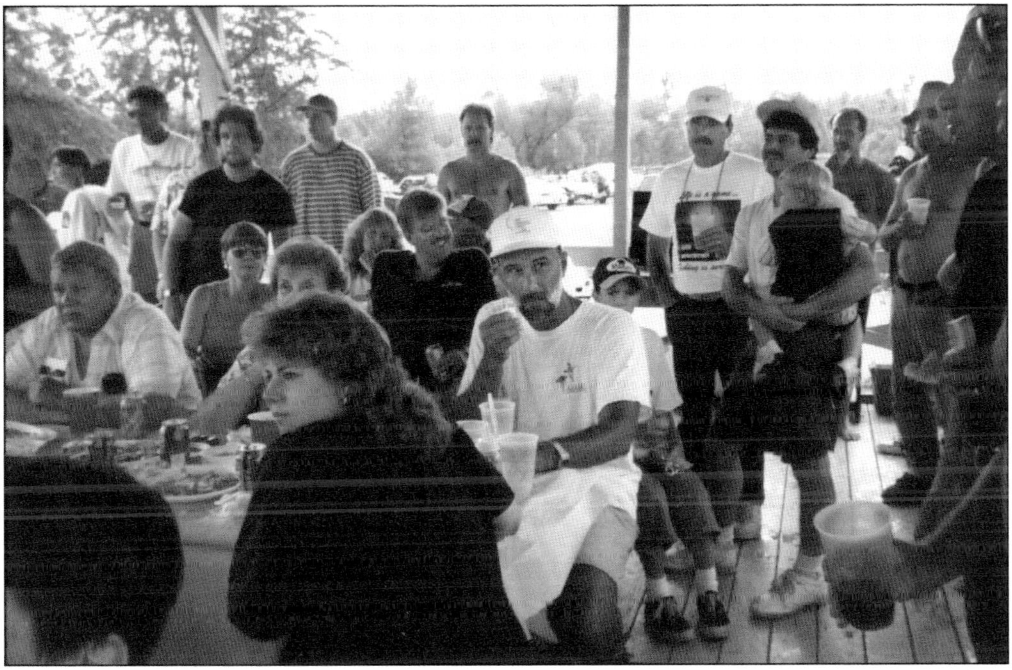

Members of the Orange Lake Fish and Game Association celebrate family day under the pavilion in this July 1998 photograph. A fishing derby for children and picnic were part of the day's festivities. (Courtesy of Edward Stump.)

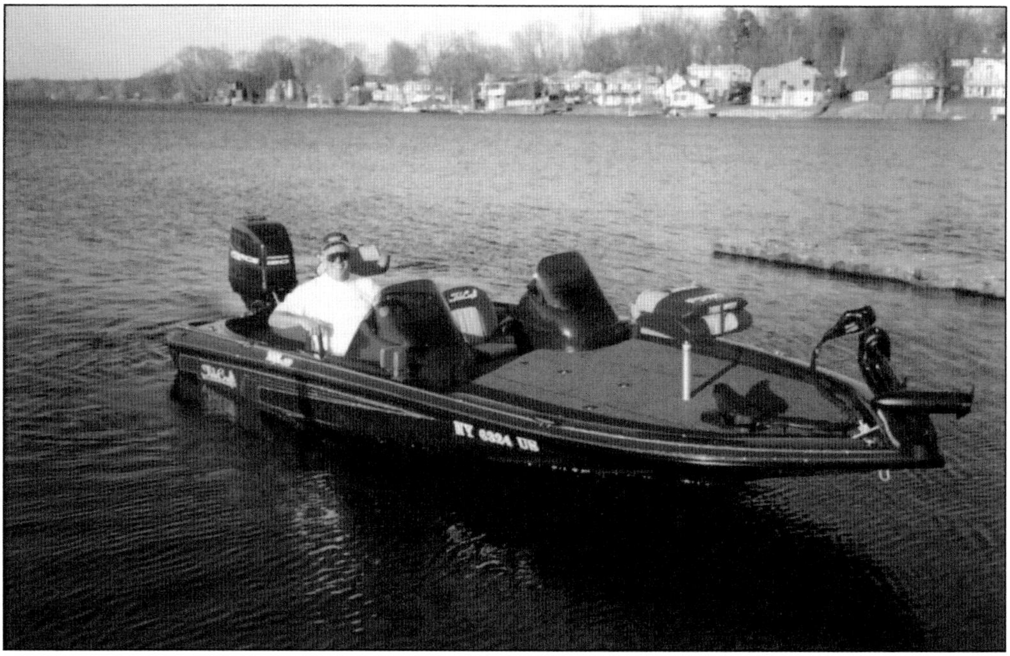

The longtime president of the Orange Lake Fish and Game Association, Edward Stump, shows off the modern bass-fishing boat the club purchased in the fall of 2002 for tournament fishing. Stump, in his tenure as president, has provided a balance between the New York State Department of Conservation, the Homeowners Association, and his association. (Courtesy of Edward Stump.)

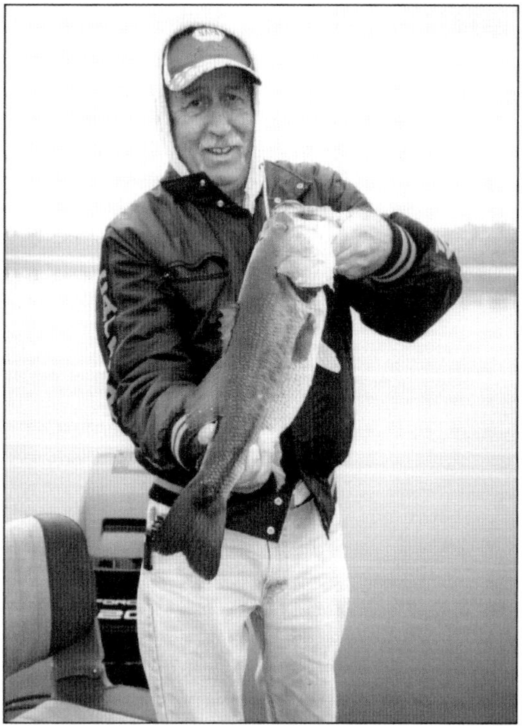

Another senior member of the club, Joseph Roy, proudly displays his four-and-a-half-pound bass, caught at the lake in the summer of 2005. In 1946, the association opened its membership to resident sportsmen from Orange, Ulster, and Sullivan Counties. There are currently 50 to 60 active fishermen and hunters in the group. (Courtesy of Edward Stump.)

Nine

A New Frontier

By 1952, the population of the Orange Lake community numbered almost 500. Many summer residents had enlarged and winterized their homes. New homes were built on former farmland. As a result of this population growth, some problems developed.

Thomas Chadwick and other mill owners still controlled the water level of the lake, leading to dangerous conditions, especially in years of drought. The Orange Lake Civic Association was established in 1952 to combat some of these issues. In a petition sent to Chadwick and the other owners in 1954, it stated, "The low level of the water has affected our water supply, wells, killed fish and our property values and fire protection are also affected." For more then 20 years, the association successfully acted as the go-between for the homeowners, resolving most problems caused by low levels of lake water. Lowering the level of the lake is now controlled by Orange Lake Resources, a group of lake residents.

Other commercial establishments came to the lake in order to meet the needs of the residents. They included a motel, a small market, and an ice-cream shop.

But the most serious threat to the lake surfaced as the population continued to increase. A seaweedlike substance began taking over the lake. For many years, state and local conservation officials were unable to find the cause of the problem. With scientific advances came an answer. Phosphates and nitrates from septic systems, fertilizers, detergents, runoff from roads, and even a waste water treatment plant in the watershed area were causing algaelike plants and fish kills. The quality of lake water was deteriorating quickly.

The Orange Lake community, after a 20-year struggle with town officials, voted and approved a centralized sewer system for the community in 1992. Water lines were also installed at the time. These, along with other measures taken by lake residents, have improved the quality of the water and insured lake water for years to come.

As the *Newburgh Telegraph* stated in 1891, "Orange Lake has a bright future before it."

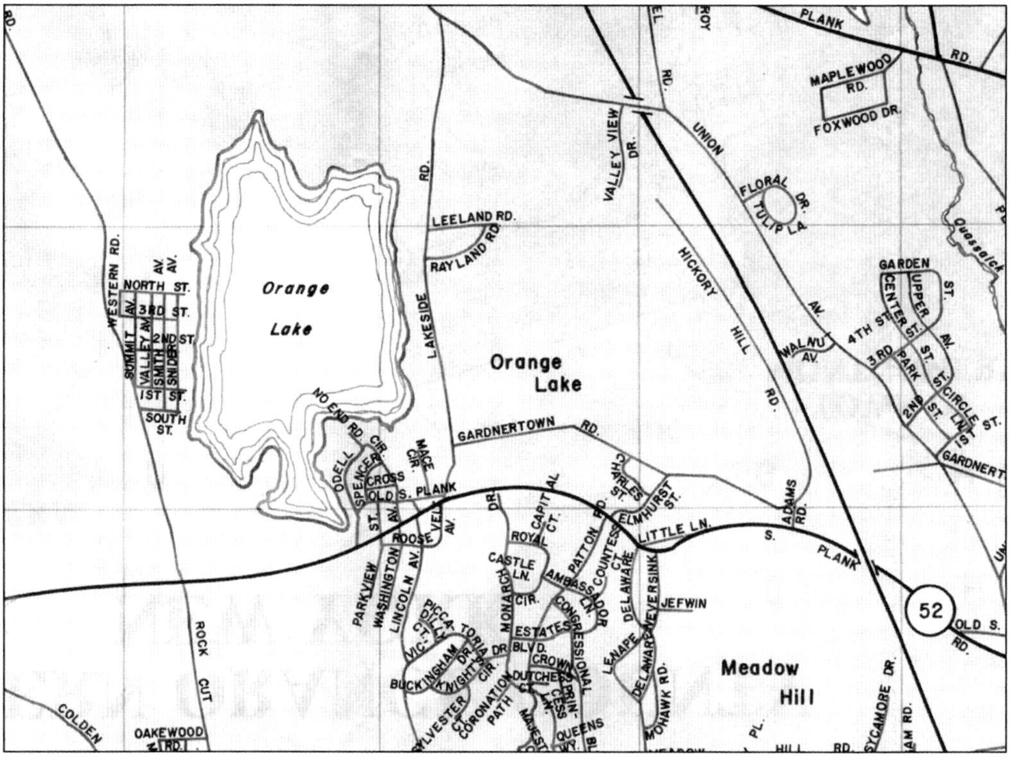

This area map was published in 1985. It shows the development of the Orange Lake area; the former Patton farm, the original Meadow Hill housing development, to its south; and part of the Gardnertown section of the town to the right. (Courtesy of John J. Lease.)

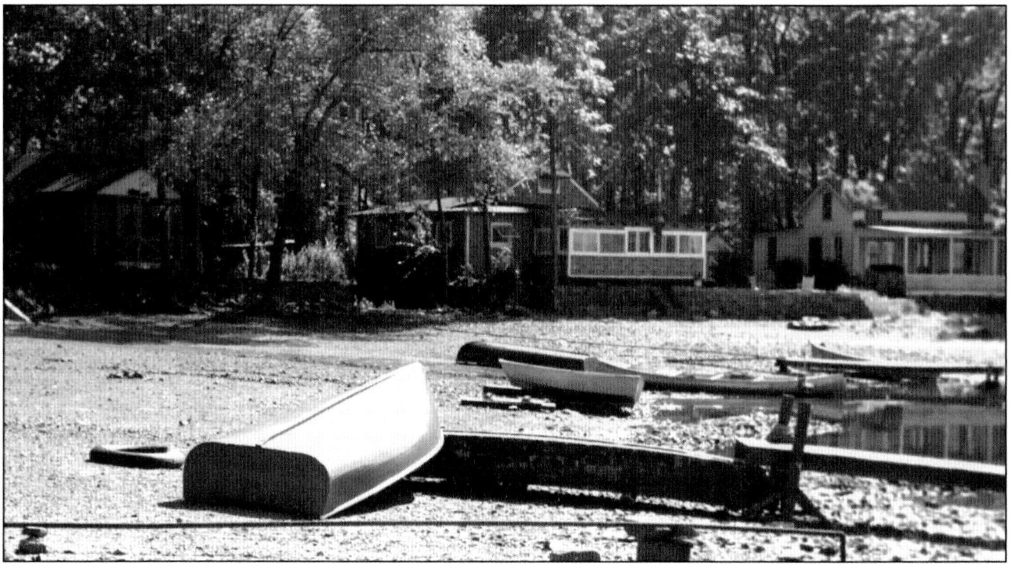

The lake bottom is fully exposed in this 1952 photograph. The third cottage from the right is still a seasonal dwelling. The sluiceway is between this cottage and the one on the far right. Made of concrete, its trough allows more water to be funneled out of the lake than the natural drainage. (Courtesy of Charles Bivona.)

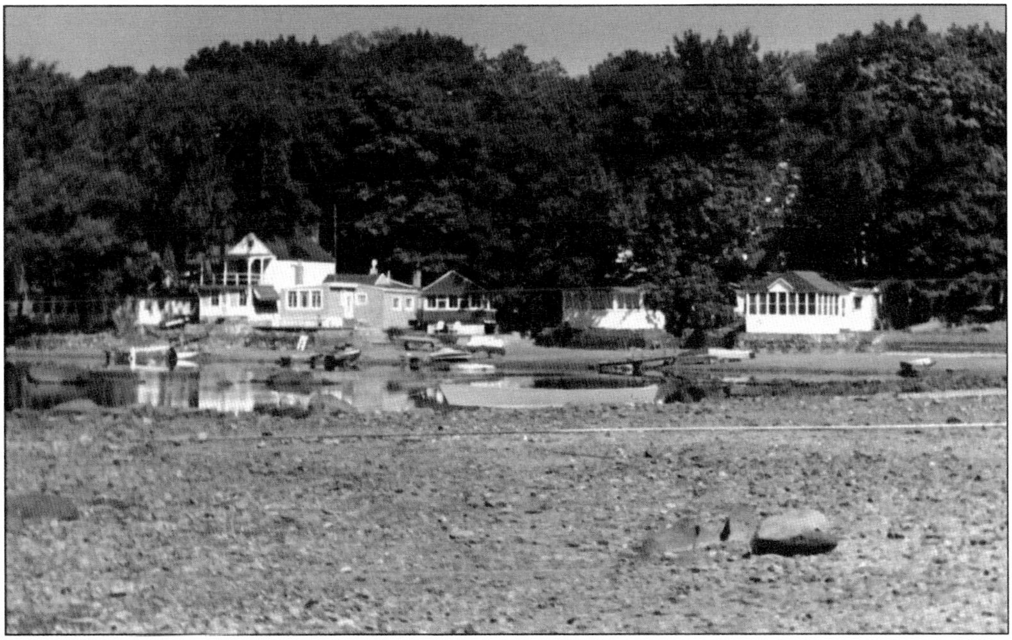

The early 1950s were very challenging years for lake dwellers. Drought and continued use of lake water by the mill owners made living conditions extremely difficult. The pipes extending from the lake to the shore carried water for washing and other chores. (Courtesy of Charles Bivona.)

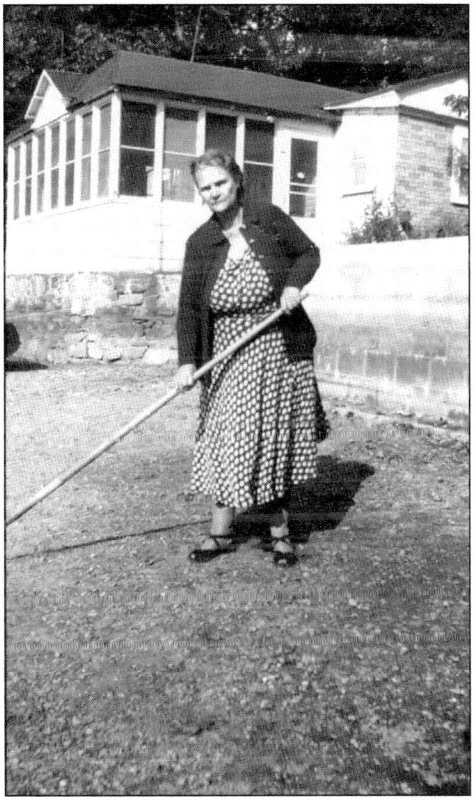

Margaret Gee took advantage of the low water to rake the large rocks from the swimming area in front of her home. In a note accompanying the picture, she writes to her grandchildren, "Grandma was getting pretty tired and I'm sure I look it in this picture." (Courtesy of Karol Gee Gibson and Kathy Gee Kobeliski.)

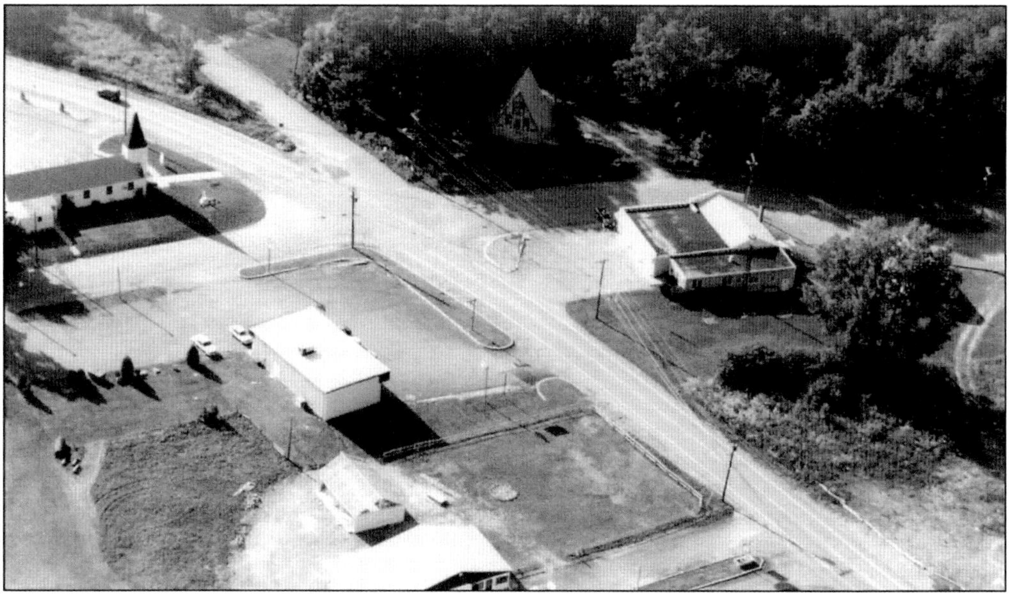

In this aerial photograph, Lakeside Road runs horizontally across the diagonal Route 52. At the bottom front is the office of the Orange Lake Motel, followed by an outbuilding at the motel. A small grocery is on the corner behind that building and the Dan Leghorn Engine Company is across the street on the opposite corner. Our Lady of the Lake Chapel is the last building on the top left. (Courtesy of Victoria Palkovic.)

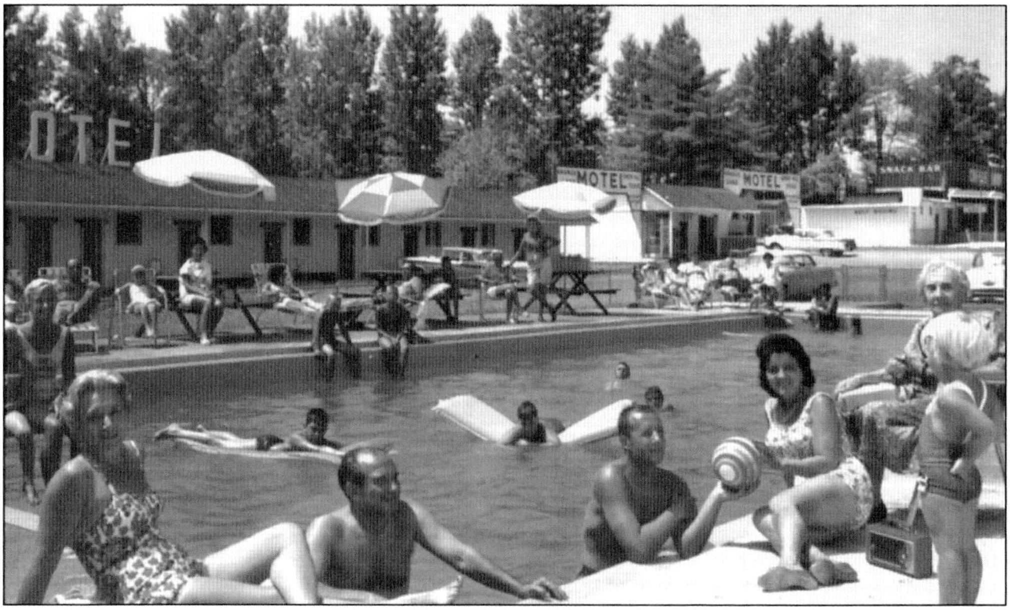

The Orange Lake Motel was a family-orientated motel when it opened in the 1950s. In this postcard view, it advertised that the motel was "only 60 miles from New York City, has a filtered swimming pool and access to the lake for fishing and boating." "Modern rooms, efficiencies, and cottages" were available for daily, weekly, or monthly rates. (Courtesy of Paul Yablonsky.)

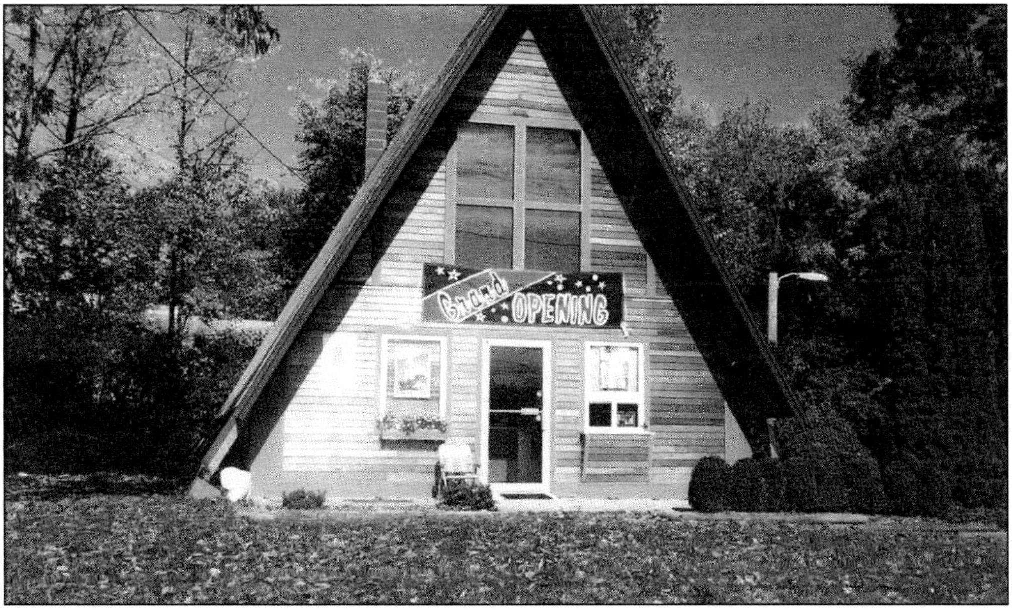

A style of building popular in the 1960s known as an A-frame was built on the corner of Lakeside Road and Route 52 around that time. It originally housed a hardware store but also was home to a conservative bookstore and needlework store. This photograph is from another incarnation of the store as an ice-cream shop called Vikki's Kool Delights. (Courtesy of Victoria Palkovic.)

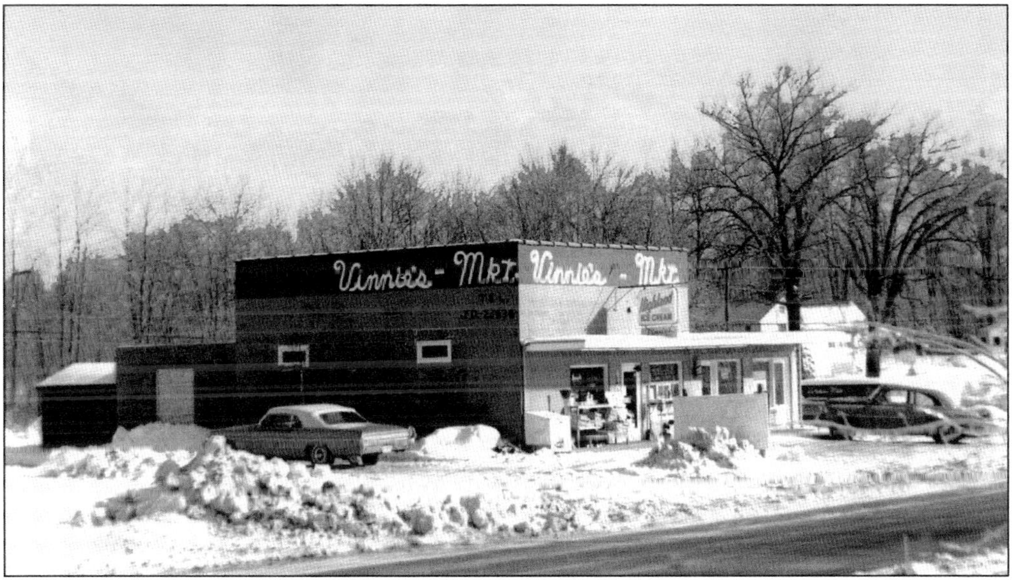

Vinnie's Market was located on Route 52, just west of Lakeside Road. It was owned and operated by a lake-home owner from the mid-1950s through the 1960s. (Courtesy of Vincent Forriester.)

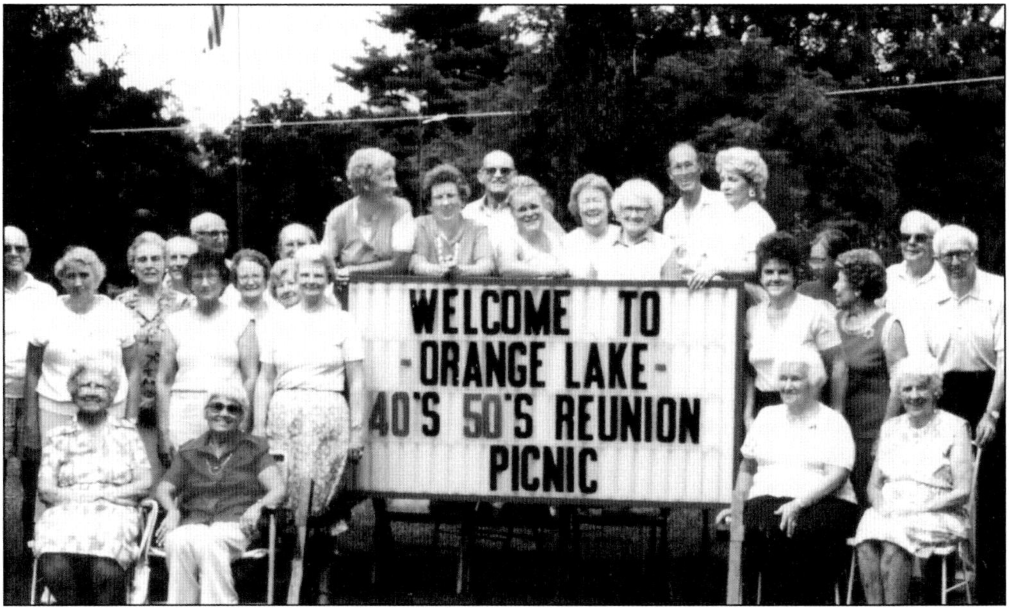

Longtime residents of Orange Lake held a picnic reunion in the 1960s in Walden. Some still lived in the area but others traveled long distances to come. Pictured in the first row are Mary Lawrence, Bernice Harris, unidentified, and Blanche Herring. Others in the background include Ann Innis, Dorothy Revelle, Helen Gage, Marguerite Harris McDermott, Igmar Kaltenbach, Mildred Reinhart, Francis McDermott, and William Herring. (Courtesy of Ilene Patton Siegman.)

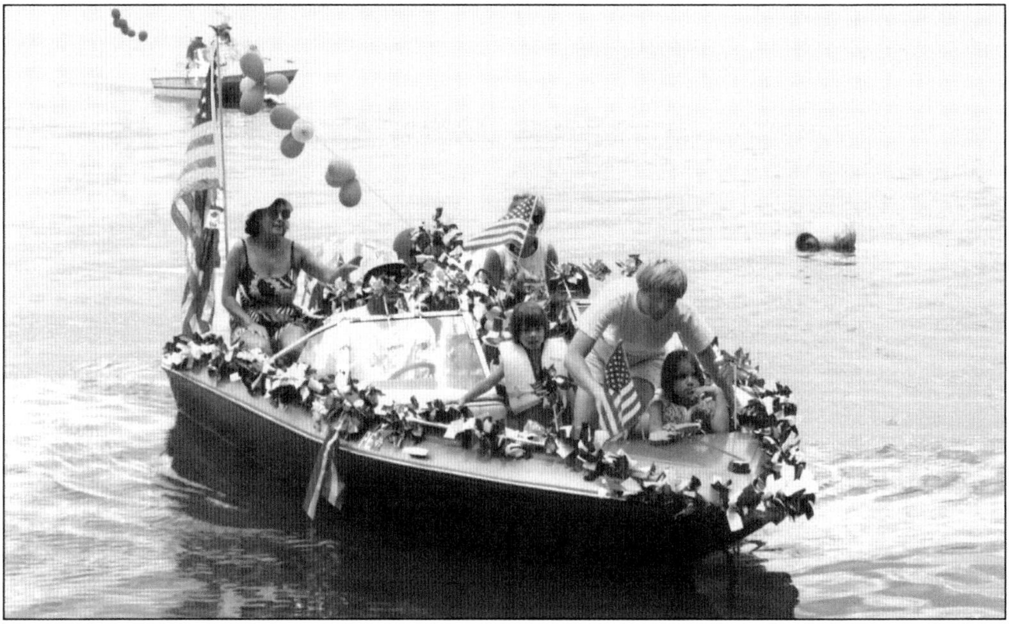

Begun in the early 1970s, the Fourth of July boat parade sponsored by the Orange Lake Civic Association is one of the highlights of the season. Some lake residents spend days decorating their crafts in patriotic colors and symbols in anticipation of the event. (Courtesy of David McDermott.)

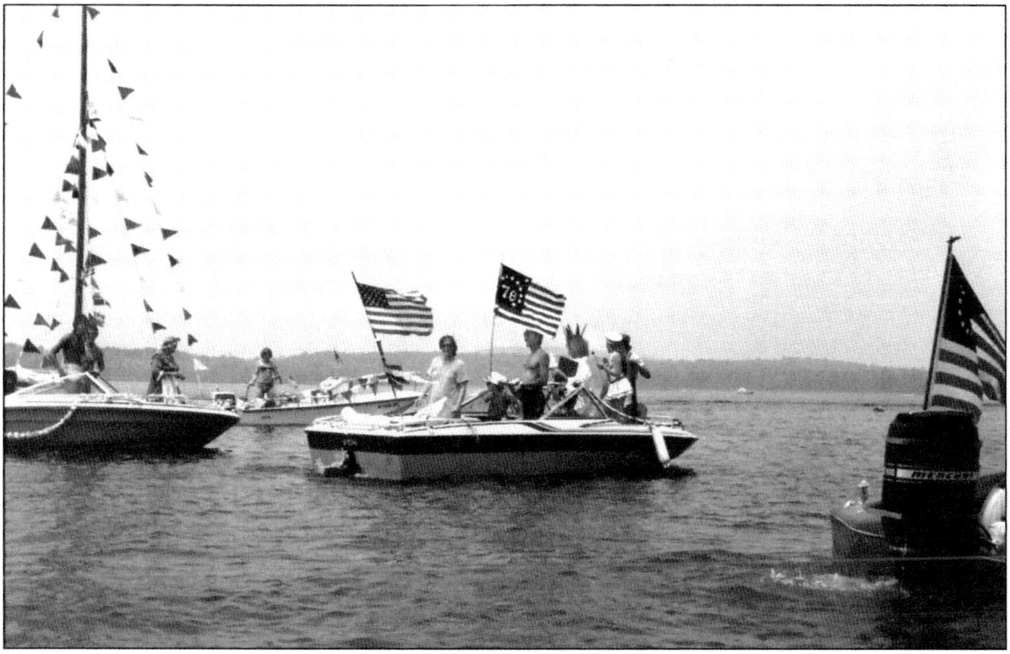

Another boater enjoys the day's festivities in this 1976 photograph. The Fourth of July has become the busiest day at the lake recently. Homeowners around the lake host many picnics and parties, and the lake is filled with pleasure craft of all kinds. (Courtesy of Sheila Gage Nugent.)

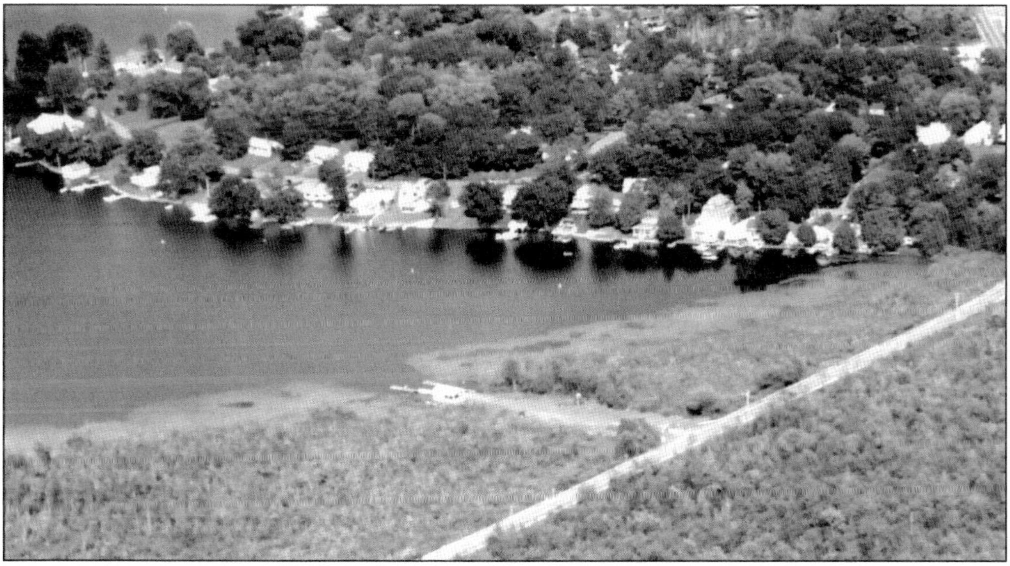

The aerial photograph pictures the year-round homes at the south end of the lake. Route 52 can be seen in the foreground as well as the pavilion of the Orange Lake Fish and Game Association. (Courtesy of Edward Stump.)

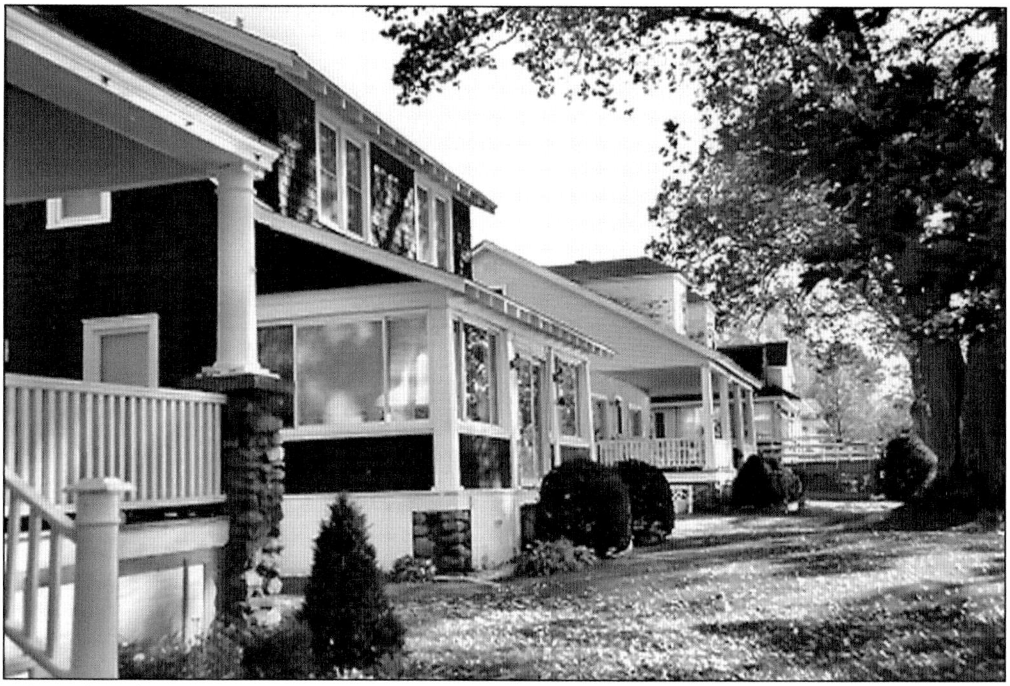

When these homes were built about 80 years ago, the developer, A. Lincoln Miller, required that they be constructed with a 100-foot setback. The restriction remains in place today, with only one homeowner who bypassed the regulation and added a deck. (Courtesy of Arthur Nugent.)

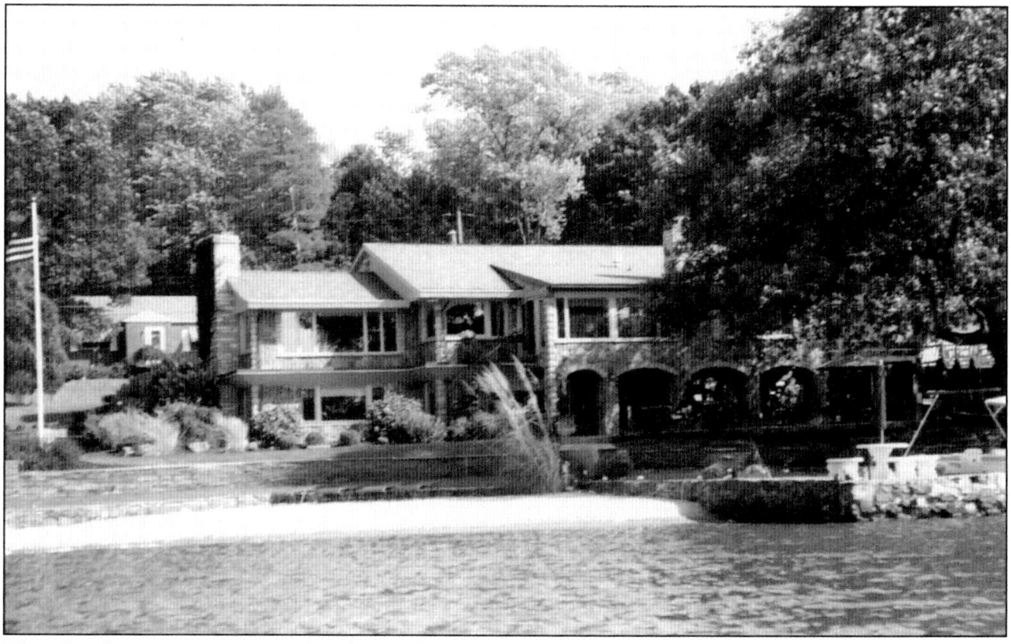

This fine home now sits on the shore of an ecologically sound Orange Lake. The stone wall at the far right is one of the few vestiges of the amusement park. It is believed to be the part of the wall where the boathouse stood. (Author's collection.)

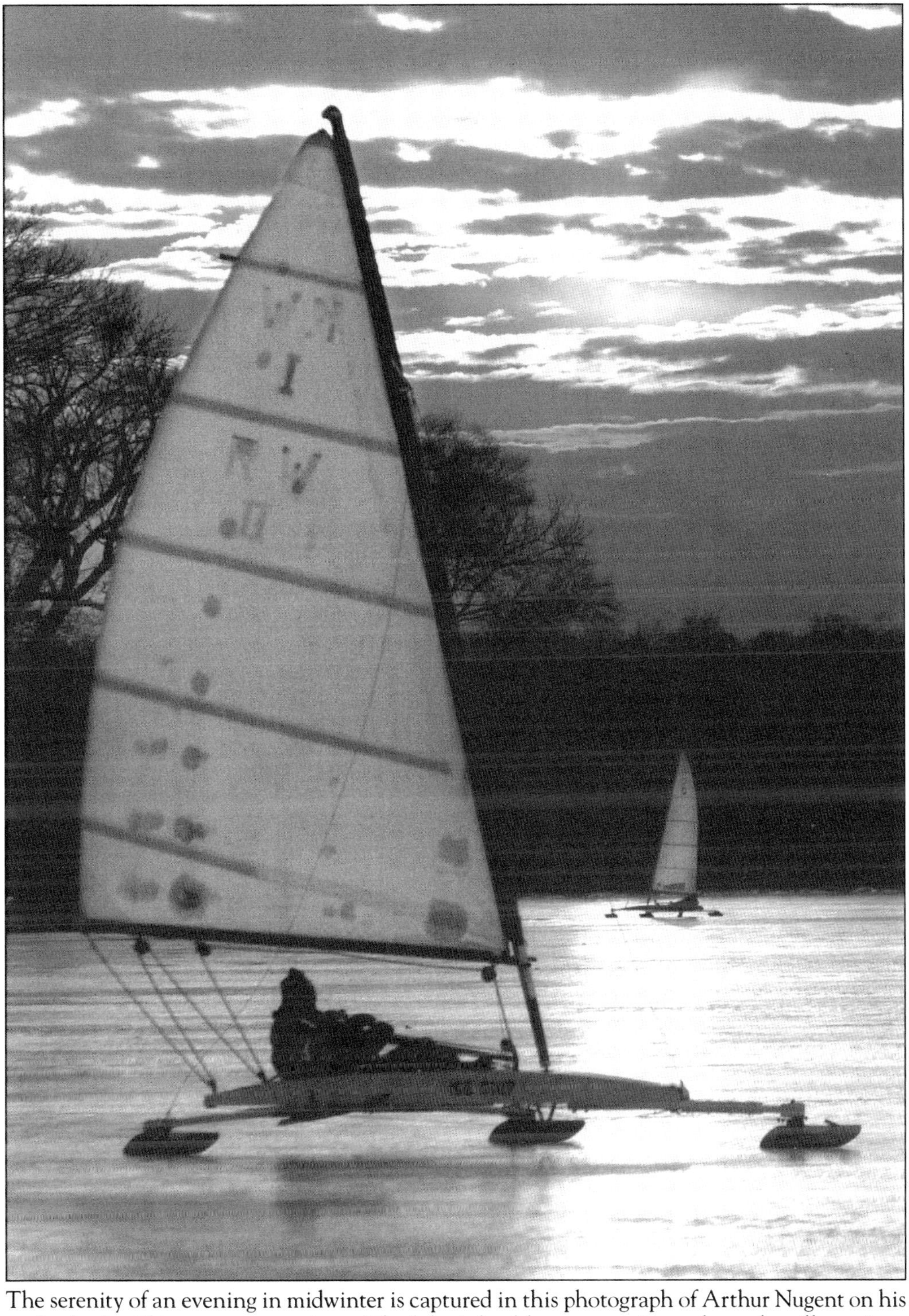

The serenity of an evening in midwinter is captured in this photograph of Arthur Nugent on his craft, the *Ice Chip*, one recent winter. The lake is healthy once again, and people will continue to share its beauty and enjoy its bounty. (Courtesy of the Times-Herald Record, photograph by Jeffery Goulding.)